NEBRASKA FOLKLORE

Louise Pound

NEBRASKA

FOLKLORE

UNIVERSITY OF NEBRASKA PRESS

LINCOLN AND LONDON

First Bison Book printing: 1989
Most recent printing indicated by the first digit below:
  2   3   4   5   6   7   8   9   10

Library of Congress Cataloging-in-Publication Data
Pound, Louise, 1872–1958.
Nebraska folklore / Louise Pound.
   p.   cm.
"Bison."
ISBN 0-8032-8724-0
1. Folklore—Nebraska. 2. Nebraska—Social life and customs.
I. Title.
GR110.N2P6 1989
398'.09782—dc20
89-32799 CIP

♾

BE IT RESOLVED That the Modern Language Association offers its congratulations to Louise Pound on the achievements of her long and useful career. Educated chiefly in her native Nebraska, with a doctorate *en passant* from Heidelberg, Miss Pound has used Nebraska as a base from which she began long ago to send out messages of learning to astonish a nation of scholars unused to the company of ladies who knew quite as much as they did. In books, in articles, in reviews, in lectures, and in editorial work, particularly on the journal *American Speech,* of which she was a founder, Miss Pound has made innumerable contributions to the study of the ballad, folklore, linguistics, and American literature. By her constant encouragement and assistance to younger scholars she has multiplied her value to our profession. Miss Pound's learning and her shrewd judgment have been recognized from coast to coast and beyond the seas. Furthermore, in those communities where she has lived, people have discovered with pleasure that a scholar may be, in addition, a social creature, a wit, and, *mirabile dictu,* a champion in athletic sports. If the Modern Language Association has tarried overlong in electing a woman to highest office, it has done well in selecting Louise Pound for the first honor.

BENJAMIN BOYCE, *Duke University*
Chairman, Resolutions Committee

Seventieth Annual Meeting of the Modern Language Association of America, Chicago, December, 1955.

These studies were collected and edited by Dr. Louise Pound shortly before her death, June 28, 1958. Except for correction of typographical errors, they are presented here as she prepared them for publication.

For permission to reprint copyrighted material we are indebted to the following publications: *California Folklore Quarterly, Western Folklore, Nebraska History, Southern Folklore Quarterly,* and *Modern Philology.*

UNIVERSITY OF NEBRASKA PRESS

Contents

Foreword

In 1949 the University of Nebraska Press published the *Selected Writings of Louise Pound*. It is altogether fitting that ten years later the Press publish a selection of Miss Pound's studies in Nebraska folklore. For much of the fifty years that Dr. Pound was actively engaged in teaching at the University of Nebraska she was regarded as one of the ranking scholars on the University faculty. As her reputation grew it became generally acknowledged that no person, while at the University of Nebraska in the capacity of student or faculty member, had gained such a large measure both of recognition and distinction.

The editor of the volume of selected writings, and Dr. Pound's long-time colleague on the English faculty of the University of Nebraska, Professor Lowry C. Wimberly, remarked most appropriately in a prefatory note that Miss Pound's writings had been mainly incidental. That is, in her teaching, her pioneering in a number of scholarly fields, her editorial activity and other ways, she expressed her major interests. Only a comparatively small portion of her time and energy was devoted to writing. Often the writing was "incidental," in that it was prepared as a paper to present on a scholarly program, or material written upon invitation for a specific purpose. While Professor Wimberly's estimate that Dr. Pound's writing was incidental to her total career is accurate, both the quantity and quality of her writings belie the statement. She wrote extensively on the many subjects that attracted her interest and study at different periods in her life.

Dr. Pound made a lifelong career of excelling in any pursuit that engaged her attention, from sports to scholarship. Thus it is not surprising to find her widely recognized as an authority in the field of folklore. Both as a teacher, training such well-known scholars as B. A. Botkin, and as a writer she attained eminence among students of folklore.

She was vitally interested in life and happenings close about her, and the study of the folklore of her area became increasingly important among Dr. Pound's intellectual interests. This is amply indicated by the relative recency of publication of most of the selections that appear in this volume. The decision to collect her writings on Nebraska folklore is a well-conceived testimonial to her deep-rooted and continuing interest in her native state.

The writings of Dr. Pound in Nebraska folklore have brought to the attention of a larger audience interesting and colorful legends and stories from Nebraska that had not been adequately studied or preserved in written form before Dr. Pound worked with them. The collection and publication of these accounts in this readily accessible form is a real addition to the literature of the state. Students of our nation's folklore will welcome the book. It will be of even more value and interest to Nebraskans of this and future generations.

W. D. AESCHBACHER
Director,
Nebraska State Historical Society

NEBRASKA FOLKLORE

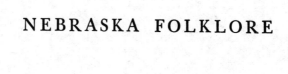

Nebraska Cave Lore

———————————— 𝄞 ————————————

Superstitions, legends, and fairy stories have always clustered about caves. Yet there seems to have been less special collection of such lore than of other phases of folklore. In the mass of studies turned out, on innumerable topics in so many fields, collectanea of cave lore have played a minor role. There appears to be less of it than that of seas, streams, fountains, and woods. It belongs, in any case, to local rather than to general lore and it has its own special interest and deserves its own recording. Nearly every striking or picturesque cave develops its individual story or stories, and its discoverer too deserves chronicling when he can be determined. There are holes all over the earth, caverns of various shapes, large and small, some amazingly beautiful, others drab and dull. In general legend, these have been inhabited by all sorts of strange creatures, giants, ogres, monsters; in German story typically by dwarfs. Polyphemus, the one-eyed giant being from whom Ulysses saved himself, lived in a cave near Mount Aetna. There is a cave in which winds were restrained in the first book of Virgil's *Aeneid*. In *Beowulf* Grendel's mother has a subterranean dwelling and the dragon guarding the hidden treasure issued from a cave. Hartley Alexander records a Haitian legend telling of the origin of man in a cave [1]

---

[1] Hartley Burr Alexander, *Latin American Mythology,* The Mythology of All Races Series, XI (Boston, 1920), 28.

1

and another telling that the sun and moon were born in caves. Water too issued from caves. Coleridge's Alph, the sacred river, "ran Through caverns measureless to man Down to a sunless sea." In the American West, giants and ogres and dwarfs are replaced by Indians, train robbers, and horse-thieves in need of hideouts, and by men concealing or looking for buried treasure. In older days, no doubt, legends would have arisen concerning the government gold underground in Kentucky. They may, indeed, yet appear if they have not done so already.

Caves are not often associated with Nebraska, a region of prairie and hill and rather sparse woodland. Its caves are not numerous nor are they famous. Yet for just these reasons it may well have initial treatment in an article that is not of geological or mineralogical or archaeological stimulus, or merely an uninquiring popular presentation of legends and factual narrations, but is devoted to the folklore of caves of a single state.

Nebraska has no large caves that are nationally known and sought out, and hence sometimes commercially profitable. There are no Mammoth Caves such as Kentucky's with its 150 miles so far explored, no Cave of the Winds such as that at Manitou, Colorado, or that at Hot Springs, South Dakota, where a strong current blows in and out alternately. It has no ice caves such as exist in Montana and Colorado; no amazing Carlsbad Caverns such as Arizona's, of which nearly 40 miles have now been explored. It has no caverns such as those of the Yellowstone region or the Black Hills or the Ozarks. Nor are any of similar well-deserved celebrity likely to be discovered here in the future. Nebraska's caves do not abound in crystals, stalactites, stalagmites, and fossils and they have no glamorous reds, yellows, purples, and pastel shades to excite the wonder of visitors. Two (those at Nebraska City and Lincoln) are electrically lighted in a minor way, but no elevators are needed nor guides for visitors. Yet search reveals more interesting caves in Nebraska than might be expected and more lore concerning them. Surely such lore deserves chronicling before historic fact has been utterly lost and before dates and personages become yet more confused and tall tales taller.

Following is a survey of the Nebraska caves with which I am

yet acquainted, those that are best known. Some are the work of natural forces in the past and some have been excavated or tampered with by man.

Three Eastern Nebraska Caves

Pahuk Cave

In a discussion of Nebraska caves, leading place should go, it seems to me, to Pahuk (Pahook, Pah-huk, Pawhuk, Pohuk) Cave on the Platte River near Fremont, known in the past among the inhabitants of the region as Elephant Cave. It has loomed large in Pawnee Indian lore. Unusual mystery and legend have gathered about it, though all that remains of it now is a gash in a clay bank at the side of a road along the Platte. The road was opened up or at least widened in recent times. It runs between Fremont in Dodge County and Cedar Bluffs in Saunders County. The gash is easily seen from the road but is pretty much dirt filled. Even for one on hands and knees progress is blocked. Few persons in Fremont remember much about Pahuk Bluff or the cave below it. Possibly the slit in the bank reveals the original entrance; just as possibly it does not. According to Dr. Gilbert C. Lueninghoener, geologist at Midland College, Fremont, the cave was one big chamber only. Externally the opening in the bank and the near-by bluff, which is 60 feet high above the Platte, seem uninteresting; but in the light of their role in Indian days they are not. In 1927 no little effort was made before the Chamber of Commerce of Saunders County to have Pahuk Bluff marked as an historic spot. Among those urging this were Dr. A. E. Sheldon, Secretary of the Nebraska State Historical Society, and Captain Luther H. North, pioneer scout and frontiersman of Columbus.

The central seats of the Pawnee Indians when the white man first came to Nebraska were along the Platte and Loup rivers. There was an Indian village on the summit of Pahuk Bluff. General John M. Thayer, later Governor of Nebraska (1887 through 1890), held council with the Pawnee there in 1854. When the Indians were moved elsewhere, their village was burned, perhaps by them, perhaps by others. Pahuk Bluff was selected as the site of "Neapolis," the projected capital of Nebraska, by an act of the Territorial Legislature of 1858, an act later declared void. The Pawnee tribe was that most advanced in culture of the Indian tribes in Nebraska. Their legends have been gathered by several scholars, notably George A. Dorsey.[2] Some of the Pawnee tales, too, are remembered by Mari Sandoz from her talks with an old Pawnee. Pahuk, it seems well established, was the sacred or holy place of the Pawnee. It was to them, said A. E. Sheldon in an address,[3] what Mecca was to the Mohammedans and Mount Sinai to the Christians. The site of Pahuk has been definitely fixed as the bluff across the Platte from Fremont. It may be seen clearly from the roadway of the Union Pacific or from the bridge of the Northwestern Railway crossing the Platte. The bluff rises abruptly on the south bank of the river a short distance east of the bridge. The ethnologist, M. R. Gilmore, then Curator of the Nebraska State Historical Society Museum, later Curator of Ethnology, Museum of Anthropology of the University of Michigan, went there in August, 1914, with Chief White Eagle of the Skidi Tribe of Pawnee, who pointed out the place to him.[4] Others made the same identification.

In the Pawnee religion, only less powerful than their main deity Tirawa and the gods of the heavens were those of the earth. These were ruled over by lodges of Nahurak or Animals, of which loci there were about five. Here the animals gathered together in council to promote or to harm the fortunes of human beings. The animals had many powers, such as that of changing men to animals or birds or the converse. Under

---

[2] George A. Dorsey, *Pawnee Mythology,* Vol. 1 (Washington: Carnegie Institute, 1906) and his *Traditions of the Skidi Pawnee,* Memoirs of the American Folklore Society, VIII, 1904.

[3] Letter, A. E. Sheldon to the Board of Commissioners of Saunders County at Wahoo, Nebraska, June 17, 1927. See also his address "The Pawnee Nation and the Battle of Battle Creek" given at a meeting of the Chamber of Commerce, Battle Creek, Nebraska, November 16, 1939. Typed MSS., Nebraska State Historical Society.

[4] Gilmore gives the site at "½ of n. e. of sec 22 and west ½ of n.w. ¼ sec. 23, twnp 17 north range east." See M. R. Gilmore, "The Legend of Pahuk." Typed MS., Nebraska State Historical Society.

their tutelage the favored persons were enabled to fly like eagles, swim like turtles, live like the coyote, and perform sleight of hand. In these lodges of the Pawnee the young aspirants for the supernatural powers of the medicine men were guided and there were taught by leaders or errand men or messengers who served as liaison beings between the gods and men. Supreme among the Pawnee lodges was Pahuk. In its underground chamber were learned from the wild animals and birds their mysteries and magical powers and the virtues of different roots and herbs. The aspirants thus favored took back to their people the wisdom and the healing gifts they learned there. An illustrative sentence showing the high status of Pahuk is the following, from a story told by Beaver Kitkehahki, who inherited it from his father, who was keeper of the Beaver medicine, the origin of which the story explains:

> They [the medicine men, the animals] sent the Magpie to all the lodges and went to Pahuk last, for there was the lodge that was really the head of all the other lodges.[5]

The name Pahuk, according to Dr. Gilmore, literally means headland or promontory but sometimes the Pawnee spoke of it as Nahura Waruksti, Sacred Ground or Wonderful Ground, because of the mystery and awe with which the place was invested in their minds. The statement has been made that Pahuk was to the Pawnee the center of the universe and the place of the origin of man. Mari Sandoz is one of those recalling this from a Pawnee source.

A recurrent legend concerning Pahuk was summarized by Dr. Gilmore who says of it, "From White Eagle I obtained the narrative which I here set forth in as good a rendering as possible in English of his version of the myth." The translation was made, at the time of establishing the site of Pahuk, by a young Pawnee named Charles Knifechief. He adds, "There are

---

[5] From "The Medicine Child and the Beaver," Tale 77 in Dorsey's *Pawnee Mythology*, pp. 241-254. Other references to Pahuk may be found in Tales 78, 85, 86, 89. See also in *Traditions of the Skidi Pawnee,* Tale 59, "Scabby Bull and the Wonderful Medicine Man," p. 231.

other versions extant as told by other narrators but differing in no essentials." Dr. Gilmore's summary runs as follows:

A young son is killed by his father and his body thrown into the Platte. He is finally restored to life by the decision of the animals. Each animal taught his particular remedy and all the songs pertaining to the ritual of healing. He returned to his people, having been told to use these remedies given him by the great powers of Heaven.

The corresponding Pawnee tales told by Dorsey are all very long and detailed.[6] At this point a letter from Captain Luther North may be cited:

The Hill, Pahuk Bluff, which he [A. E. Sheldon] recommends marking as a historic site is according to a legend of the Pawnee the home of Nah-hoo-nack and the ghost animals. Their home is deep down in the hill and the entrance is from below the water of the river. There is a long tunnel to go through before you come to the opening of the house and at the door as Guards are a huge rattlesnake and a gigantic grizzly bear. Any one entering must pass between them and if they show the least sign of fear they would never be heard from again.

I know a very good story of a young Pawnee who was supposed to have been in this house.[7]

Captain North added that the story was too long for him to try to tell it in his letter. It seems probable that it was a variant of that known to Dr. Gilmore and those recorded by Dr. Dorsey.

In June, 1948, Althea Marr Witte of Fremont gave me this information as told to her by Dr. G. C. Lueninghoener of Midland College:

The cave, which is nothing but a small slit now, was of clay and had only one large chamber. The only legend I know is of Chief Pohuk. The story goes that the parents of their baby who later was Chief Pohuk threw him into the Platte river and abandoned him because he was such a small, weak and sickly

---

6 Dorsey, *Pawnee Mythology,* I, section III, "The Origin of Medicine Ceremonies of Power."

7 Preserved in the Library of the State Historical Society, Lincoln.

baby. The animals such as the beavers, woodchucks, squirrels and turtles rescued him and cared for him. They nursed him to health, brought him food, and taught him many things. Because he was so close to nature he grew to be very wise and strong and in time became one of the greatest chiefs of the Pawnee tribe.

The latest tale I have heard concerning Pahuk cave was from a woman living in a shack on the low ground between the bluff and the river. She said she had heard that two boys "had been caught in it and as a result it was dynamited." She said she did not know whether this was true, being herself relatively a newcomer, and so far no one has verified her story to me.

Lincoln Cave

The conspicuous sign on the high ground that is the site of the Lincoln cave reads on one side "Notorious Old Cave" and on the other "Robbers' Cave." The cave is described as follows in the entry concerning Lincoln in the Federal Writers' Project *Guide to Nebraska:*

The Cave, 11th and High Streets . . . is a series of caverns and winding passages in an outcrop of Dakota sandstone. The walls scratched with names, initials and dates, are streaked in ocherous yellow and hematite reds and browns.

In Pawnee legend it was in the "Nahurac" spirits' cave that medicine men held mystic sacred rites, and neophytes were proven and initiated. A snowbound wagon train used its protection; and after the Indian scare of 1862, settlers lived in it all winter. In 1863, when a stone quarry was started by three men who had acquired the title to the land from the Government, the removal of the cap rock destroyed the original entrance to the cave. In 1906 when the caverns were being cleared of debris so as to be used as a mushroom garden, stories of hidden treasure brought so many visitors to the place that plans were changed and the cave was kept open for sightseers and picnics.[8]

---

[8] Federal Writers' Project, *Nebraska: A Guide to the Cornhusker State* (New York, 1939), p. 197.

This information in the *Guide* probably derives mainly from the present owners of the place who came to Lincoln in the 1880's.

The Lincoln cave had no doubt the usual origin of caves, through the action of water on sandstone or limestone. It may have been one of the five loci that were sacred to the Pawnee. Indian knowledge and utilization of the cave for certain rites is quite possible. But I have found no references to it in Pawnee lore, as I did for Pahuk. There were Indians of the Pawnee, Otoe, and Omaha tribes about in Lancaster County in early days; but I know of no traces of an Indian village or burial mounds in the vicinity. It is quite possible, for that matter, that the starting of a little quarrying (little is all there could have been) on the site opened up the cave for discovery. Nor can I find sources for the story of the snowbound wagon train nor for the story that settlers lived in it all the winter of 1862 during an Indian scare. There were mild Indian scares from time to time in Lancaster County in the late '50's and early '60's, but none of special interest in 1862 or in other of these years unless 1864. The cave had but one chamber then and that none too large. It would have been a dusty, unpleasant, and, indeed, dangerous place, not easy to enter and quite dark. Removal nearer other settlers and nearer water would have been wiser.

My father came to Lincoln in 1867 and my mother in 1869. They knew the region well and its history; yet they were silent as to Indian knowledge of or use of the cave and as to the refuge of settlers there, so close to their own day. The cave had little celebrity until after 1906. The stories about it as a hideout of robbers and horse-thieves in the '70's and '80's, mentioned in the Federal *Guide to the City of Lincoln* (1937) always amused my mother. She said it was used as a beer cellar by a near-by brewery of her time. Among others, Pearl J. Cosgrave, daughter of Judge P. J. Cosgrave, testifies that her mother too was amused by the stories of robbers and horse-thieves associated with the cave. The Federal *Guide to Nebraska* says nothing of the use of the cave for storage by brewers; but that it was so used is stated by the present owner and is entered in the Lincoln *Guide*. This seems well established. In 1869 two brewers bought the site and hired a laborer to enlarge the cave for the purpose of storing beer and malt underground, in old-world fashion. A laborer is said to have spent three years off and on digging the chambers and passages out of sandstone with pick and shovel and wheelbarrow. The caverns are fairly large now. Some of the enlarging was done after 1906 when debris was cleared out and the place made accessible as a picnic grounds. In 1873 the brewers became bankrupt in the financial collapse and the cave was given up.

As for the robbers and horse-thieves said to have occupied the cave in the late '70's and the '80's, their presence there is very doubtful, their origin probably commercial. Members of the Pound family were all on hand then and never heard of them. Horses could not well be concealed in or outside the cave. So near the thriving Lincoln of those days, with its growing university, the presence of horse-thieves and robbers and their use of the brewers' old storage cave would have been known. Trouble would have arisen concerning them. My father was a judge and, of all persons, would have been likely to hear of their operations. Dwellers in a house on the site or near it were known to us, and never reported robbers in the neighborhood.

In summary, the Indian rites supposed to have been held in the cave, though possible, are unauthenticated. After the historic Pahuk cave near Fremont became known, and its role in the life of the Pawnee Indians, somewhat the same role was sometimes claimed for the Lincoln cave but without basis of fact. The stories of hidden treasure there have never been accepted as having a basis in fact. Belief in the use of the cave as a dwelling place for safety in winter by pioneer settlers, or use of it as a hideout of Jesse James (he has been assigned several such hideouts in Nebraska), and a later tale stating that a portion of Coxey's Army found lodging there in the winter of '93-'94 (mentioned in the Lincoln *Guide*), all these belong no doubt to folklore. Members of Coxey's Army crossed Nebraska in 1894, but there is no record of the stay of a group in Lincoln; and if there was, the cave would have been a hopelessly cramped and unpleasant lodging. The present owner who "arrived in the '80's" said nothing of it when I heard him recount the history of the cave. Possibly one or two of the Coxey itinerants were about the place but the "Army" did not lodge there. The utilization and enlargement of the cave by brewers is the only story connected with it that can be established.

At its lowest point the cave is said to go to a depth of about 82 feet from the top of the bit of high ground that is its location. It may cover in all its passages and chambers perhaps 700 feet, said the owner. It is worth visiting as it winds through sandstone walls into its present five chambers. High school picnics, college initiations, and various other events have been held in it. It is lighted here and there by mild electric bulbs, and its depth and irregularity make it a weird though dusky and dusty setting for those wishing something of the sort. That legends of various types should have arisen about it seems inevitable and, to me, not regrettable.

John Brown's Cabin and Cave

The most publicized of Nebraska's caves is the so-called John Brown's Cave, or Cabin and Cave, at Nebraska City. It is over a mile from the Missouri River at the right of State Highway 2 leading to the city and the river. Nebraska City was incorporated December 20, 1857; it was on the edge of free territory and in steamboat days was the busiest and most important city in the area. The river was crossed at Brownville and at Nebraska City, usually the latter. Nebraska City served as a second stop after Nemaha City on the Underground Railway when fugitive slaves were brought from Missouri through Kansas to be ferried over or carried over the ice from Nebraska to Iowa. From about 1854 to 1861 or a little later it was an important station in the successive hiding places in which the freed slaves and their convoys might rest in comparative safety. There are supposed to have been several of these hiding places in Nebraska City, a barn, for example, and a cave in a pasture, these perhaps changed from time to time for safety.

However dubious may be Brown's connection with the John

Brown Cabin and however few or numerous the slaves he brought there, it is beyond question that he was in Nebraska City many times, passing through it on his journeys from the east by way of Chicago to Kansas and return. An interesting paragraph from the Nebraska City *News* of February 12, 1859, tells of what proved to be Brown's last appearance in Nebraska City. More will be said of this, a unique expedition in his midwestern years, later:

> John Brown, Captain John Brown, of Osawatomie . . . passed through this city late last Friday evening at the head of a herd of stolen niggers taken from Southern Missouri, accompanied with a gang of horsethieves of the most desperate character. They had a large number of stolen horses in their possession—two of which were taken and are now held by the deputy sheriff of this County.
>
> There is an appropriateness and fitness in nigger stealing being associated with horsethieves that the rankest black republican cannot fail to appreciate.

The so-called Brown cabin is now a small museum free to the public. It is advertised as the "oldest wooden structure now in Nebraska." It is of brown cottonwood logs and according to its historian and late owner, Edward D. Bartling,[9] it was built by Allen B. Mayhew, its first occupant, in 1851. When the state highway was put through in recent times, the cabin was moved about 25 feet to the north, was placed on a foundation of natural limestone and was somewhat changed or restored by Bartling in minor ways. An earthen cave for storage was excavated near it, as is sometimes the practice nowadays, though refrigeration has done much to end such caves. Bartling says that when the house was moved it was placed over the original cave site. The "cave" is now much like a 10 x 12 cellar to the cabin. The entrance (or perhaps it was the outlet), now just outside to the east, was originally, it is stated, in a ravine about 75 feet west of the cabin and hidden in the underbrush; traces of it are supposedly still to be seen there. Accounts vary. Those knowing the early days have affirmed that there was originally no con-

---

9 Edward D. Bartling, *John Henry Kagi and the Old Log Cabin Home.* (Published by author, Nebraska City, 1938, 1940, 1943.)

nection between the cabin and the cave;[10] others state that the cave was a tunnel running directly under the Mayhew home and entered by a trap door in the cabin;[11] others that a cistern was enlarged to form the cave.[12] Since the cabin was moved in recent times and is said to be now over the original cave site, it could not have been over it originally. The cistern testimony is probably erroneous too.

Brown's best biographer, Oswald Garrison Villard, stated the following concerning the last appearance of Brown in Nebraska City, that told in the newspaper item of 1859 quoted above. The last lines deserve special attention.

> On the 19th of December, 1858, began one of the most picturesque incidents in John Brown's life ... his incursion into Missouri and his liberation of slaves by force of arms. While as already recorded Brown had taken two slaves out of Kansas to freedom before this wholesale liberation and was throughout his life and ever-ready agent of the Underground Railroad, he was at no time especially interested in this piecemeal method of weakening slavery. It was to his mind wasting time, when a bold attack might liberate five hundred or a thousand slaves.[13]

Whether or not Brown had previously taken more than two or three slaves out of Kansas to freedom,[14] his arrival with the group of Missouri slaves chronicled in the Nebraska City newspaper of February 12, 1859, was his only expedition of the kind. The operations of the Underground may have been pretty steady before, during, and after his coming to Kansas; but

---

10 N. C. Abbott, Omaha *World-Herald*, October 27, 1929.

11 Nebraska City *News*, November 14, 1874.

12 Wayne Overturf, "John Brown's Cabin at Nebraska City," *Nebraska History* magazine, XXI (April-June, 1940), 93-97, "After the battle of Osawatomie the cistern at the Mayhew cabin was converted into a cave." See also a letter from Eugenia Rowan (aged 80) in 1938, mentioned by Bartling, *op. cit.*, p. 10.

13 Oswald Garrison Villard, *John Brown: A Biography Fifty Years After* (Boston 1910), p. 367.

14 Villard notes that Brown's son, John Brown, Jr., freed two slaves in 1856, but they were returned to their masters. *Ibid.*, pp. 150-151.

Brown himself devoted his activities to other matters than "piecemeal" rescues. After reaching Canada with his group of freed slaves in 1859 he planned the Harper's Ferry debacle in which his leading men were killed and he himself was captured and, on December 2 of that year, was hanged.

Villard's biography supplies a chronology of Brown's movements from his departure for Kansas till his death.[15] It is important to note from it his visits to Nebraska City, when they occurred, and who was with him. He first arrived in Kansas October 7, 1855. The probable date of his leaving Topeka for Nebraska is July 23, 1856. He reached Nebraska City soon thereafter. Those in his party are enumerated by Villard.[16] No fugitive slaves were with him on this trip. He arrived at Topeka on his return journey, August 10. On October 8, after the battle of Osawatomie, he narrowly escaped capture by Lieutenant Cooke near Nebraska City and went on to Tabor and Chicago. This time a fugitive slave was along. A. B. Keim places this liberation in 1855,[17] but Brown did not leave Kansas for Nebraska in that year. Brown's son, Jason, gave the following account:

> We crossed the river at Topeka. We had a one-mule team and a one-horse covered wagon. The mule team was full of arms and ammunition that father was taking out to Tabor. . . . In the covered one-horse team was a fugitive slave covered with hay, father lying sick, Owen, John and I. Owen, John and I walked all we could to save the horse. . . . We finally got both wagons together at the ferry at Nebraska City and camped. Next morning we crossed the river by rope ferry, into the southeast corner of Iowa. When we landed we let the contraband out of the hay, fixed him up as best we could, and traveled on to Tabor. There Owen stopped and the Negro there found work.[18]

---

[15] *Ibid.*, p. 672.

[16] *Ibid.*, p. 222.

[17] A. B. Keim, "John Brown in Richardson County," *Transactions and Reports of the Nebraska State Historical Society*, II, 109-113. Keim tells of Brown's headquarters in Falls City but says nothing of the Nebraska City cave in Otoe County.

[18] Villard, *op. cit.*, p. 262.

Note the word *camped* in Jason Brown's account of their stay
at Nebraska City. Brown started back to Tabor about October
27, 1856, but did not return to Nebraska and Kansas. Instead
he went again to Chicago and on east. In the fall of 1857 he
again reached Nebraska and proceeded to Topeka where he
stayed a few days, then started back to Nebraska City on November 17. Again there were no fugitive slaves in the party.[19]
He arrived at Tabor about November 22 and journeyed east
again. During his brief stay in Tabor, Brown offered to take
his men, go to Nebraska City, and rescue from jail a slave who
had run away and had lost his arm when captured, if the Tabor
people would pay his actual expenses. He promised to put the
slave in their hands, but they were afraid of the consequences
and did not give him the means.[20] Brown left Boston on the
last of his journeys to Kansas on June 3, 1859, and was in
Lawrence on June 26. On December 20, 1858, came his raid
into Missouri described by Villard. He entered Nebraska February, 1859 (this was his last day in Kansas), crossed the Missouri
River at Nebraska City, reached Tabor with his slaves on February 4, and on March 12 saw them ferried over to Windsor,
Canada.

Of much interest and special pertinence is a letter from Belpre,
Kansas by E. F. Mayhew, son of Allen B. Mayhew who built the
cabin. It was written in 1925 in response to an inquiry from
N. C. Abbott of Nebraska City.

The cave you speak of on my father's farm was dug in the
fall of 1856 and used for storing potatoes. It was later enlarged
to three rooms and used for storing wine only one season. . . .
There was never a Negro in it while my father owned it that
we know of. However, there was a Negro woman at our house
one night on her way north. She and the ones instrumental
in bringing her there had been directed by John Kagy. At
another time Kagy brought 14 Negroes there for breakfast one
morning. It was at this time that the officers and some men
from Missouri came to the house after him. Although my
father told them he was upstairs they were afraid to go after

19 *Ibid.*, p. 308.
20 *Ibid.*, p. 311.

him, knowing he was armed. . . . My father told them not to bring any more Negroes there, as it was only making trouble. . . . I lived in the log house from the time I was about 6 until I was about 12 years old. We moved into another about 1860.[21]

This testimony accounts for the cabin and the cave till 1860 or perhaps 1859 or possibly, if Mayhew's date is *very* vaguely given, till 1857. The Mayhew son should know whereof he writes. Any of the three Pound children, brought up like the Mayhews, in or near a small prairie town, would have explored a cave so close to their home and would have known of the goings on there, whether in the daytime or night, this when they were between the ages of six and twelve.

If Allen B. Mayhew, helped by his father-in-law Abraham Kagy, dug the cave and the Mayhews lived in the cabin from 1851 till 1860 or thereabouts, it would seem that if the cave was ever a hiding place for freed slaves it must have been after John Brown's death. The Kagys were strong abolitionists. John Henry Kagi (he preferred to respell the name in the Swiss way), brother of Mayhew's wife, was an exceptionally able young man. At one time he was the Kansas correspondent for the New York *Herald Tribune,* and he was one of John Brown's chief advisers and assistants. He surely visited his sister at the cabin more than the one time when he brought the slaves to be fed and was asked not to do so again. Kagi was killed, however, at Harper's Ferry at the age of twenty-four. This link between the cabin and freed slaves did not exist after 1859. John Brown may have been with Kagi several times; but the cabin was never his headquarters and it is not probable that he ever led slaves there, in view of the younger Mayhew's statement and of Villard's records of Brown's movements.

There was, then, a cave near the log cabin in the years between the Osawatomie event in the spring of 1856 and Brown's last visit to Nebraska in February, 1859, the year of his Harper's Ferry disaster. That he was ever in the cabin more than casually, if that, or that Negroes were hidden in the cave in his lifetime has not been established.

---

[21] Omaha *World-Herald*, October 22, 1927.

A puzzling testimony at variance with that of E. F. Mayhew is that of John H. Blue, editor of a Nebraska City newspaper, the *Chronicle*. Blue wrote on October 27, 1874, that is, fifteen years after Brown's death:

> The Nebraska City cave was dug after the battle of Osawatomie, in which John Brown lost a son, and he reverted to more secretive methods of removing slaves from the south. Bands of renegades were organized at strategic points and friends of Brown in Nebraska City organized a "Vegetarian Society" under which guise they drew in the more fanatical abolitionists. The Vegetarian Society members lived up to the name of their organization, so to speak, by declaring that the cave was dug in which to store fruits and vegetables for winter use. The cave, however, never harbored food until long after the Civil War and people other than the slave runners moved on the land.

This seems inaccurate since the cave was dug in Allen Mayhew's day and, if the Vegetarian Society used it, it must have been after the Mayhews had moved and after Brown's death in 1859. Doubtless, however, the Underground was still operating after Brown and J. H. Kagi died.

Mrs. Lena Linhoff who lived in the cabin in 1886 said that on the door casing in the basement leading to the cave were written not fewer than fifteen names of Negroes. This is hardly of help in determining whether, if ever, Negroes were in the cave while John Brown was alive. And one wonders how she determined certainly, so many years after the Civil War, that the names were those of Negroes.[22]

Finally, here is contemporary lore of the cave as familiar to Robert Brust, a student from Nebraska City attending the University of Nebraska in 1948:

> Perhaps the most interesting legend centers around an old log cabin which is built over an underground tunnel. The cabin and cave are called Tom Brown's [*sic*] Cave. During the Civil War the cave was used as a part of an Underground Railroad system which smuggled slaves to Canada and freedom.
> Many people that have visited the cave have sworn that they

---

[22] Bartling, *op. cit.*, p. 8.

have heard the joyous singing of the slaves. The singing is caused by the wind blowing through the crevices of the tunnel and it caused a low moaning sound which gives the effects of Negro singing.

Whatever is or is not the "historicity" of the John Brown Cabin and Cave, it is clear that considerable folklore has sprung up about them. The cabin was owned by Edward D. Bartling, recently deceased, from the 1880's till 1948. In his pamphlet history of it, *John Henry Kagi and the Old Log Cabin Home* (1938, 1940, 1943), he gives many facts but there are many omissions and he is vague concerning essentials. The cabin may fairly be called John Brown's Cabin in these days, I suppose, for it is now a small John Brown Museum; but John Brown never lived in it nor controlled it, may never have visited it, and it seems unlikely that slaves were ever in it during his lifetime. If they were it could have been but once, that in the expedition of the year of Harper's Ferry, 1859, provided the Mayhews had left it by that time. Even if the Mayhews were no longer occupants as early as 1857, Brown had no fugitive slaves with him to house there in his Nebraska visit of that year. It seems certain that no reliance may be placed on statements such as that in the Federal *Guide to Nebraska* ("Here John Brown of Ossawatomie had runaway slaves . . . . A score of fugitive slaves at a time were secreted in the dungeon rooms,") or that in Bartling's pamphlet ("During the troublesome days following the Missouri Compromise John Brown and his followers aided hundreds of slaves to escape from Missouri,") or that of N. C. Abbott in his sympathetic and well written newspaper article ("There is no doubt that John Brown brought hundreds of slaves to Nebraska on their way north").

Caves of the Niobrara Region

The upper Niobrara River of northeast Nebraska, called *L'Eau Qui Court,* "Running Water," by early French explorers and traders, flows onward through the sandhill region beyond Valentine in Cherry County till it reaches the Missouri in Knox County on the border of South Dakota. Mari Sandoz, native and laureate of the sandhill country, has supplied lore of several caves of the so-called Nebraska Panhandle and eastward. The caves of the region are usually of sandstone with strong limestone characteristics and soft formations beneath. Buffalo Springs Cave and Fly Speck Billy's Cave, for instance, are in sandstone.

Buffalo Springs Cave

Miss Sandoz has given me the following account of this cave. She recalls mention of it, she says, somewhere in anthropological literature of the Sioux, but we are unable to identify the place.

"Old timers used to tell of seeing buffalo herds hit the dry bed of the Platte in late summer looking for water. Finding no water but smelling it underground, the great herds milled around on the sandbars until it welled up around their hoofs. These buffalo springs, as they were called there, were common and temporary, but Deer Creek which flows north of the sandhills into the Niobrara river, starts in a cave that the Indians say was made by the buffalo. It seems that in the Great Dry Time, long before the White Man came, there had been no rain for so many moons that the people were dying of thirst and hunger, the rivers just dusty gullies and the thirsty buffalo gaunt as the empty parfleches in the tipis. When it seemed as if everything but the buzzards must die, an old buffalo cow threw up her head as though she smelled something, and led off into sandhills, the weak herds struggling after as fast as they could; the Indians too. At a sandy spot against a big hill, the cow stopped and the herds milled around her, bellowing and pawing, until suddenly water came up around their hoofs. By the next morning the buffalo spring had washed back under the hill, making a cave, the water boiling up strong and clear and cold and flowing away in a creek that found its way to the dry bed of the river, the first water there for months.

"After that other springs appeared and soon it was raining again, the Dry Time almost forgotten. But the Indian youths went over to that hill for their puberty fastings that were to bring them the guiding vision if they lay long enough on the blown-out top in sun and darkness. Afterward they came down and drank the water from the cave and made their sweat lodge

with the scrub willows that had sprung up. The Indians brought
their sick and injured here too, for the medicine water from
the cave. My father used to tell us of hunting deer with one
of his old Oglala Sioux friends who wouldn't let him shoot
any deer they found drinking at the little stream where it left
the cave or resting in the buck brush near by. Not even if they
were short of meat.

"There is a story that when Conquering Bear was shot in the
Grattan fight down on the Platte river in 1854, the Indians
tried to get him to Buffalo Springs Cave, certain that he would
not die if he could be bathed in the river. They reached the
Niobrara and moved down it as fast as their gravely wounded
chief could endure, but when they were within a day's travois
travel, the old man could go no farther."

Road Agent's or Fly Speck Billy's Cave

According to Mari Sandoz pretty much the whole Panhandle
country of Northwest Nebraska has been searched over and
dug into for hidden gold stolen from Black Hills stages back in
the '70's and '80's by road agents, or, as easterners would call
them, highwaymen. "Usually," she says, "the amount named
for the buried caches is $300,000, and sometimes the thieves
were said to have been three men, perhaps including a not very
heroic robber called Fly Speck Billy. They were said to have
hidden out in a cave in the Niobrara bluffs and to have fallen
to quarreling among themselves over the division of the gold.
Sometimes one or two, or even all three of the men died, it was
said, from the shooting resulting from the quarrel. In any case
the gold was always assumed to be buried a short distance from
the cave, either before the fight or afterward by the surviving.
The marker by which the place could be recognized later was a
line of three small pine trees standing like horsebackers along
the top of the bluff above. There were three such trees not far
from the place Old Jules homesteaded in 1884. By then there
had been regular invasions of treasure hunters. After two of
the three trees had been cut down, perhaps by some settler
needing the poles, the substantial stumps and the remaining
tree seemed to serve very well as a lure for the shovel men.

"There was a cave too within half a mile of our place and this was supposedly the place of the quarrel. Mostly the digging was between the cave and the trees, not on our land. But my father used to go up to watch a while, with his Winchester along, of course, since he never left the house without it. Usually the men reached nervously for their revolvers when he suddenly appeared beside them. He used to tell of these encounters and laugh so hard he choked. 'Hell, go ahead. People have been digging here ever since I came to the country,' he usually told them. But not once did any of them take him up on his invitation to come down to the house for supper.

"The diggings usually blew in before many months, or, if they were deep enough to endanger stock, somebody would go up and throw enough dirt into them to make them safe. But the cave was cool and moist and a fine place for the boys of the region to explore, and for picnickers to go to or to flee to in a shower. Often at night there were lights there; matches struck, or even a fire started that was shielded inside but somehow reflected a little into the dark. The more superstitious and fanciful saw ghosts around there late at night, from the road of course. The dead men haunting their booty, it was said. Several times men talked of utilizing them in the search for the $300,000, but it didn't work out. Several times, too, fleeing bad men were said to be hiding there, and the local joke for a time was to elect the most timid man of the community constable and then tell him to go arrest the hideouters in Billy's cave. For a while a local chicken thief used the cave to hide his loot, and for several years afterward the cave stank in bad weather and was full of chicken feathers. As late as 1942 I received letters from people still hopeful about Fly Speck Billy's Cave as the key to the lost gold. I often wondered how anyone could be certain that, if the treasure ever was there, it hadn't been dug up and carried away, say, by the two men who came poling a raft down the river, with maps and compass, a big bull dog, and two 30-30 rifles.

"The last time I saw the cave was in 1931. It had fallen in, making a washed gulley, but there were some rather recent diggings around it, with a lot of wind-exposed potsherds scattered over the turned-up earth; evidence of a much earlier occupancy than Fly-Speck Billy's or anybody else's with $300,000 of Black Hills gold."

There are stories of the cave where the body of Crazy Horse, the Sioux chief, was said to have been hidden for about a month after he was killed at Fort Robinson in September, 1877. Memory of the site of this cave, if there was one, has been lost. In the Crawford and Crow Butte regions in Sioux County are several caves said to be Indian hideouts. Doc Middleton's cave, supposedly his secret headquarters, is in the Niobrara River canyons north of O'Neill. Doc (David C.) Middleton was a cattle rustler, gambler, ex-convict, and performer in Buffalo Bill's Wild West Show. He died in a county jail in Wyoming where he was confined for bootlegging. And of course there is a Jesse James cave farther east in Knox County, beyond the mouth of the Niobrara, where he is said to have concealed himself when he lived there with Indians. This is probably to be associated with Devil's Nest near Crofton. This region of rough meadow and woodland was described in the journal of Lewis and Clark who camped here in 1804. Calvin Ravenscroft of Kennedy in Cherry County reports that on the Snake River where it flows into the Niobrara is a cave, now cemented over to some extent, in which was said to live a man who thought he had discovered perpetual motion. He shut himself in the cave to try to perfect his machine.

Other Caves

Big Bear Hollow

East of Winnebago and near the northern end of Memorial Park in Thurston County is a wooded indentation of special interest discussed in 1934 by Ora Russell of Decatur.[23] It is surrounded by hills and sheer cliffs of white Dakota sandstone. According to a fairly well-known legend, in a cave in one of these hills lived Big Bear, a mysterious creature half man and

---

[23] Lincoln *Journal and Star*, December 9, 1934.

half bear, given to descending on Indian villages and carrying away women folk through magic power. Big Bear was protected by other black bears invested with magic against which the arrows of the Indians were futile. Once he stole an Indian girl who was on her honeymoon with her husband. The latter trained two young bears as ferocious fighters. Against these, Big Bear's protectors lost their magic. Big Bear himself was killed by the Indian and Indians again hunted in the hollow.

Barada Cave and Robbers' Cave

Barada Cave not far from Falls City is a hollowed-out place under a limestone cliff, made by the action of water. Tradition has it that this cave sheltered horse-thieves. Its name comes from the small town of Barada which was named from an early settler, Antoine Barada (1807-1887), about whom legends and tall tales of his great strength have grown up. Robbers' Cave is on this side of Holy Fireplace Point near the Winnebago Indian agency in Thurston County. It is now only a small recess in the bluff overlooking the Missouri River. The Federal *Guide to Nebraska* describes it as once the hideout of river bandits: "When an unsuspecting trapper was seen floating his season's catch down the river, the bandits would assail him and take his furs. At one time the opening of the cave formed a right angle and it was necessary to crawl on hands and knees to enter it. Now erosion and the destructive work of vandals have changed it. The James brothers are said to have evaded capture on one occasion by hiding in this cave after attempting to rob a bank in Northfield, Minnesota." [24]

Dripping Fork Cave

Dripping Fork Cave, on the Platte, mentioned in John D. Hunter's *Manners and Customs of Several Indian Tribes West of the Mississippi* (Philadelphia, 1823), may not have been in Nebraska. No records or traces of it are now to be found. Despite its picturesque name, Hunter's reference to it is the only one that remains.

---

[24] Federal Writers' Project, *op. cit.*, p. 263.

Ponca Cave

The so-called Ponca Cave, the creation of two imaginative newspaper men, has been given considerable space in the Nebraska press. There were a few columns about it in the Lincoln Sunday *Star* of July 5, 1925, under the heading "Ponca Residents Recall Discovery of Cave of Prehistoric Beasts and Plants." The authors were Harry I. Peterson and William Huse, the latter the historian of Dixon County of which Ponca is the county seat. Their tall tale was repeated in the Lincoln *Sunday Journal and Star*, March 28, 1948, twenty-three years later.

Ponca is in northeast Nebraska, near where the Missouri River rounds the corner bordering South Dakota and Iowa. About 1915 fossil remains such as shark teeth and turtle shells were uncovered there, and a large fossil fish, now in a Chicago museum, was blasted from the bluffs along the river. Local legends and tales seem to have started up after this event; Messrs Huse and Peterson's tale is the tallest. They associated their story with no specific site at Ponca but claimed that it had been lost. Their yarn tells of vast caverns, prehistoric skeletons, and gigantic fossilized animals beneath the northern part of Dixon County. It narrates the marvelous subterranean travels of "Professor Jermiah Perrigoue, who liked geology and liked to dig along the bluffs for fossils, minerals, and petrifications."

In 1876, Perrigoue found a great hole or an abandoned mine shaft 85 feet deep. He went through a fissure in the rock about 150 yards, then turned sharply to the left. Below him he saw to his amazement a gigantic cavern, a room supported by enormous trees reaching to 300 feet, their leaves turned into a canopy of stone. In this ancient forest he found petrified worms, a gigantic bird, terrible reptiles, a pterodactyl, dinotherium, megatherium, plesiosaur, ichthyosaurus, and paleotherium. Some of these creatures seemed to have been engaged in a death struggle before their demise. Other features of the great cavern were a subterranean river and a waterfall. Perrigoue penetrated more than two miles from the entrance and spent more than two days before retracing his steps. Finally, "Near the entrance where he had enlarged the fissure he encountered the dread fire-damp, and to his utter horror he saw the gauze of his miner's lamp had taken fire and was shooting up flames. In desperation he tried to extinguish them and finding it impossible he hurled the lamp far from him and scrambled up the shaft. He had barely reached the upper world before a terrible explosion heaved the ground, the shaft disappeared and this extraordinary sarcophagus was eternally sealed."

Shelter Caves

Shelter caves, the once-inhabited homes of subterranean earth-lodge dwellers, have been found in many parts of the country, in the Ozarks, for instance, and in West Texas. Dr. Earl H. Bell, formerly anthropologist at the University of Nebraska, discovered a number of these in the 1930's in Cheyenne and Morrill counties, and there are shelter caves along the Platte and the Republican rivers also. These have been little individualized, have had little prominence, and little lore has arisen about them. They have not been taken into account in this paper, a paper intended to emphasize folklore rather than archaeology, geology, or tribal history.

This ends my present list of Nebraska caves and my account of the lore associated with them. It is not intended to be exhaustive even if my space permitted it. No doubt there are many other minor caves in Nebraska around which stories or yarns or legends have clustered that deserve chronicling by county historians. I have tried to include all those that are best known.

Cave lore seems to me a timely subject just now, when we are reminded daily that we live in the atomic age and may all eventually have to take shelter underground and become cave dwellers.[25]

Read in part before the Western Folklore Conference at the University of Denver, July 15, 1948. Reprinted from *Nebraska History*, XXIX (December, 1948), 299-323.

---

[25] A National Speleological Society was established in 1939, to stimulate interest in caves and to record the findings of explorers and scientists within and without the Society. Properly enough it subordinates folklore to adventure, discovery, and scientific findings. Its tenth Bulletin, 1948, initiates in its 136 pages the treatment of the caves of a single state, Texas, a state peculiarly rich in caves of special interest and importance which has had less attention hitherto than it deserves.

Nebraska Snake Lore

Snakes are peculiarly uncanny writhing creatures. No wonder that fantastic superstitions and tales cluster about them. They have always played a conspicuous role in various types of lore, magical, medicinal, pseudo-scientific, even Scriptural, and among advanced as well as savage peoples. The fateful serpent of the Garden of Eden was no unique figure. Older literature, oral and written, has told of human beings transformed into snakes, or having snake habits, or of snakes taking on human characteristics. The use of the viper in medicinal practice was mentioned in Pliny's natural history of the first century A.D. It is surprising how many curious beliefs concerning snakes, some recalling mediaeval science or the aboriginal practices of the jungle, yet abound over the United States. A display of these as they persist into our twentieth century has a certain interest, an interest that is anthropological or sociological as well as reptilian, even though made for one state only. Nebraska lore is not so abundant, certainly not so barbaric, as that found among uneducated whites and Negroes in southern states. But more widespread bits of snake lore are to be found within its limits than would be guessed by those who have never canvassed for it.

My collectanea come directly from Nebraskans, mainly of course from dwellers in less settled regions and smaller towns. They are mostly personally contributed. Snakes are infrequent in cities and fewer superstitions regarding them are handed on by city dwellers. The entries in the following pages have been supplied by both lettered and less lettered contributors. They are reproduced verbatim, or, as nearly as may be, in the words of the informants. They are as complete as I could make them but can hardly be exhaustive. The folklore field, as is well known, is an ever-shifting one, with variants springing up constantly and new matter entering.

The population of Nebraska is mixed, though basically from the British Isles. Pioneers came to the Middle West from many states, bringing with them traditional matter from their old homes. They were joined by immigrants from Old World peoples such as the Scandinavian, German, Dutch, Bohemian. Relevant evidence may sometimes be recorded but it would be futile to attempt to track the origins and wanderings of the mass of superstitions, beliefs, and sayings yet existent in the state.

As regards the attitudes toward their lore of Nebraska informants, more of it is accepted than one might think; much of it is handed on with complete faith in it. A surprising number of the strange cures reported are in actual use in certain regions or in certain families. But a majority of the superstitions or sayings are repeated by skeptics who hand them on but look upon them as mirth-provoking and preposterous.

My concern has been to present traditional Nebraska snake lore and that only. Manufactured "tall tales" about snakes, yarns by humorists or journalists, or evolved in competitive narration I have not tried to collect, though no doubt many of these exist. Nor have I tried to include the lore of foreign groups in Nebraska, such as Mexican, German, Swedish, Dutch, preserved by them in, or translated from, their native languages. And I have not tried to include Negro lore. It has its special interest and is often far more colorful than that of the white population. But other states have far larger Negro populations than Nebraska and would afford better hunting ground. Nebraska Indian lore, too, is a separate subject and deserves separate attention.

Special acknowledgment of indebtedness should go to my colleague, Dr. Ruth Odell, to Pauline Black Holtrop and Louise Snapp when graduate students, to Margaret Cannell of the

Agricultural College staff, to successive generations of under-graduate students attending the University of Nebraska, and to many pioneer residents of the state and their descendants. I am also indebted to Richard B. Loomis of Lincoln, who is well versed in snake life and snake ways and who supplied many factual details.

Snakes and Cures

The most striking section of Nebraska snake lore has to do with the curative powers associated with snakes, notably the rattlesnake. It was with this snake, naturally enough, that the prairie pioneer was most concerned. For this he most needed remedies, and he found them in what was most available, such as poultices of animal grease or lard or of prairie plants. The medical use of snakes now surviving, it is to be hoped, for civilized countries only in folklore, can be traced as far back as the elder Pliny and the Greek physician Pedacius Dioscorides in Europe and the founders of Chinese medicine in Asia. The old and widely established prescription of remedies having a revolting smell or taste or revolting associations, this lasting even into modern times, is supposed to have had its origin in the effort to get together nauseous messes that would drive from the soul of primitive man a devil that had slipped in, perhaps when his mouth was open when he slept. Hence were handed down such curatives as angleworm oil, tincture of frog, grease of a black dog, hog's hoof tea, asafoetida, tar, bitters, and the use of the toad and of the viper. That belief in the medical value of the viper persisted in common credence is shown by statements such as the following from an advertisement in Addison and Steele's *The Spectator* of eighteenth-century England:

> Whereas the Viper has been a medicine approv'd by Physicians of all nations; there is now prepar'd the Volatil Compound of it, a preparation altogether new . . . the most Sovereign **Remedy** against all **Faintings, Swoonings, Lowness of Spirits, Vapours,** etc.

The Volatil Compound of Viper was used no doubt by ladies

and gentlemen in the days of Pope and Swift. In the Middle West the viper has been replaced by the rattlesnake as a curative agent.

Remarkable as are some of the Nebraska cures supposed to be efficacious, there are of course many that are just as remarkable, or yet more so, in other states or in the Old World, from which most of our lore except for the prairie cures is a legacy.

Curative Powers

Application of a snakeskin will cure a headache.

A snakeskin is good for rheumatism.

Put a piece of snakeskin in your pocket to cure rheumatism.

A snakeskin around the head will cure fever.

Rattlesnake rattles will cure a headache if held against the head.

Carry rattlesnake rattles in your hatband to cure headache.

Wear the rattles of a rattlesnake in your hat to cure rheumatism.

Let the baby chew rattlesnake rattles to help his teeth through.

Put a rattlesnake rattle in a tobacco bag and hang the bag around a child's neck during teething.

When a baby is fretful while teething, string three large rattles of a rattlesnake on a red cord and put it around the child's neck. Do not remove the rattles until the child is through teething.

A snake head bound on a bruise will effect a cure.

The bite of a rattlesnake will cure tuberculosis.

The warm intestines of a rattlesnake are especially curative for pneumonia.

Wrap a snake around the neck and allow it to creep off and a goiter will disappear.

Snake oil, like the eighteenth-century Volatil Compound of Viper, served or serves as a cure-all. Itinerant medicine peddlers appeared in Omaha and elsewhere as late as the 1930's selling snake oil, supposedly from Indian formulas; "Indian Snake Oil will cure everything but is especially good for rheumatism and rejuvenation."

Cures for Snake Bites

You must kill the snake if its bite is to be healed.

To cure a snake bite cut the snake to bits and bind it on the wound.

To cure a snake bite cut the snake in half and bind it on the wound.

Kill the snake, cut it, and apply the pieces on the wound.[1]

If a snake bites you, kill the snake and cut it into pieces and you will not be poisoned.

For a rattlesnake bite, in an emergency, beat cockleburrs to a pulp and apply a poultice.

Cut the outside prickles off the cactus found in the Sandhills and mash the inside of the plant and apply it to the bite as a poultice. Keep it moist with water and change it as often as it becomes warm.

Mash the roots of the milkweed and apply to a rattlesnake bite. Also give the bitten person the milk internally.

Make a poultice of tansy boiled in milk.

Apply fresh cow manure to a snake bite.

A snakeskin will draw the poison from a rattlesnake bite.

Apply hog lard to the wound. Heat the lard and have the patient drink all he can.

Apply a mixture of turpentine and gunpowder to a rattlesnake bite to cure it.

Soak the bite in coal oil for a long time.

Pack mud on a rattlesnake bite to cure it.

Bury the part of the body bitten by the snake in the ground and soak the earth with sweet milk.

Whiskey taken internally is a popular snakebite remedy: "Drink all the whiskey you can, the more the better."

---

[1] Pauline Black Holtrop, "Nebraska Folk Cures," University of Nebraska *Studies in Language, Literature and Criticism,* No. 15, 1935, p. 32, testifies that "A man from Thomas County who was bitten by a rattlesnake immediately cut off the snake's head and then split open its body, cutting it into three-inch pieces. These he applied at once to the wound, discarding each piece as it became saturated with the poison. The snake was not used because of any charm that the man associated with it but as a poultice in an emergency."

Tobacco juice will cure a snake bite. Tobacco served on the whole as the most popular poultice for a snake bite.[2]

Puncture the skin around the bite with the sharp points of the soapweed to let the poison run out.

Keep jabbing the swollen places with a sharp knife until the black blood and water come out. This will be the poison.

Scarify the flesh as deeply as the fangs went and make at least two incisions. Then apply table salt.

Apply the warm flesh of an animal, especially the intestines, to draw out the poison.

Split a live chicken and place on the snake bite to draw out the poison.

If there are any chickens available, cut one open either after it has been killed or while it is still alive, and put it over the snake bite. Before long the chicken will be all green from the poison which it has drawn out. It takes nearly a dozen chickens to draw all the poison from the wound.

Kill an animal, preferably a cow, and slit a hole in the abdomen. Bury the bitten area in the middle of the animal. Leave it there until the carcass becomes cold and then remove. The poison from the bite will be drawn out.

When a horse is bitten by a rattler take a sharp knife and scarify the wound until it bleeds freely. Cut the tips from five or six blades of soapweed, stick them all around the wound and leave them for 24 hours.

Drench a bitten animal with warm lard out of a bottle to cure a snake bite.

The familiar advice "When bitten by a snake suck the wound and spit out the blood and saliva" is the soundest of the folk cures reported and that reported most frequently. It is recommended in the manual for Boy Scouts.[3]

---

2 Mrs. Holtrop also reported that the late Captain Lute North of Columbus, Nebraska, a resident of the state since 1856 and a well-known personage in his region, told of a man he once saw cured of a rattlesnake bite by the application of tobacco. Another man chewed quantities of it and kept the hand well-poulticed. The man who was bitten recovered from the bite but the man who chewed tobacco for the poultice became very ill.

3 Madge E. Pickard and R. Carlyle Buley, *The Midwest Pioneer, His Ills, Cures, and Doctors* (Crawfordsville, Indiana, 1945), note no instances of the

Weather Signs

Some persons seem to think that snakes may serve as rain-making charms, or may contribute to the control of rain. Sometimes those who pass farms observe dead snakes hung on bushes, fences, or barns, apparently as rain-making agents.

When a snake is killed and hung up it will rain. The higher the snake is hung the harder it will rain.

If you hang a snake on the fence it will bring rain.

If you hang a snake on the fence it will rain until it is taken off.

If a snake is hung on a fence on its back it is a sign of rain.

It is a sign of fair weather the next day if a snake lies on its back.

If a snake lies on its back it is a sign of rain.

It is a sign of clear weather if a snake lies on its back in its death throes.

If a snake leaves the water for higher ground it will rain.

If snakes or toads are around dwellings it is a sign of stormy weather.

If frogs or snakes come about the house it will rain the next day.

If snakes cross the road in unusual numbers it will rain.

Snakes crossing your path mean a long drought. Snakes migrate to wet regions.

If when tossed up a snake alights on its back, it will rain. If it does not alight on its back do not expect rain.

Snakes waken when they hear thunder.

Warm spring weather is sometimes referred to as "snake time."

Luck

Good Luck

It is good luck to kill the first snake you see in the spring.

It is good luck not to kill the first snake you see in the spring.

---

use of snakes as curatives but say of snake bites (p. 42): "Snake bites offered a wide choice of remedies, from white plantain boiled in milk, ash bark tea, alum water, or whiskey internally applied, to incisions and applications of salt and gunpowder, black ash leaves, crushed garlic juice, or salt and tobacco."

Bull snakes in the yard bring good luck.

Keep a bull snake in the yard for good luck. Bull snakes are never to be killed.

Kill a snake when you see one and you will have good luck.

The rattles of a rattlesnake will bring good luck.

If you kill a rattlesnake keep the rattles for good luck.

Rattles carried around the neck bring good luck.

Rattles carried anywhere bring good luck.

Bad Luck

Expect to have bad luck if a snake crosses your path.

It is very bad luck if a rattlesnake crosses your path.

It means bad luck if you kill a snake.

You will have bad luck if you do not kill the first snake you see in the spring.

"Bull snakes climbing trees mean bad luck."

Dreams

If you dream of a snake it is a sign that a friend is betraying you.

Dream that a snake bites you and you will hear of the death of a friend.

Snakes in dreams signify enemies.

To dream of a snake you do not kill means that you have an active enemy. If in your dream you kill the snake you will become friends with your enemy.

If in your dream you kill the snake that has bitten you, you will conquer your enemy. If the snake gets away you will be conquered.

Dream that a snake bites you and you will have trouble with a friend.

If you dream of a snake you will hear of the death of a friend.

If you dream of snakes you will get money the next day.

If you tell the snake dream, you will quarrel with the person to whom you told it.

Report a dream about a snake and you will quarrel with some one.

Preventives

A snake will not cross over a rope, especially a horsehair rope.

Make a horsehair circle or ring to keep snakes away for they will not cross it.

Campers in a rattlesnake country coil a horsehair rope about them at night to keep snakes away. This practice is said to be still relied on occasionally. "A rattlesnake has been known, however, to squirt his poison over the rope upon the sleeper." (Horsehair rope around a person is not reliable protection. If a snake is placed inside a coil of rope it promptly crawls over it. But, to some extent, snakes do avoid crawling over objects, or crawling uphill.)

Keep hogs on a farm to drive away snakes. Hogs will kill rattlesnakes.

If you live in the rattlesnake region, keep hogs on the farm, as the hogs will smell out the rattlesnakes and kill them. "This is believed by many farmers." (Hogs and others animals, as deer, do kill a great number of snakes.)

Kill and cut to pieces a snake that bites you and you will not be poisoned.

Carry a rattlesnake's rattle in your pocket and it will prevent smallpox.

If you do not kill the first snake of the season your enemies will torment you.

Snakes and Animals, Birds, Insects, Plants

Hogs will kill snakes. Thus they keep snakes away from farm buildings. (See under Preventives.)

If there are hogs on the farm all the rattlesnakes will leave, as the hogs can smell out the rattlesnakes and kill them. "This is believed by many farmers."

A cat will warn you that a snake is around, for it will sit unmoved and watch a snake until some one comes to kill it.

A dog bitten by a rattlesnake will crawl into a mud hole and stay there for a time to draw out the poison.

If a cow goes dry it is because a "milk snake" has sucked it. One contributor testified that "a milk snake was seen sucking a cow, in Pennsylvania, while the cow was in its stall. This, I believe, is not a superstition." ("Milk snakes" are of no great height, have small teeth that no cow would tolerate, do not carry milk stools, and have never been known to drink milk.)

Snakes and prairie dogs are amicable companions.

A snake and a prairie dog will lie down together amicably in the same burrow.

Snakes and prairie dogs and owls are supposed to live amicably together in their holes in clay banks. (Snakes inhabit prairie dog burrows but not in amicable companionship. Sometimes they do so to eat the young of a prairie dog, or baby owls. Sometimes also for hibernation.)

"Snake doctors" or "snake feeders," i.e., dragonflies, warn snakes of danger.

So long as the head of the snake remains, a "snake doctor" can renew a dead snake's vitality.

There are always snakes close to "snake flowers." "These are wild iris," a contributor suggested; but other plants go by the name, as viper's bugloss, white dead-nettle, stichwort, starflower, white campion.

Snake Death

If you kill a snake it will not die until sundown.

If you kill a snake it will not die until sunrise.

If you kill a snake it will move (wiggle, wriggle) its tail until sundown. One contributor commented that he found by testing it that this is not true. Another reported that "It is true that if you cut a snake's tail off close to the head, it will be a long time before the body becomes motionless." (It retains motion and activity for some time, if stimulated.)

A snake cut in pieces will come together again.

If you cut a snake in two pieces the two pieces will get together and crawl away.

Cut a snake in two and, no matter where the two parts are, the head will go back, find the tail, and attach itself to the tail.

Some snakes if struck will break into pieces and later join into entirety again. Such snakes are called "glass snakes." (The "glass snake" is actually a lizard. Two-thirds of its length is usually a brittle tail. It can generate a new tail which looks as if it was put on. But it cannot get its old tail back.)

If any vitality yet remains in a snake, the "snake doctor" (dragon-fly) can bring it to life again.

If you kill a rattlesnake and cut it into two parts, young will crawl out, because the mother snake eats her young for their protection. (There is no authentic testimony that a mother snake eats her young, or swallows them for their protection, or that in either case they remain alive.)

Poisonous snakes follow the trail of their killed mates, perhaps to avenge them.

A bull snake will kill a rattlesnake but will die itself of the poison.

A rattlesnake will bite itself and die if surrounded by cactus thorns by a road runner. (A variety of bird noted for running at great speed. Road runners sometimes hang up on cactus snakes and lizards they kill. Road runners are not found in Nebraska.)

Habits and Characteristics

Some snakes have stingers at the end of their tails. They sting instead of bite.

A rattlesnake will strike twice its length.

A snake eats but once a month. (Snakes eat about every week, or whenever their last meal is digested.)

Poisonous snakes are born alive. "Other snakes are hatched from eggs." (Poisonous snakes are born alive, except the coral snake from the Southeast United States.)

The shape of a snake's head is supposed to determine whether or not it is poisonous.

The number of its rattles is an indication of the years of age of a rattlesnake. (The number is an indication of the snake's sheddings, which is from one to four times a year. When a rattler sheds, it gets a new segment or rattle on its tail.)

A rattlesnake does not poison itself when it strikes itself. (It poisons other rattlers but not itself.)

Snakes will not bite when they are in the water. (They will bite but not strike.)

Once a snake strikes, its fangs drop out and it cannot bite until they grow in again. (Partly true. Snakes have a series of new teeth in different stages of development beside each tooth. When a tooth is lost, one of the successional series takes its place. They shed their fangs when they shed their skin, and at fairly regular intervals.)

Rattlesnakes lay eggs. (True for most species of snakes.)

A rattlesnake will never strike a small child. "Dad, when a small child, played with one." [4]

A rattlesnake will not strike a person from the rear. "To go fishing once we had to cross a prairie dog town which, as are all such towns, was infested with rattlesnakes and owls. To protect ourselves we tied a half of stovepipe on the front of our legs and walked safely through, relying on the saying that the snake would not strike after we had passed."

A hoop snake will swallow its tail and roll down hill.

If when rolling down hill a hoopsnake releases its tail and strikes its stinger into a tree, the tree will die.

If the hoop snake while rolling down a hill rolls into any living thing, the thing will die.

"Whoopsnakes (sic) are so poisonous that a tree will die if they bite it."

Some snakes are supposed to be able to enter a hen house and suck eggs.

---

4 Compare, Pickard and Buley, *The Midwest Pioneer*, etc., p. 78: "About the only thing the child did not have to worry about was snake bite, for that just naturally could not happen to him until he was seven years old. Then, when bitten, if he did not approve of good liquor or gunpowder, he could draw on a toad to draw out the poison. If the toad died another was tied on. When the toad lived all the poison was out. Carrying an onion in the pocket provided insurance against snake bite, but if one were bitten, it was necessary for him to eat the heart of the offending reptile if he would gain further immunity. Spitting into the mouth of the snake would kill it and prevent serious harm, or the curse of Adam ('God created everything and it was good; save thou alone, snake, are cursed; cursed shalt thou be and thy poison') might be put upon it, and then it would sneak away and die of shame."

Snakes go blind during dog-days. (Now usually counted from July 3 to July 11.)

Snakes go blind in the late part of summer.

Rattlesnakes do not bite and poison people during the months of fall. They are supposed to bite only during the spring, when they shed their skin and are blind. (Rattlesnakes do go blind when they shed their skin, which is when it becomes too tight for the growing body beneath. This is usually from four to six times a year, depending on the food supply. It may be in spring, summer, or fall.)

A side winder will kill any living thing it touches.

A blue racer will chase you if you run from it but will flee if you turn on it.

Blue racers will chase you. If you cut them into pieces they will join together again. (Blue racers will follow, not chase a person. The popular explanation is that they do so from "curiosity.")

Snakes have hypnotic powers. They are able to hypnotize small game, as birds, rabbits, frogs. Some believe that they can hypnotize human beings. "I have been hypnotized by a large bull snake in the field," one contributor testified. Perhaps this belief is to be explained by the fact that the victims are overcome by fear. W. G. Simms, *The Yemassee*, 1835, describes in vivid detail, Chapter XX, the hypnotizing of his heroine, Bess Matthews, by a rattlesnake.)

When frightened, some species of snake swallow their young to protect them. (This may be partly true, but the later release of them and the "protection" are legendary.) [5]

---

[5] John J. Strecker ("Reptile Myths in Northwestern Louisiana," *Publications of the Texas Folk-Lore Society* IV, 1925, 42-52, also "Reptiles of the South and Southwest in Folk-Lore," V, 1926, 66, and his "Dragons and Other Reptiles Real and Imaginary," *Baylor University Contributions to Folk-Lore,* No. 3, 1929, 66) lists leading snake myths, mostly from Negro sources. He includes the myth of the coach or whip snake which whips its victims with its tail, the joint snake which breaks into pieces when struck, the hoop snake which rolls, the stinging snake, the milk snake, the thunder snake (with legs) and others. He raises the question whether snakes ever really swallow their young and seems to hold that this is another snake myth and catalogues it as such.

Sayings

Animal reference always looms large in proverbial lore, especially as a source of comparison applicable to human beings. Domesticated animals play a prominent part, such as the pig, hog, mule, ox, lamb, hare, horse. So do birds, insects, and the snake. Snake similes, used for disparagement, have a conspicuous place.[6]

> As cold as a snake.
> As crooked as a snake.
> As deadly as a cobra.
> As poisonous as a snake.
> As treacherous as a snake.
> Like a snake in the grass.
> Hiss like a snake.
> Lower than a snake's belly.
> Madder than snakes in haying.
> Nourish a viper in the bosom.
> If it was a snake it would have bit you.
> Sew on Friday and you'll get snakes in the house.

Miscellaneous

Pull out a human hair, place it in a glass of water, and it will turn into a snake within two weeks.

Pull out a horse hair and place it in a rain water barrel and in two weeks it will turn into a snake. (I have heard many persons affirm this with unshaken conviction. Perhaps the belief has its basis in some chemical action of the hair during the two weeks of its immersion. There is a so-called "hair snake," but it is really a worm. It frequently appears in water or near water plants but it does not come from human hair or horse hair.)

If you suck the poison from a wound from a snake bite, your teeth will fall out. (Those who have bleeding gums when they suck poison from a wound are definitely likely to find their teeth loosening.)

---

[6] See Louise Snapp, Proverbial Lore in Nebraska, University of Nebraska *Studies in Language, Literature, and Criticism*, No. 13, 1933.

Stepping on a dead snake will make sores break out on your fingers.

Stepping on a dead snake will make sores break out on your feet.

A bull snake is believed to kill rattlesnakes.

A bull snake will kill a rattlesnake but will die itself of the poison.

A bull snake will tease a rattler until the rattler strikes at him. The bull snake dodges. The rattler misses him and on the return will hit and poison himself. (Mistaken identity may explain this belief. Bull snakes do not kill rattlesnakes but king snakes do kill other snakes. There is some resemblance between king snakes and rattlesnakes.)

Two snakes can each grab the other's tail and swallow it until both snakes disappear.

"Keep the rattles from a rattler in a violin and it will play better. My grandfather had such a violin." (Compare, "The town fiddler practiced there with snake rattles in his violin to make the tone clearer . . . ." *The Last of the Bad Men,* a biography of Tom Horne by Jay Monaghan, 1946, p. 43.)

A few contributions of strange lore imported into Nebraska, coming from groups not taken into account in the preceding pages, are:

"Snakes are the abiding place of devils. You cannot kill them except with some instrument in the form of a cross." (From a German family arriving in Nebraska in the 1920's.)

"A rattlesnake having a poison sac in its mouth must remove it to drink, in order to keep from poisoning itself. If you steal the sac the snake goes wild with anger and dashes itself against the rocks." (Told as fact by a Mexican from San Antonio.)

"To keep Negroes wearing their shoes they are told that snakes will bore a hole in their feet to get in the blood stream and consume the blood, killing the person." (Told by a contributor in Lincoln, Nebraska.)

The searcher for curious beliefs and survivals finds them naturally enough in the greatest numbers in the communities that are farthest behind our contemporary civilization and among the classes having least sophistication. Illiteracy fosters their vitality. The less well-read a person is, the larger the number of superstitions he cherishes, the more barbaric his superstitions, and the greater his credulity. That Nebraska superstitions are on the whole relatively mild may be illustrated by the following from other states:

Snake dust, made by pulverizing a dried snake, put into a person's food will grow to full-sized reptiles within that person. The blood of a blacksnake, taken warm with whiskey, will enable you to do more work than anyone else.
Eat the brains of a snake or rat to bring skill in conjuring.
Take a dried one-eyed toad, a dried lizard, the little finger of a person who committed suicide, the wings of a bat, the eyes of a cat, the liver of an owl, and reduce all to a powder. Then cut up into fine pieces a lock of hair from a dead (natural) child, and mix it with the powder. Make a bag of a piece of sheet that has been used as a shroud, put all the material into it and put it into the pillow of the intended victim when nobody is aware of your action. A few feathers run through the top will expedite matters.[7]

Read at the Fourth Annual Western Folklore Conference at the University of Denver, July 20, 1944. Reprinted from the *Southern Folklore Quarterly*, X (September, 1946), 163-176.

---

[7] This complicated voodoo conjuring charm is from New Orleans. See H. M. Wiltse, *Journal of American Folklore*, XIII (1900), 211. For the preceding bits of lore, see Newbell Niles Puckett, *Folk Beliefs of the Southern Negro* (1926), 222, 322.

Nebraska Rain Lore and
Rain Making

Among weather signs and portents, rain lore plays a conspicuous role. Collectors have often assembled it. Signs of rain may be detected, according to various folk beliefs, in the position of the moon or the sun or the direction of the wind; or rain is forecast on the basis of the behavior of cattle, cats, geese, chickens, cocks, crickets, or ants. Even the leaves of trees and plants may indicate the coming of rain. Lore of this type is current everywhere, modified here and there by local conditions. In Illinois, over 250 items of rain lore have been collected in one county alone.[1] The foretelling of rain by natural manifestations, however, is not to be the subject of this paper, but rather the lore of rain making by artificial means.

When the new and rather peculiar profession of rain making arose in the late 1880's and 1890's, a profession that flourished especially in the Great Plains region, it did so with no little scientific or pseudoscientific experiment behind it. Some of the efforts put forth were genuine endeavors to supplement or to replace the older reliance on prayer by reliance on science. Other efforts were associated with hocus-pocus and attempts to victimize the public.

---

[1] Harry M. Hyatt, *Folk-lore from Adams County, Illinois.* Memoirs of the Alma Egan Hyatt Foundation, New York, 1935.

The Background

Attempts to produce rain by human action began, of course, long before the nineteenth century, among primitive peoples in their incantations, rituals, and sacrifices to deities. Nearly every Indian tribe had the belief that its medicine man could produce rain. One of the fullest accounts available of Indian rain making is that of George Catlin who wrote about the Mandan Indians, a Siouan tribe. His nineteenth letter tells of the "Rain Makers." The rain-making ritual was intricate and the tribal rain maker a dignitary. The mystery apparatus involved the burning of wild sage and other aromatic herbs "that their savoury odors might be sent forth to the Great Spirit." A leading feature was that ten or fifteen young men willing to try to make it rain or accept the alternative of suffering the disgrace of fruitless effort were called upon in turn to spend a day on the top of the medicine lodge while incense was burned below. The youths, with shields on their arms and bows and arrows in their hands, in loud voices invoked the spirits or threatened the clouds. If the first youth did not bring rain he retired in confusion and disgrace, and it was the turn of the next one. Catlin comments that when the Mandans undertook to make it rain they always succeeded, since their ceremonies were continued until the Rain God was responsive and the rain came.[2]

Civilized man, too, in all periods has called on divine powers for relief. Groups are still brought together now and then to pray for rain. A United Press newspaper special for June 13, 1945, from Metter, Georgia, told that the mayor had ordered all stores and offices closed from 11:30 to 1:00 P.M., so that everyone could pray for rain to end a drought that had severely damaged the tobacco and corn crops in the region. On such group occasions the religious-minded take the lead, the skeptical remain a little apart; and sometimes rain comes.

In nineteenth-century America many theories of rain making

---

[2] George Catlin, *Illustrations of the Manners, Customs and Condition of the North American Indians* (London, 1876). See also, for the Mandans, John Frost, *The Indians of North America* (1845), p. 109.

were advanced, and these brought in their wake various attempts to supply the rain which would end the drought and save the crops. Rain makers appeared in the Plains region in the latter half of the century, reaching the Kansas-Nebraska region in the 1890's. Attempts were made over a period of years and in many places before it was conceded that theories of rain making belonged not to the field of science but to that of lore, to which they are now relegated.

In 1870 Edward Powers of Delavan, Wisconsin, a civil engineer, published *War and the Weather, or the Artificial Production of Rain,*[3] the first elaborate treatment of an older idea. Powers' theory may be termed the concussion theory. It was his conviction that rain could be produced by noise or concussion. In his book he tried to demonstrate by means of statistics that great battles are followed by rain. He failed, in 1874, to get Congress to authorize a test of his theory, yet it proved long-lived and influential. It was his assumption that was responsible for most of the bombardment of the skies and the general "foolish fireworks" of the 1890's. In 1945 one still heard, "It always used to rain on the Fourth of July. That was because of the firecrackers and explosives shot off." Even in World War I the incessant rains in Flanders were ascribed to the continuous bombardment. I heard several well-educated persons remark, during the rainy spring of 1945, "Surely the war in Europe must have had something to do with our unusual rainfall." On May 31, 1945, a newspaper special (NANA) from New York City, by Lawrence Perry, stated that Dr. Benjamin Parry, chief of the United States Weather Bureau, had said in reply to a telephoned question: "No, bombing and gunfire have had nothing to do with a May rainfall. . . . If I kept a list of the persons who ask me this question I would use up a lot of energy and stationery, for the fallacy that gunfire causes rain is one of the leading popular misapprehensions." Nebraska is thus not the only state in which this folk belief still lingers.

James P. Espy (1785-1860), whose theory published in his

---

[3] The first edition of Powers' book was printed in Chicago in 1871, but most of the edition and the plates were destroyed in the great fire. The second edition was printed in Delavan in 1890.

Philosophy of Storms in 1841 brought him the title of "The Storm King" and who became meteorologist to the United States War Department in 1842, and to the Navy in 1848, stated that "a very large prairie fire will cause rain." [4] He held this belief with great tenacity and in a special letter of 1845 proposed a plan for the bringing of rain by means of fire. Edward Powers repeated Espy's notion in stating, "It is well known that the burning of woods, long grass, and other combustibles produces rain." [5] This idea, too, has passed into lore. Yet a statement which I heard in my youth, "A very large prairie fire will cause rain," is still current on the Plains. Indian tribes of South America, it has been reported, were accustomed to setting fire to the prairies when they wanted rain.

Major J. W. Powell's *Report on the Lands of the Arid Region,*[6] included an article by G. K. Gilbert which furnished disproof of the theory that the increased rainfall of the decade might be attributed to the laying of railroad tracks and the installation of telegraph lines. "When the railroads and the telegraph wires were first thrown across the Plains they offered hope of increased rainfall. In this theory was involved the idea that rain would be produced through the agency of electricity in the wires and perhaps by the electrical current running through the rails." [7]

In 1880 General Daniel Ruggles of Fredericksburg, Virginia, patented a process for producing rain by firing aerial explosives.[8] Ruggles' invention was illustrated and described in the *Scientific American.*[9] His expectation of generating moisture

---

4 See Mark W. Harrington, "Weather Making Ancient and Modern," *Annual Report of the Smithsonian Institution to July, 1894,* pp. 260-262. It was Espy who laid the foundation of weather forecasting by establishing daily weather observations and compiling weather maps. His *Philosophy of Storms* (Boston, 1841) has a section on "Artificial Rains."

5 *Scientific American,* LXIII (1890), 384-385.

6 John Wesley Powell, *Report on the Lands of the Arid Region* (2nd ed.; Washington, D.C., 1879), pp. 57-80.

7 Walter Prescott Webb, *The Great Plains* (Boston: Ginn & Co., 1931), p. 377.

8 Patent No. 230067, July 13, 1880.

9 *Scientific American,* XLIII (November 27, 1880), 106, 302.

by great explosions from balloons was probably an outgrowth of Powers' concussion theory. It was Ruggles' position that brought on the elaborate Dyrenforth experiments in Texas in 1891 and 1892, of which more later. A second method patented was that of Louis Gathman of Chicago in 1891.[10] It was based on the assumption that the sudden chilling of the upper atmosphere by releasing compressed gas would bring rapid evaporation. Carbonic acid gas was to be set free on the section of air from which the precipitation of rain was wished.

A folk belief current on the prairies was that smoke from the chimneys and cabins of settlers might cause rain. And in 1892 Lucien I. Blake of the University of Kansas had a dust theory for the artificial production of rain. His article, "Rain Making by Means of Smoke Balloons," was printed in the *Scientific American*.[11]

A belief current in the decades when the rainfall seemed to be increasing was that the great increase in the absorptive power of the soil wrought by the cultivation of the soil and the growing of crops caused the greater rainfall and would cause it to continue. This belief was promoted by men of standing such as Professor Samuel Aughey of the University of Nebraska who stated it in his *Sketches of the Physical Geography and Geology of Nebraska* and in his discussion of the "Physical and Natural Features of Nebraska," the initial article in the *History of the State of Nebraska,* 1882. Aughey's scientific prestige made the theory acceptable, and the railroads then existent (except the Union Pacific) took over enthusiastically the idea that the land had increasing agricultural possibilities. This belief was also encouraged by Charles Dana Wilber of the Nebraska Academy of Sciences, and by Orange Judd, editor of *The Prairie Farmer* published in Chicago. It was given circulation nationally and in Europe. William E. Smyth, an editor of *The Irrigation Age,*[12] wrote, "The arid region will be the seat of the future agricul-

---

10 Patent No. 462795, November 10, 1891. See *Report of the Smithsonian Institution* (1894), p. 263.

11 *Scientific American,* LXVII (1892), 420.

12 *Congressional Record,* 52d Cong., 1st Sess., p. 6504; quoted by Charles Lindsay, *The Big Horn Basin* (Lincoln, Nebraska, 1932), p. 173.

tural development of the United States. It will be money in the pockets of every farmer and fruit grower to make his few acres as near like a model for the new settler as possible." Orange Judd was invited to speak at the Nebraska State Fair at Lincoln in September, 1885. He said confidently:

When enough of the sod over a considerable region is brought under the breaking plow, a change comes over the entire country. Rains fall more frequently and more abundantly. Today in the cultivated counties rainfall is greater and more frequent than it was when they were first settled. As this goes on toward your boundary, the whole state of Nebraska will be in a new condition as to its rainfall and its fertility.

In 1878 C. D. Wilber wrote, in the annual report of the Nebraska State Horticultural Society, of this doctrine of the westward extension of rainfall through the advance of agriculture. One section of the report is entitled "How Deserts May Be Controlled." Wilber predicted that "the agencies of civilization now in action are such as will secure a complete victory over the wilderness and waste places of western territory."[13] Yet officials of the United States Weather Bureau had warned people persistently for decades that climate is nowhere subject to permanent change either in temperature or in rainfall.

A belief held especially by the Latter-Day Saints was that rainfall had increased and that it was a mark of special favor to them from the Divine Providence.[14] We have seen that many still hold the belief that rainfall may be achieved by prayer.

Another belief of long standing was that the planting of trees would foster rainfall, though this is not borne out by the statistics of forestry. At the session of the Nebraska State Horticultural Society at Lincoln, January 18, 1883, its president, Samuel Barnard of Table Rock, stated, "The fact is well established that the cultivation of timber has the effect of equalizing the rainfall throughout the growing season by providing a porous surface to absorb the rain, by breaking the force of the wind,

---

13 In Wilber's book, *Nebraska and the Northwest* (1881) chapters iv and v deal with annual rainfall. The last sentence of chapter iv and the subtitle of chapter v are "Rain follows the plow."

14 Webb, *op. cit.*, p. 377.

and by preventing the rapid evaporation from the surface." [15] This idea still has wide currency on the Plains. When Arbor Day was established by the Government, it was not with the belief that tree planting would bring greater rainfall. Yet many expected this, as many now expect it of the gigantic shelter belts which, along with resettlement and federal help, were planned for the relief of drought sufferers in the 1930's. Tree planting is beneficial and deserves for its own sake all the encouragement it may have. I prefer to think of the shelter belts not as promoting rainfall but as reforestation, and believe that they preserve to some degree moisture in the soil and help to preserve soil contours. I hope it was for these reasons that they were built, not because of a lingering folk belief that they would do away with drought.

The most ingenious suggestion to produce rain by trees came before the National Irrigation Congress at El Paso in 1904. William T. Little, editor of a paper at Perry, Oklahoma, but formerly of Texas, presented a paper entitled "Tree and Plain." His reasoning was as follows: High winds on a level plain accelerate evaporation. The experiments of King of Wisconsin have shown that evaporation is retarded on the leeward side of a grove of trees or windbreak. The higher the windbreak and the greater the velocity of the wind, the greater is the retardation. It was estimated that the retardation stood in about the ratio to the height of the obstruction as 16 to 1. Therefore a windbreak 30 feet high would benefit an area 480 feet wide. In the Great Plains the prevailing winds blow south and north. Therefore a series of board walls 30 feet high and 480 feet apart, built across the wind from Mexico to Canada, "from Gulf to British domain, could but be a solving." But since this may be impracticable, the same effect may be had by planting trees for windbreaks. True, all the air will not be deflected, since some will pass through the branches, but this will be compensated for by the reduced evaporation incidental to the tree growth. Ponds could also be formed, presumably parallel with the wind-row hedges, and the evaporation from these would increase the

---

[15] Addison E. Sheldon, *History of Nebraska*, I, p. 50.

humidity and the likelihood of rain. A plan such as this would become "the alpha and omega of both sub-humid and semi-arid farming." In conclusion, Little appealed to his hearers for co-operation in building "a yet greater West to this end, that the general government financially recognize artificial tree wind-breaks on sub-humid prairies and semi-arid plains, as has the paternalism of internal improvement fostered levees and irriga-tion structures." [16]

Basic for all these theories was the assumption that moisture in abundance exists in the sky. It is to be coaxed down by magic, incantation, or prayer, or to be jarred down by noise or concussion. Or it may be that oxygen or hydrogen, which in combination precipitate into rain, may be set loose by the proper combination of chemicals, helped perhaps by electricity, or even by fire or smoke or dust. To their upholders these theories seemed to be scientific but they have not been accepted by scientists.

Attempts at Rain Making

The theories of Edward Powers and Daniel Ruggles brought many experiments in the late 1880's and early 1890's, especially in the Great Plains region. The largest-scale experiment was government financed and took place in Texas in the years 1891 and 1892. On the motion of an Illinois senator, C. B. Farwell, it was provided that under the Forestry Division of the United States Department of Agriculture $2,000 should be expended in experiments having for their object the artificial production of rain by the explosion of dynamite. The De-partment of Agriculture selected R. G. Dyrenforth of Wash-ington to head the undertaking. In contemporary accounts he is referred to as "General" Dyrenforth or as "Major" Dyren-forth, but he seems to have been a patent and corporation lawyer, not a military man. Experiments were carried on for two years. For the first year $7,000 was finally appropriated,

---

16 *The Official Proceedings of the Twelfth Annual Irrigation Congress Held at El Paso, Texas, Nov. 15-16-17-18, 1904* (Galveston 1905), pp. 285-291. See also, for summary, Webb, *op. cit.,* p. 379.

and for the second, $10,000, of which, however, only about $5,000 was expended and the remainder returned.

The intention was to produce rain by violent and continued concussions, both on the earth's surface and in the air, and there were three lines of operations, each two miles in length and one-half mile apart. The first line consisted of a large number of ground batteries by which heavy charges of dynamite and rack-a-rock powder were to be discharged at frequent intervals. The second line was to be of kites flown high, with connections by electric wire, by means of which dynamite cartridges were to be carried up and exploded. The third and principal line was to be of explosive balloons, to be exploded at elevations greater than those attained by the kites, at one or two-hour intervals throughout the operations. . . . The second line was operated less successfully, high winds rendering kite-flying difficult, also breaking the electric wires; as a consequence this line was not operated to the extent proposed.[17]

The first experiment was in August near Midland, Texas, in 1891. The second Dyrenforth experiment was made near San Antonio in November, 1892. Professor A. MacFarlane of the University of Texas was present as an invited guest during the experiments. Dyrenforth's final report was qualifiedly favorable. Professor MacFarlane's account [18] was distinctly unfavorable. Dyrenforth was referred to thereafter by the newspapers and the citizenry as "Major Dryhenceforth."

Theories and practical attempts at rain making reached Nebraska, as they did many states in the Plains region, in the last decades of the century. The dry years and crop failures of the late 1880's and early 1890's put an end to the roseate theory of increasing rainfall as the country grew more settled and more trees and crops were grown. In those years the long-suffering homesteaders might well have felt receptive to nearly anything that promised hope of relief. Hence efforts were more numerous in this region than elsewhere. Kansas was probably

---

[17] George E. Franklin, "The Work of the Rainmakers in the Arid Regions," in *The Official Proceedings of the Twelfth National Irrigation Congress,* pp. 424-425.

[18] In the New York *World,* December 4, 1892.

the scene of greatest activity, eclipsing Texas, though its experiments were not on so vast as scale as those of Dyrenforth, and the commercial motive played a more conspicuous role. Kansas rain-making activities have been well chronicled by Martha B. Caldwell for the Kansas State Historical Society.[19] There was some activity in Colorado and in California, and Nebraska certainly had its share. Two professional rain makers, both serious experimenters, lived in Lincoln, my home town. In Nebraska 1894 was the great year of rain-making activity, despite the doubtful results of Dyrenforth, and there was much experimentation with chemicals and gases as well as with explosives.

In the panhandle of the northwest section of the state, the "Rain God Association" was formed in 1894 to raise—and it did raise—$1,000 to buy gunpowder. From Long Pine to Harrison on a hot July day, on high peaks known as "Rain God Stations," at the prearranged second, gunpowder was discharged in a steady cannonade. No rain fell, however.[20] I tried to learn full details of the Rain-God attempts from the regional newspapers of the day; but most of those that I examined, those in which I expected to find references or comment, dealt with only political matters and included but few local items. The other pages were filled with syndicated matter. Of the newspapers published in Valentine, Chadron, Crawford, and other likely towns, the Nebraska Historical Society archives lacked most of the issues for that year.

Rain-making apparatus was set up not only in the Panhandle but in many other parts of the state, with cannonading leading as the rain inducer. Following are some illustrative items from newspapers of 1894.

July 2, 1894. O'Neill, Nebraska got a ton of dynamite to make the rain come. The dynamite was fired simulating thunder near town in hope that the jarring noise would cause rain. Two professional rainmakers came soon and were to have

---

19 Martha B. Caldwell, "Some Kansas Rainmakers," *Kansas Historical Quarterly*, VIII (August, 1938), 306-324. See also J. P. Walton, in *Kansas Academy of Science*, February 12, 1894.

20 Addison Erwin Sheldon, *Nebraska Old and New* (1937), pp. 359-360.

been given $1,000 if they "made" it rain. It rained hard a few hours after their time limit was up.[21]

Apparently O'Neill tried it again the next month. The Valentine *Republican* for August 3 had: "Rainmakers in all parts of the State are now playing in hard luck"; and on August 4: "An attempt to make it rain at O'Neill by the use of fierce explosives failed to fetch a drop."

Special from Loup City, July 4, 1894: C. L. Drake, the local rainmaker commenced operations in a blacksmith shop about 9 o'clock this morning and at 12:30 rain commenced. It came down in a steady downpour for an hour and a half. It was the first we had had for several weeks and farmers were becoming discouraged.

July 15, from Ravenna: The Ravenna News avers that five out of seven rainmaking experiments in that section proved successful.

July 19, from Columbus, Nebraska: Rainmaker Jewell of Lincoln arrived tonight on the Burlington and will proceed in the morning for Platte Center, where he is under contract to furnish a copious general rain in 24 hours. Should he be successful he will receive $700.

July 26, from Hastings: The rainmakers are having a sorry time of it. The end of the five days in which they were to bring rain is approaching and prospects of the promised precipitation are not more flattering than before their arrival.

July 29, from Hastings: The rainmakers gave up in disgust and left in the St. Joseph and Grand Island evening train for Madison where they hope to have better success than they had here.[22]

Martha B. Caldwell quotes from the *Jewell County Republican* of Jewell, Kansas, an item for which I have found no record in Nebraska sources: ". . . a rainmaker at Minden, Nebraska, was . . . unlucky. Upon his failure the citizens tied him to a telegraph pole, turned the hose of the fire department on him and showed him how it could make it rain."[23]

---

[21] *Nebraska State Journal*, Lincoln, July 2, 1894.

[22] *Ibid.*, July 15-29, 1894.

[23] *Jewell County Republican*, Jewell, Kansas, August 24, 1893.

Mari Sandoz tells in *Old Jules,* seemingly as a yarn, that in eastern Nebraska "a Pawnee Indian promised a shower for $10, a soaking rain for $20. Some one gave him a jug of whiskey and the rain pounded the grass into the ground. It was a good story, told not without envy." [24]

The Rain Makers

The four leading rain makers who operated in Nebraska were Frank Melbourne, Clayton B. Jewell, Dr. W. F. Wright, and Dr. William B. Swisher. Melbourne, known as "The Rain Wizard" and later as "The Rain Fakir," [25] was the most famous of the four and the one who operated most widely. He was also the man most obviously in his profession for revenue. Said to be an Australian, he came to Cheyenne in the autumn of 1891 and contracted to make the rain fall, taking money for it. The Cheyenne *Daily Leader* for September, 1892, stated: "The firm believers and the doubting Thomases were all forced in out of the wet, and those unable to find shelter were drenched to the skin." In the spring of 1893 he circulated a pamphlet, "To the People of the Arid Regions," giving testimony that he had produced rain in Ohio, Wyoming, Utah, and Kansas. He charged $500 for a "good" rain—one that would reach from fifty to a hundred miles in all directions from the place of operation. Associated with him was his "manager," Frank Jones. Melbourne's catalogue and correspondence are part of a collection of the Wyoming State Department of History. He seems to have operated in Nebraska as well as in Kansas and Colorado. A telegram to him from Bertrand, Nebraska, read: "Can you come here at once and prospect for rain. Wire conditions." Another telegram read: "Our money is raised. Name earliest date you can be here and await reply." From Grand Island, Nebraska, came another telegram: "Wire your price for one-inch rain." This was followed by: "Don't come until so ordered."

24 Mari Sandoz, *Old Jules* (Boston: Little, Brown & Co., 1935), p. 149.

25 For Melbourne, see Alvin T. Steinel and D. W. Working, collaborator, *History of Agriculture in Colorado . . . 1858 to 1926* (Fort Collins: State Agricultural College, 1926); "The Rain Makers Appear," pp. 260-262.

Melbourne and Jones worked in eastern Colorado in the summer of 1892, says Steinel, and in the neighborhood of Logan, Phillips, and Sedgwick counties, and in Keith County, Nebraska. He was to cause rain not less than 0.15 of an inch at Holyoke, Julesburg, and Fleming within seventy-two hours. He was to get six cents an acre for wetting the cultivated lands. On the day of the week set for the rain a few clouds appeared, but no rain fell. Late the next afternoon there was a slight sprinkle. A contemporary account says, "Before enough rain fell to quench the thirst of a grasshopper the rain ceased."

Melbourne confessed ultimately that his claims were fraudulent. "The American people like to be humb___ ed," he declared, "and the greater the fake the easier it ___ ___ work." It was discovered that the dates he fixed upon were identical with those in the long-distance forecasts of Irl R. Hicks who made them from St. Louis for many years. Hicks published an almanac which had a large rural circulation, and his weather forecasts were believed to have a scientific foundation. If Melbourne went wrong on his dates the prophecies of Hicks were responsible. Melbourne always announced that he kept his rain-making formula a secret. His method seemed to have involved burning chemicals on a raised platform in open country. Martha Caldwell calls him "Professor" Melbourne.[26] His reign as the "King Rain Maker" was not long, however. In 1894 or 1895 he was found dead in a hotel room at Denver. His death was attributed to suicide.

A second well-known rain maker was Clayton B. Jewell [27] who came to be known, like Melbourne, as "The Rain Fakir." A Kansan, the chief train dispatcher for the Rock Island Railway at Goodland, Kansas, Jewell operated chiefly in Kansas and neighboring regions with one unsuccessful engagement in California.[28] A visit to Columbus, Nebraska, was mentioned in the newspaper special from that city, which wrongly ascribed him to Lincoln. After Melbourne's visits to Kansas, Jewell ex-

[26] Caldwell, *op. cit.,* p. 315.

[27] For Jewell, see *ibid.,* p. 320, and also George E. Franklin, *op. cit.,* pp. 425-427.

[28] Franklin, *op. cit.,* p. 426; and Webb, *op. cit.,* p. 382.

perimented in rain making, believing he had discovered Melbourne's formulas, and for a time he seemingly had success. In the dry May of 1893 the officials of the Rock Island Railway offered him the chance to experiment on a more extensive scale. The company placed at his disposal the electric batteries along the track from Topeka to Colorado Springs, for he thought electricity greatly helped in rain making. The Rock Island also furnished him with balloons for trying the concussion theory. He lived in a freight car partitioned off as his laboratory. The trans-Plains railroads would have profited greatly by the success of rain-making endeavors, and it is not surprising that they financed the experiments. Mark W. Harrington quotes a high official of a railroad company who wrote on August 22, 1893, in answer to an inquiry:

> While these experiments have been made by a couple of employees of this company, we can say but little about them ourselves. These parties claimed to be able to cause rainfall by artificial means, and we have furnished them with materials together with transportation facilities more or less all the time since the early part of May, they having experimented in some eighteen or twenty different locations, and in each case we have had more or less rainfall. In nearly every instance we can but feel there is something in their claim. . . . they are either very fortunate in reaching the different points where they have experimented just in time to have rain storms, or they have certainly hit upon the right thing in the way of rain making.[29]

Jewell and a helper experimented first at Goodland with chemicals valued at $250. In a few days their efforts were followed by a heavy rain throughout the county and, still later, by a more general rain. Next, the pair proceeded along the railroad, stopping at various places for experiments, some successful, some not. The boxcar in which they had started out was replaced by a car especially constructed for them by the railroad. A trip through Iowa and Illinois ending in "Kansas Week" at the World's Fair was planned, but Chicago was not enthusiastic over the prospect. Miss Caldwell relates that the

---

[29] Harrington, *op. cit.*, p. 267.

Chicago *Times* warned Jewell that he had better not "give an exhibition of his abilities as a Pluvian influencer at the World's Fair. . . . Chicago does not believe much in rainmaking, but if Jewell fools around the fair grounds and it should rain, it will be too bad for Jewell, that's all." [30] No account seems to survive of his visit to the fair, if he made one. His experiments were free at this time, unlike those of Melbourne and those of the three rain-making companies that had been established at Goodland.

In the spring of 1893, experiments were begun by the Rock Island on a larger scale. After their initial efforts it was intended that contracts be made and successful rain making be charged for. Three cars were started out by May, 1894. Jewell's methods were based chiefly on the hypothesis that volatile gases charged with electricity and sent high in the air would chill the atmosphere and bring a condensation of vapor. He used four generators in his work, making fifteen hundred gallons of gas an hour. Meantime opposition arose for various reasons. There was too much rain in some places. Some farmers complained of wind and cold weather. Others held that the dry weather was Divine punishment for man's impertinence in trying to take control of the rainfall. By the end of July, rain making had died out, supplanted by increasing enthusiasm for irrigation.

One of the two leading rain makers of Lincoln, Nebraska, was William F. Wright, usually termed "Doctor" Wright. Whether the title was rightly his or was honorary like Dyrenforth's military title and Melbourne's "Professor" I do not know. The Lincoln *Journal* [31] says of Wright that he claimed credit for 0.03 of an inch of rain after he had been trying to obtain rain for several days. The rainfall which he said his bombardment had brought on was so slight that it was of no practical benefit. After his first trial on a Wednesday night he fired at intervals and on Friday was still firing. He had funnels on most of his guns in order to induce a spiral current when the shots were fired, but the funnels were blown away

---

[30] Reprinted in the Goodland *News*, June 29, 1893. See Caldwell, *op. cit.*, p. 320.

[31] Lincoln, *Nebraska State Journal*, August 4, 1901.

by the force of the concussion and were then discarded and the bases alone used. Wright is said to have tried unsuccessfully to obtain legislative aid. His plan was to "construct a huge gun or cannon of some sort, which would be shot into the sky." Recalling his activities some years later in an interview,[32] John F. C. McKesson, a son-in-law of Dr. W. B. Swisher who worked with Wright, said that E. E. Blackman of the State Historical Society "once helped to carry a big black box up into a vacant barn." The box was supposed to contain rainmaking material or equipment, and "to this day he does not know the magic which drew down rain within the specified 24 hours."

Wright was the author of a book, *The Universe as It Is*, the last section of which deals with "Artificial Rainfall." It was locally published in 1898, but the printing establishment issuing it burned, thus destroying the plates from which only twenty copies had been printed. A copy of the book, perhaps Blackman's copy, supposed to be the only one extant, is in the library of the State Historical Society. The book is well written and well printed and reads like the carefully prepared work of a thoughtful student. I cannot think that Wright was a fraud. Certainly he was no Melbourne. He placed his reliance, as did Dr. Swisher, on the explosion of gases rather than of gunpowder. He wrote in his last chapter:

> It is not to be expected that one or two men operating at one point, with inadequate apparatus and a few chemicals, would be able to produce any very marked results. . . . A sufficient number of men, equipped with the right instruments and materials, stationed at proper intervals throughout the county and state, all working harmoniously under a well directed system, would soon remove all doubts as to the practicality and success of the undertaking.

Wright thought rain making superior to irrigation and rainwater superior to water from wells and streams, and advocated a "state or national system to produce rainfall whenever and wherever needed." In a footnote he stated that "National Ir-

---

[32] Lincoln, *Nebraska State Journal*, date uncertain.

rigation under State and National Control" was the title of a
work soon to be issued by him, containing a more complete
explanation of the philosophy of artificial rain production and
fuller details of the processes necessary to put the system into
successful operation.[33] Wright always retained his faith in the
ultimate success of man in controlling rain.

The second Lincoln, Nebraska, rain maker was Dr. William
B. Swisher, a surgeon in the Union army and later a pioneer
doctor in Nebraska. His daughter, Dora Swisher McKesson, and
granddaughter, Mrs. Hubert Walker, still live in Lincoln, and
to them I am indebted for considerable information.

Of the three rain-making companies founded at Goodland,
Kansas, after Melbourne's visit there the earliest formed was
the Inter-State Artificial Rain Company, established in 1891.[34]
A central station was organized from which "rainmaking
squads" were to be sent out. The reported success of the Inter-
State Company brought, early in the next year, the formation
of the Swisher Company of Goodland, chartered January 13,
1892, with a capital stock of $100,000; this company made con-
tracts for doing business. The Swisher Company relied mainly
upon chemicals with which Dr. Swisher had been experiment-
ing. His success was reported to be equal to that of the Inter-
State Company and his money reward to be good. The third
company, the Goodland Artificial Rain Company, was chartered
February 11, 1892. All three companies claimed to use the Melbourne methods. Contracts were made in many places and
competition between the companies developed. At one time
the Inter-State Company offered to furnish rain for the crop
season for $2,500, the Swisher Company for $2,000, and the
Goodland Company for $1,500. For a good rain in Jewell
County, a single rain, the first company got $400. In a telegram
from Lincoln, July 26, 1892, Dr. Swisher claimed: "Rain as
per contract. Time 48 hours." In the same month Dr. Swisher
had a contract at Colby, Kansas, but lost his pay since the rain
was not in the stated amount. According to A. E. Sheldon,[35]

---

[33] I have found no trace of this book and doubt that it ever was published.
[34] Caldwell, *op. cit.*, pp. 311 ff.
[35] Sheldon, *Nebraska Old and New*, p. 359.

Dr. Swisher was one of those "employed by the Rock Island railroad to travel in a special car fitted with rainmaking apparatus. He was to operate in Nebraska and Kansas and to produce rain along the Rock Island right-of-way." Melbourne was in Kansas too, but lost prestige to the Goodland companies, and they in turn lost prestige to Jewell, when he entered the field. Dr. Swisher went back to Lincoln with his chemicals. In Lincoln he made an agreement with a real-estate man, J. H. McMurtry, who owned a number of farms in the vicinity, to bring rain within three days. McMurtry promised to pay him $500 if one-half inch of rain fell. Shortly after the rain maker began his work there fell a drenching rain of one-half inch. McMurtry claimed that it came from natural causes, but Dr. Swisher took the matter to the courts, and McMurtry was forced to pay the $500.

According to Swisher's son-in-law, McKesson, Swisher and Wright worked out their theory together and produced rain. Throughout the dry summer of 1894 they worked in various parts of the country and apparently with success. One noteworthy instance was in Mexico, where rain followed Dr. Swisher's effort. The two men operated together only for that summer. But "wind made results uncertain," blowing the gases elsewhere from the place where precipitation was desired. Moreover Dr. Swisher was religious minded and "felt more and more that the plans of nature and Providence should not be tampered with. And so the black box was put away." The mysterious black box, said McKesson, "was merely a receptacle for two large earthen jars from Germany. As hydrogen and oxygen combined in the proper ratio produce water, we felt there was a deficiency in one or the other." They manufactured hydrogen and put it into the air to start a nucleus of water which might result in more. The first operations took place on Swisher's farm at Emerald near Lincoln. Two hundred people had subscribed to a fund for the work. Later, the two men operated elsewhere in Nebraska and in Kansas. McKesson stated to his interviewer that their efforts were "followed in every instance by rain."

Rain making must have been a profitable profession while it lasted. The largest profit came from selling the rain-making secret formula and the right to operate in a designated region. Melbourne did this, and so did one or two of the Goodland companies. Whether farmers believed in any of the systems is a question. Several operators were sent out at the same time by the different companies. If one company brought rain money was made.[36] The contracts read always, "No rain, no pay." If it did not rain those who contracted for it were out nothing, and if it did rain they thought the benefit worth what was paid for it. Newspapers generally were skeptical. The rain makers were accused of studying the weather forecasts and of being "out of chemicals" if the signs were not auspicious. And, in any case, the rain makers were never brought in until there had been a long drought. After 1894 little is heard of rain making. In the drought of the 1930's—1936 was a record period of dryness—rain makers did not reappear. Instead, came only occasional reversion to prayer and song.

In the middle decades of our twentieth century and still continuing, scientists such as Irving Langmuir and Vincent Schaefer of the General Electric Laboratories at Schenectady and Bernard Vonnegut of Cambridge have made further experiments and investigations in weather modification, cloud physics, cloud seeding, and their results have been better authenticated and better rewarding than the nineteenth-century efforts.

Perhaps it should be added, in conclusion, that there is one

---

[36] I am indebted to Professor Levette J. Davidson for the following special to the *Rocky Mountain News*, Denver, Colorado, January 1, 1892. It is headed "Artificial Rain. A Proposition to Furnish Rain for Several Counties."

"*Holyoke, Colorado, December 31.*—H. W. Wakeman of Philips County has been in correspondence with the Inter-State Artificial Rain Company of Goodland, Kansas. The secretary of that company has visited Holyoke and has left a proposition to give four test rainfalls any time during the months of April, May, June, or July, as the committee shall select. The proposition embraces three counties in Nebraska, namely, Perkins, Chase, and Dundy, and five counties in Colorado, Washington, Logan, Philips, Yuma and Sedgwick. A mass meeting of the citizens of Philips County held at Holyoke last Saturday elected a committee and raised over $200. There will be another meeting next Saturday. The cost of the four test rainfalls will be $2,400. Each county's quota will be $300. If this proposition should prove acceptable to the people of the above-named counties Mr. Wakeman will take the trouble to visit them and exhibit the plan in detail. This much may be said here, that the proposition is on the basis of 'no rain, no pay.' "

method of rain making that does not fail, according to current Nebraska folklore, and the saying is probably to be heard elsewhere in the central states: "Wash and polish your car and you may be sure rain will follow."

Reprinted from the *California Folklore Quarterly*, Vol. V, No. 2 (April, 1946), 129-142, published by the University of California Press.

The Nebraska Legend of Weeping Water

— ⚘ —

Lore of Streams and Lakes Arising from Tears

The small Nebraska stream known as the Weeping Water, *L'Eau qui pleure* of early French explorers and traders, arises in Cass County in southeastern Nebraska, passes through the towns of Weeping Water and Nehawka, and flows into the Missouri between Plattsmouth and Nebraska City. Somewhat too large for a creek, though possibly larger in an earlier day, it is not large enough to be termed a river. Its name is poetic and suggestive and a legend now well established has become associated with it. Tales of bodies of water originating from tears, as in the Nebraska story, are far from unusual in folklore. A few are recorded from Greek mythology.[1] In an Irish tale a father sheds "three drops of grief" for his dead son and these become three lochs. In another Irish tale a king's daughter died of shame and her foster mother's tears made Loch Gile.[2] In a third Irish tale a saint's tears produced a fountain.[3] In Oceanic tradition the mother of a Maori

---

[1] W. S. Fox, *Greek and Roman Mythology*, "The Mythology of All Races" (Boston, 1916), I, 257.

[2] J. R. McCulloch, *Celtic Mythology*, "The Mythology of All Races" (Boston, 1918), III, 135.

[3] Charles Plummer, *Vitae Sanctorum Hiberniae* (Oxford, 1910), p. cl; and Rev. W. J. Rees, *Lives of the Cambro-British Saints* (1853), p. 481.

hero deity is said to have wept at the action of her son, her tears falling to earth and flooding it, thus overwhelming all men.[4] An instance in the Finnish *Kalevala* tells how the mother of the beautiful Aino weeps about her daughter's fate and her tears flow on and ever.

> As the tear drops fall and mingle
> Form they streamlets three in number,
> And their source the mother's eyelids,
> Streamlets formed from pearly tear-drops,
> And each streamlet larger growing
> Soon became a raging torrent. . . .[5]

In the mythology of the North American Indians there are examples of bodies of water originating from tears. Professor Stith Thompson's *Tales of the North American Indians*[6] presents stories of floods caused by tears, usually the tears of a disappointed suitor or a jealous husband. In his *The Folk Tale* Professor Thompson writes:

As for stories of deluges, it is often extremely hard to tell whether we are dealing with an aboriginal idea or with some modification of the tale of Noah as learned from missionaries or other Europeans. Of the flood tales which have the appearance of being aboriginal there are good examples in every part of the continent. Sometimes these are obviously related to each other, and sometimes they are clearly independent stories, perhaps frequently the reflection of some actual catastrophe. Interesting causes for these floods are sometimes related. Rather widespread is the notion that the flood is caused by tears, often those of a disappointed suitor. This concept is found with great frequency among the Plateau tribes and on the North Pacific Coast, and even over into Siberia. Its distribution shows that this is a very definite tradition, obviously disseminating from some center, probably the North Pacific Coast.[7]

---

[4] R. B. Dixon, *Oceanic Mythology*, "The Mythology of All Races" (Boston, 1916), IX, 38.

[5] *The Kalevala: The Epic Poem of Finland*, translated by John Martin Crawford (Cincinnati, 1898); rune 4: "The Fate of Aino."

[6] (Cambridge, Massachusetts, 1929), p. 287, n. 57b.

[7] Stith Thompson, *The Folk Tale* (New York, 1947), p. 313.

The so-called Nebraska Legend of Weeping Water has existed in printed and oral form for at least eight decades. Many questions arise concerning it. How did it start? Among Indians or white men? If the latter, were they French or English? How old is it? Who handed it on? How fixed is its form? These questions are of interest, especially to Nebraskans, whether final answers may be arrived at or not. The Nebraska legend of a stream having its origin in tears seems unique in that the cause of lamentation is a massacre resulting in the extinction of two warring groups. There is a frustrated suitor present in some forms of this legend; but the basic tragedy is not his, although he too is slain. The suitor seems to have been a literary addition.

The Nebraska Legend of Weeping Water

The first printed mention of the Weeping Water tale occurs, so far as may be determined, in a poem "The Weeping Water," by Professor Orsamus Charles Dake, the first professor of English Literature at the University of Nebraska.[8] Professor Dake was born at Portage in Livingston County, New York, was graduated at Madison University, Hamilton, New York, and became among other things a teacher, editor, and ordained clergyman. In 1863 he organized Brownell Hall, Omaha, a girls' school. In 1865 he went to Fremont, where he organized a church. He was a professor at the University of Nebraska, which was founded in 1869, from 1871 until his death in 1875. He published a small volume of 165 pages entitled *Nebraska Legends and Other Poems* in 1871.[9] The initial poem, about 800 lines of blank verse, is "The Weeping Water." Preceding the poem, printed on the page opposite the opening lines, is the following brief statement of the legend which the author says in his preface is one of the two legends he "developed."

The Omaha and Otoe Indians, being at war, chanced to meet on their common hunting ground south of the Platte

---

[8] A. C. Edmunds, *Nebraskans: Pen Sketches with Photographs* (Lincoln, 1871), pp. 297-300; also account by A. E. Sheldon, *Nebraska History*, VI (April-June, 1923), 42-44. Dake's poem is reprinted in full in this issue.

[9] (New York: Pott and Amery, Cooper Union, 1871.)

River in Nebraska. A fierce battle ensued, in which all the male warriors of both tribes being slain, the women and children came upon the battle-field and sat down and wept. From the fountain of their tears arose and ever flows the little stream known as the Ne-hawka or the Weeping Water.

Dake's preface, dated 1870, states:

In the development of the two Nebraska legends I have treated my Indian characters as noble, and possessed of true sentiment. A brutal savage is not a poetical subject, and, except under rare conditions, has no business in poetry. If the Indian, like his human brethren of more favorable opportunities, has his worse side, he also has his better. Until corrupted by intercourse with the whites, his nature is simple, affectionate, childlike. Certainly he is no worse than the old pagan Greeks of Homer and the dramatists, who were separated into little tribes, forever at war, and whose common occupation was the sacking of towns and the carrying off of defenceless women for concubines. Every inducement, therefore, that could urge an ancient poet to portray pre-historic peoples as chivalrous and of a sustained dignity should impel a writer of today to do likewise. Elemental poetic conditions do not change.

These statements imply that Professor Dake knew an already existent legend of the stream. The next poem in the little volume, "The Raw Hide," was founded on a mid-century incident often mentioned as historic,[10] supposed to have taken place in Nebraska, and now of legendary associations.

---

10 The story of the flaying of a white man by Indians after his casual shooting of an Indian woman has been told with variations since Gold Rush days. It is narrated as fact not legend in John B. Dunbar's "The Pawnee Indians," *Magazine of American History*, IV (April, 1880), 257, and by Captain R. W. Hazen, *History of the Pawnee Indians* (1893), pp. 29-31. The victim is said by Hazen to have been Seth Estabrook, one of a band of gold seekers headed for California in 1850. It was termed historical also by W. O. Dodge of Fremont (Omaha *World-Herald*, October 19, 1925) and by E. W. Smith of Hooper and J. E. Mathews of Fairmont (*Nebraska State Journal*, March 19, 1926). Dr. Cass Barnes in his *The Sod House* (1930), p. 27, foreword by A. E. Sheldon, is more doubtful of its authenticity. The site of the incident is said by all these persons to be Rawhide Creek just east of Fremont. The magazine *Nebraska History* (VI [1923] 121), prints an account by H. J. Miller who testifies that the incident occurred on the Little Blue River

The initial poem reflects the author's Homeric knowledge and stimulus and his religious training. On the whole "The Weeping Water" does credit to Nebraska's pioneer professor of English literature. Lofty speeches of the Homeric and Virgilian type take the place of dialogue, and the narrative is studded with elaborate similes in the manner of the classic epics.[11] The author supplies a love story, not mentioned in his prefatory summary, of the Otoe youth Sananona and Nacoumah, the daughter of the Omaha chief, Watonashie. When their union is forbidden by the Otoe chief Shosguscan, the spirited Sananona leaves his tribe to go among the Omaha. It is this situation that brings on the tribal conflict ending in the destruction of the warriors of both sides. When all is over, the bereaved women steal across the battlefield searching for their husbands, brothers, sons.

> They sat them down through lingering painful hours
> Of the dim night, and, without utterance, wept. . .
> But all the tears of children and of wives,
> In a green hollow of the lonely hills
> He gathered in a fountain, that the sun
> Dries not in summer heats, but crystal pure

---

in 1858. He says his account was written for Mrs. Miller by Mr. Long, a member of the small party involved, which was on its way to Pike's Peak. In the same magazine (XIV [July-September, 1933] 190), Adam William Schoup gives the location of the happening as near Lodge Pole and says it took place in connection with a train of about 200 going west on the Oregon Trail. Perhaps, like the scalping of white men, such an incident could have taken place anywhere in Indian days. Whether or not the tale has historic basis, it is widespread and not only among Nebraskans. The same tale is told about the naming of Rawhide Creek near Torrington, Wyoming, and of many other places west of the Missouri River. A. E. Sheldon suggests in his foreword to Dr. Barnes's book that it might have been told so widely and so often in order to forestall overt acts by thoughtless white men passing through regions occupied by Indian tribes.

[11] Examples are the lines beginning: "As when an eagle whets his murderous beak . . ."; "As when along some blown Alaskan vale a herd of Caribou drags forth its length . . . ." Too modern for the theme is:

> ". . . As one
> Who, whirling through the country by a train
> That flies the track and plunges down the steep,
> Picks himself out from shattered heaps of cars
> And smutched and mangled bodies of the dead. . . ."

O'erbrims and murmurs through the changing years.
Forever on it flows, that gentle stream,
Fountained by tears, and glides among the hills—
Ne-hawka—in a valley of its own. . . .
Until, at length, it lingers at the marge
Of the untamable Missouri flood. . . .

The poem is ambitious and it commands respect as pioneer Nebraska verse; but it tells an unbelievable event in an imitative outmoded way.

The next appearance of the legend seems to be in a *History of Nebraska* [12] published by A. T. Andreas twelve years after Dake's book. In his account of the town of Weeping Water the author includes a version of the legend which echoes the manner of Dake's poem and with a basic love story. But the narratives are not identical. It is as though the historian knew a somewhat different form of the story. Of course it is not to be expected that versions of legends handed down will always agree as to persons, groups, and circumstances involved. The Andreas *History* says:

There is an Indian tradition that somewhere near the source of the river now known as the Weeping Water, there once dwelt a powerful but peaceful tribe, governed by sound laws, ruled over by a chief as mild tempered as he was valorous, whose warriors were as straight as their own arrows, as strong and fleet as the horses they rode, whose maidens were lithe and lovely, their beauty far exceeding that possessed by any of the surrounding tribes. And it is further said that the fairest of these maidens was the chief's daughter—so fair that she captivated the heart and brain of the ruler of a still more powerful tribe upon the west, who asked her father for her, was refused, and finally succeeded in abducting the maiden while she was bathing with her companions in the deep still lake adjacent to the village.

Pursuit was made, the lodges being left in charge of the women and the infirm. The chase was a long and hard one, and the result was most disastrous, every man of the pursuers being killed in the fight that followed. For three long days

---

12 (Chicago, 1882), p. 509.

and nights those who had been left at the village waited, then started out in search of their fathers, husbands, and lovers, to find them dead upon the plains, and, finding them, to weep so long that their falling tears formed a stream that still exists—Nehawka—the weeping water.

One difference between the Andreas and the Dake story is that the tribes and persons are not named in the Andreas version. And the young hero is the chief of his tribe, as though Dake's Sananona and Shosguscan are merged into one character. Another difference is that the youthful chief abducts the daughter of the chief of the rival tribe instead of leaving his own tribe.

I shall mention here but two of the many brief contemporary oral accounts I have collected.

The most elaborate and detailed account of the legend is that of Professor J. C. Lindberg of the State College at Aberdeen, South Dakota. It is too long to be quoted in full. There is no love story as in the Dake and Andreas versions. Each of two hostile tribes claims territory in the southeastern Nebraska region as its ancestral hunting ground. Upon the same night each tribe planned to surprise and overpower the other. At early dawn each found itself face to face with the enemy. Deadly and sustained conflict resulted in the annihilation of one of the tribes and only a handful of the other remained to tell the story. Those left in camp held a council and decided to go en masse to bury their dead.

There were tears, many tears. After they had buried their dead another council was held at which it was decided that each year upon the anniversary of the battle the whole tribe should journey to the scene of the slaughter and lament their dead heroes. This custom was dutifully kept up till the white man appeared upon the scene and pushed the Indians farther west. But meanwhile a great many tears had been poured out, so many, indeed, that a little stream was formed and made its way down the valley. The bed of the stream is very uneven and broken by many little falls and because of this (as well as from the origin of the stream) there is a constant murmuring and complaining and so it was christened the Weeping Water. It was in these complaints that the water heard the following voice.[13]

A poem of three eight-line stanzas, evidently of Professor Lindberg's own composition, follows, of which more will be said later.

The latest printed version I shall quote appeared in the *Nebraska History* magazine in 1936, a prize essay by Roberta Williams of Nebraska City.[14] The essay concerns the disappearance of the old town of Wyoming, near the Weeping Water. It was founded in 1855, and when it had lost importance changed its name in 1882 to Dresden. Under the sidehead "Indian Legend" Miss Williams tells that the Indian legend gave the name to the stream and seems to imply that it was in general circulation.

> Doubtless, too, the Weeping Water flows over its rocky bed with the same mournful sound that the two early explorers [Lewis and Clark] heard. There is a legend that two Indian tribes met in battle several miles above the point where Wyoming was later to be, and that nearly all the warriors were killed. The Indian maidens shed so many tears for their lost braves that it started a tiny stream. Each year they returned to mourn. The stream grew, and flowing over the uneven, rocky surface, made a mournful sound as though it had caught the lament of the Indian maidens. The tribes began to call it *Nehawka,* Weeping Water. When the French traders came they heard the lament of the stream and repeated the name, saying *l'eau qui pleure.*

Professor Dake's was not the only poem to be associated with a Nebraska river. If his epic narrative was Homeric, that of E. E. Blackman, Curator of the State Historical Society Museum (1902-1942), *Niobrara's Love Story: An Indian Romance of Pre-Historic Nebraska; of the Fabled Ancient Empire of Quivera,*[15]

---

13 *Nebraska History,* V (1922), 57-59.

14 *Nebraska History,* XVII (1936), 80. Miss Williams was the winner of an essay contest offered by the Sons and Daughters of Nebraska. In the latest oral version of the legend I have found (1947), a tribe of Indians is massacred by white men rather than by another tribe.

15 Printed at Roca, Nebraska, 1900.

which he published in 1900, was in the pattern and verse form of Longfellow's *Hiawatha* of 1856. It tells the story of Keha Paha, the valiant youthful hunter, and Niobrara, daughter of King Tartarax, who named the Niobrara River in northwestern Nebraska after her. Like Dake's, it is a creditable poem of an imitative type. I have not found that any legend of the Niobrara River arose from this narrative, perhaps because of the later date of its composition and because of the less haunting, though musical, character of the stream's name.

To return to the Weeping Water, Professor Lindberg's poem is in the manner neither of Homer's *Iliad* nor of Longfellow's Indian poem but is an attractive lyrical lament. Here are the first and last stanzas:

> Though all nature around us is smiling
> There's a note of despair in the song.
> Come tell me, no longer beguiling,
> Come tell me the tale of thy wrong.
> Then a murmur as soft as the breeze,
> Yet weird as the sighing of waves—
> "I'm grieving the death of my kinsmen,
> I'm grieving the death of my braves." . . .
>
> Now the sun in its glory is shining,
> And the shadows of evening unfold.
> No breezes the tree-tops are fretting,
> And the cloudland is purple and gold;
> Still the soul-rending wail of the mourner,
> An echo from countless graves;
> "Revenge me, revenge me, my kinsmen,
> Revenge me, revenge me, my braves."

A third poem on the Weeping Water legend is a ballad in eleven rhymed quatrains composed, according to his father, I. N. Hunter,[16] by the Rev. A. V. Hunter of Boston. It is entitled "The Legend of Weeping Water." It runs in part:

> Long before the white man wandered
> To these rich Nebraska lands

---

[16] "Recollections of Weeping Water" (in which the ballad is quoted in full), *Nebraska Pioneer Reminiscences* (Cedar Rapids, Iowa, 1916), issued by the Nebraska Society of the Daughters of the American Revolution.

Indians in their paint and feathers
  Roamed in savage warlike bands. . . .

Then one day the war cry sounded
  Over valley, hill and plain.
From the North came dusky warriors,
  From that unknown vast domain. . . .

Awful was the scene that followed,
  Yells and warwhoops echoed shrill,
But at last as night descended
  Death had conquered; all was still.

Then the women in the wigwams
  Hearing rumors of the fight,
Bearing flaming flickering torches
  Soon were wandering in the night.

There they found the loved ones lying,
  Calm in everlasting sleep.
Little wonder that the women,
  Broken-hearted, all, should weep.

Hours and hours they kept on weeping.
  'Til their tears began to flow
In many trickling streamlets
  To the valley down below.

These together joined their forces
  To produce a larger stream
Which has ever since been flowing
  As you see it in this scene.

Indians christened it Nehawka,
  Crying water means the same.
In this way the legend tells us
  Weeping Water got its name.

At this point, the oral prose version of an old settler may
be reproduced. The late Thomas S. Allen, a brother-in-law of
W. J. Bryan, gave the following account in a Nebraska newspaper.

When I was a boy we lived on the banks of the stream Weeping Water and we had for neighbors several families that had settled in and around the village of Weeping Water in 1856. I have heard from several of those persons, and particularly Willis J. Horton, now deceased, this legend.

In the early days there was a feud between the Pawnee and Sioux Indians. One day the Pawnee and their allies, the Otoes, arranged to go to battle against the Sioux. As the warriors came from their reservations and were on the march, in the darkness of an October night, the two tribes—Pawnee and Otoe—met and mistaking each other for the common enemy, the Sioux, the battle began. When day came all the warriors were killed and it was then discovered that the allies had by mistake fought each other unto death. The squaws were filled with grief when the news of the battle reached them, and their tears formed the source of a stream called by them and their descendants Minne-boo-hoo.

The legend is that Lincoln in 1849 on a trip to the West came to the east bank of the Missouri and looking across saw a beautiful stream flowing into the river from the west. He was told that Indians called it Minne-boo-hoo. He jocularly remarked that if Minnehaha is "Laughing Water," Minne-boo-hoo should be Weeping Water. From that day on the white settlers accepted Lincoln's translation and the historic stream is now the Weeping Water.[17]

Another and more credible version of the Minneboohoo story —for the stream was called the Weeping Water long before Lincoln's day, as will be shown—is that told by Frederic William Taylor, a professor of horticulture at the University of Nebraska, 1891-1893. He said that in the days when the admission of Kansas and Nebraska to statehood was agitating the country, President Lincoln was looking at a map of Nebraska when his attention was arrested by the name Weeping Water. He commented that "If Minnehaha is Laughing Water, Weeping Water should be Minneboohoo."

[17] *Nebraska State Journal,* June 6, 1925.

L'Eau Qui Pleure in Nebraska History and Cartography

An investigation of the Indian lore preserved and available throws no light on any legend concerning the Nehawka or Weeping Water. The *Twenty-seventh Annual Report of the Bureau of American Ethnology* of the Smithsonian Institution deals with the Omaha tribe.[18] It is an exhaustive work of about 700 pages and includes among other material the traditional songs of the Omaha. There is no reference in these or elsewhere in the volume to a massacre legend. A long list of streams known to the Omaha [19] is included, but among them the Nehawka or Weeping Water is not entered. Nor is anything to be found in what is available concerning the Pawnee, Otoe, and Sioux tribes. For the Pawnee especially a large body of traditions and legends has been recorded.[20] But, of course, this negative evidence is not to be taken as proving that such a legend did not exist.

In the records of French travelers and explorers, the name Weeping Water for the stream appears at an early date. Father Marquette discovered the Mississippi as early as 1673, and he reached the mouth of the Missouri. La Salle reached the Missouri in 1682. The French carried on fur trading with the Omaha tribe in the middle of the eighteenth century. M. de Remonville, writing of the Missouri in Paris in 1702,[21] mentions fourteen Indian nations then living on the banks of the Missouri. Beginning in 1700, after the founding of Biloxi on the Gulf of Mexico, French explorers and fur traders moved up the Mississippi from Louisiana. Further penetration of the area followed after the founding of New Orleans in 1717 and of St. Louis in 1765. The Otoes were in the region about 1717, and also the Pawnee, Panamaha (Omaha), and Comanche. The

18 Alice C. Fletcher and Francis La Flesche (a member of the Omaha tribe), "The Omaha Tribe," *Twenty-seventh Annual Report of the Bureau of American Ethnology* . . . *1905-1906* (Washington, 1911), pp. 15 ff.

19 *Ibid.*, pp. 89-94.

20 George A. Dorsey, *Traditions of the Skidi Pawnee*, Memoirs of the American Folk-Lore Society, VIII (1904); also G. B. Grinnell, *Pawnee Hero Stories and Folk Tales* (New York, 1899).

21 Pierre Margry, *Mémoires et documents*, VI (Paris, 1888), pp. 175-190.

French were not supplanted by the English until the latter part of the eighteenth century. In the closing decades of the eighteenth century trappers were active on the lower reaches of the Missouri and its branches and had even ventured up the Platte.

The French explorers and traders seem to have given definite descriptive names to streams, islands, and other landmarks, to make them identifiable for those coming later. Thus the Niobrara, a fast flowing river, was *l'Eau qui court,* or "running water," on the Perrin du Lac Map of 1802.[22] This was the name for the river used by Father de Smet in the mid-nineteenth century: "My land journey commenced at Bellevue, nine miles beyond the Nebraska or Platte river, thence to the mouth of the Niobrara or *L'Eau-qui-court,* ten days' march."[23]

The same old map has *R. qui monte,* translated as "the river which paints" and named White Paint Creek on the map used by Lewis and Clark. It is now the Bazile, which flows into the Missouri in Knox County, Nebraska. *L'eau bleu* of these maps is Blue Water River, and there are names such as River Bois Blanc, White Wood, Cedar Island, Muddy Island, Long View. The Evans Map of 1755, that of Lewis and Clark, has River Qui Parle, "river which speaks," for the "Sheyenne." Obviously the Weeping Water, or river that weeps, was so designated by the French because it makes a mournful sound flowing over its uneven rocky bed. Today it is much flooded with silt in the Nehawka region and the weeping sound which gave it its name is dulled or gone.

---

[22] The so-called Perrin du Lac Map, *Carte du Missouri levée ou rectifiée dans toute son étendue,* was printed at Paris in 1802. The map is substantially the same as the Mackay Map. James Mackay went up the Missouri, representing the Missouri Fur Company, in the summer of 1795. He spent the winter in Nebraska, on the Elkhorn and Niobrara rivers. Perrin du Lac entered Mackay's discoveries on the map published in connection with his book of travels, *Voyage dans les deux Louisianes, et chez les nations sauvages du Missouri, . . . 1801, 1802 et 1803* (Paris, 1805). The Perrin du Lac Map is reprinted in the *South Dakota Historical Collections,* VII, and also in the *Missouri Historical Society Collections,* IV (1912).

[23] In letters corncerning the expeditions to the Sioux, *Life, Letters and Travels of Father Pierre-Jean De Smet,* edited by Hiram Martin Chittenden and Alfred Talbot Richardson (New York, 1905) II, 618.

The Perrin Du Lac Map gives *L'eau qua pleure,* followed by the English translation "weeping water," as flowing into the Missouri. The same entry but with the correct French pronoun *qui* is made in the so-called Indian Office Map (1755), which under the name of Evans was transmitted by President Thomas Jefferson to Lewis and Clark.[24] Thus it, too, antedates the Lewis and Clark expedition and its written records.

As for travelers, no mention of the Weeping Water region appears in the *Journal* of Jean Baptiste Truteau (Trudeau) among the Arikara Indians in 1795,[25] nor in the works of Washington Irving, George Catlin,[26] and others. There is unmistakable reference, however, in the journals (1804-1806) of Lewis and Clark, who kept a detailed log of each day.

> July 20, Friday, 1804
> a cool morning passed a large willow Island (I) on the S.S. and the mouth of a Creek about 25 yds wide on the L.S. called by the french *L'Eue qui pleure,* or the Water which cry's (weeping water), this Creek falls into the river above a Clift of brown Clay opposit the Willow Island . . .
> From this evening's encampment a man may walk to the Pani [Pawnee] Village on the S bank of the Platte River in two days and to the Ottean in one day.[27]

Patrick Gass of the same expedition has a similar entry in his journal:

> Friday July 20, 1804 we embarked early; passed high yellow banks on the south D Side and a creek called the Water-which-cries, or the Weeping Stream, opposite a willow island, and encamped on a prairie on the south side.[28]

---

24 See Raphael V. Hamilton, "Early Maps of the Missouri Valley," *American Historical Review,* XXXIX (July, 1934), 629-662; and Annie Heloise Abel, "A New Lewis and Clark Map," *Geographical Review,* I (May, 1916). Also *Report* of the American Historical Association, 1908, pp. 188-189.

25 *Missouri Historical Society Publications,* IV.

26 George Catlin, *North American Indians* (New York, 1841).

27 Edited by Reuben Gold Thwaites (1904) I, 85.

28 *Journal of the Voyages and Travels of a Corps of Discovery under the Command of Captain Lewis and Captain Clark* . . . (Philadelphia, 1911), I, xxxiv, ff.; originally published in 1807.

Opinion on the authenticity of the legend of Weeping Water has tended, in the main, toward disbelief in its existence before Dake's poem. A. E. Sheldon, Secretary of the State Historical Society and historian of Nebraska, thought it "certainly as much a work of the imagination as Virgil's story of the founding of Troy." [29] E. E. Blackman, who talked with Isaac Pollard, a pioneer who settled on the banks of the stream in 1856, not far from the present town of Nehawka, says that Pollard decided that the legend originated with Dake. Blackman adds, "I have given the legends of Nebraska considerable study for the past twenty-five years and have never found evidence that this legend originated from any other source." [30] Pollard did find, however, unmistakable evidence of Indian activities in his vicinity. J. Sterling Morton reported in a Nebraska newspaper the discovery of extensive flint mines on Pollard's farm in 1901 and 1902.[31] The stratum containing the flint is about halfway up the small bluffs which border the stream. Tunnelings were found by Pollard and a committee of archaeologists in a limestone-bordered ravine, also burial mounds on the hillside and ruins of lodges near the quarries. Evidence of Indian life along the Weeping Water is unmistakable.

These discoveries led many, such as Dr. L. R. Kunkel of Weeping Water, to believe that the legend might really antedate Professor Dake. Kunkel, in a newspaper article, writes of the relics of ancient life found along the creek and repeats the legend that

> . . . two tribes fought long years ago until all the warriors had been killed. The women made pilgrimages to this valley and wept, mourning the passage of their dead warriors until their tears made the creek known today as the Weeping Water. For years the story was thought to have been a myth, but as archaeologists study the country and dig into the many graves and

---

[29] Plattsmouth *Journal*, May 25, 1936.

[30] *Nebraska History*, VI (1923), 45.

[31] *The Conservative*, July 11, 1901. E. E. Blackman reported on them in 1902 and 1903. See also his "Nehawka Mines and Loup Valley Indian Remains." Nebraska State Historical Society *Reports*, X, *Nebraska History*, 1924.

house sites in this vicinity, the thought presents itself that perhaps this story might be true.[32]

It was Isaac Pollard who named the town of Nehawka. More
is known now of Nebraska Indian languages than in his day,
and present knowledge disposes finally of the story that the
stream was named by Indians from a massacre along its banks.
For her *Nebraska Place-Names*, Lilian Fitzpatrick was supplied
with information concerning Indian names by Dr. M. R. Gilmore, a student of Nebraska Indian languages. Her entry for
Nehawka reads:

> This town received its name in a peculiar way. When the
> government granted a post office to the farmers along the north
> branch of the Weeping Water creek, Isaac Pollard, one of the
> settlers, stopped at the post office department at Washington,
> during a trip to the east, to select a name for the new office.
> He wanted to use the Indian name for "Weeping Water," but
> the only one he could find was too hard to pronounce. Finally
> he came across the word "Nehawka" which meant something
> else, but which he thought sounded well, and so this name was
> agreed upon. Nehawka is a white man's approximation to the
> Omaha and Otoe Indian name of the creek, Nigah°e, which
> does not mean "weeping water" but means the sound of water
> as it runs over low falls, that is, "rustling water." [33]

In the entry for the town of Weeping Water Miss Fitzpatrick
says:

> The Omaha and Otoe Indian name of the creek is Nigah°e,
> from *ni,* water, and *gah°e,* the rustling and swishing sound of
> water running over low falls, or "rustling water." The *h°* is an
> *h* with a guttural sound. The name was confused by white men
> with Nih°age which means "weeping water" from *ni,* water,
> and *h°age,* weeping. The legend of "weeping water" is a white

32 Lincoln *Journal and Star,* October 13, 1855.

33 *Nebraska Place-Names,* University of Nebraska Studies in Language,
Literature, and Criticism, No. 6 (1925), pp. 32-33. Dr. Gilmore is a Nebraskan
now [1947] associated with the Museum of Anthropology of the University of
Michigan. In his "Some Indian Place-Names" in *Publications* of the Nebraska State Historical Society, XIX, 130-139, Dr. Gilmore gives many examples of Indian names that have been mistranslated.

man's tradition or invention to account for the word "weeping water," a mistranslation as stated above.

The Indians could hardly have had a legend that the stream had its origin in tears: their associations with its name were not associations of lamentation.

What do we really know, in the twentieth century, of the Weeping Water legend, told in poetic form in the nineteenth? For one thing, it is clear that the name of the stream is old. It is also clear that it was given by French explorers and traders, not by Indians. Students of Nebraska Indian languages testify that to the Indians it was not the mournful stream but the rustling stream. *Nehawka* does not mean weeping water but is a white man's approximation of an Indian name of different meaning. There is a long stretch of time from the end of the seventeenth century, when the Weeping Water already had its name, to the middle of the nineteenth, when Professor Dake wrote of it.

The Midwest plains afforded the choicest of hunting grounds for Indian tribes. The first to have entered are said to have been the Pawnee. They came earlier than the Sioux, by perhaps a century. During the hundred years that followed the entry of the Sioux, the Pawnee and allied tribes of eastern Nebraska, the Omaha, Otoe, and Ponca, warred with the Sioux. Enough massacres, recorded and unrecorded, occurred on the plains to have started legends independent of the stream called the Weeping Water by white men.

I am inclined to believe that there was a tradition of an Indian massacre before Dake wrote his preface. Why should he have stated that his Nebraska narrative was founded on a legend if it was not? The incident in his second poem, "The Raw Hide," was not of his own creation. Blackman made no claim that his poem of the Niobrara had a legendary basis. Whether the massacre legend, if there was one before Dake, was of Indian origin, the legacy of some actual massacre later associated with the stream by Indians or by whites, or was evolved by whites, from the mournful name of the Weeping Water, is impossible now to determine. But it has seemed to me of interest to trace, so far as I could, a tale appearing in historic times and now unmistakably traditional.

Read at the Western Folklore Conference at the University of Denver, July 10, 1947. Reprinted from *Western Folklore*, Vol. VI, No. 4 (October, 1947), 305-316, published by the University of California Press.

Nebraska Legends of Lovers' Leaps

---- 🐾 ----

1

In mountainous regions it is difficult not to find a precipice from which it is fabled that some human being has leaped, a knight pursued by the enemy, or a virgin fleeing from her captor. The leap may end with disaster, or the fugitive may be saved by a miracle.—A. H. KRAPPE, *The Science of Folk-Lore* (London, 1930), p. 72.

Tragic tales in which lovers leap to suicidal death have played a notable role in literature and folklore, although for some reason academic folklorists have troubled little to give them separate recording. No doubt, as Dr. Krappe implies in the quotation cited above, such legends are to be found pretty much throughout the civilized world. That they exist in less civilized regions is doubtful. Two of them, conspicuous in classical antiquity, have had literary elaboration and may have given impetus to the emergence of others of the same or similar types. There is the legend of the Greek woman poet, Sappho of Lesbos, who was at the height of her prestige about 610 B.C. Students of classical story are familiar with the tale of her hapless devotion to the disdainful Phaon and her fatal leap from the Leucadian promontory, a white rock stretching out into the Ionian sea. The promontory, now separated from the mainland, is the island now called Santa Maura; part of the cliff is still known as Sappho's Leap. The Roman poet Ovid tells of her taking the leap. And about 100 A.D. a minor Roman poet, Ptolemy Hephaestion, listed many men and women who were cured or killed by taking it, though he does not mention Sappho. Indeed, the best authorities have decided that, although long implicitly believed, this legend rests on no dependable evidence but is an invention of later times. Present-day scholars have given it up, though the story lingers. Among those treating the theme are John Lyly, who wrote a play on Sappho that was acted before Queen Elizabeth in 1584; the Austrian poet, Franz Grillparzer, in 1818; and the American dramatist, Percy Mackaye, whose play appeared in 1907. Gounod made the Sappho story the subject of his first opera.

Of special importance, perhaps, for stimulating American stories of lovers' leaps attached to definite loci was Addison's interest in the legend about Sappho. He devoted four eulogistic essays to her in the *Spectator,* in the early eighteenth century. These essays are in the following issues: No. 223, in which Addison tells the legend; No. 227, in which he reverts to it, adding historical and geographical details; No. 229, which includes translations of a fragment by Sappho; and No. 233, which lists, as did the Roman poet, persons (he names seventeen) who in the forty-sixth Olympiad leaped from the promontory in order to cure themselves of their desperate love. Some lived, some died.

A second lover's leap in classical story is that of Hero in the fateful tale of Hero and Leander mentioned in Virgil's *Georgics* (iii, 258). The tale is supposed to have existed earlier in song and art, but Virgil's seems to be the first literary allusion to the youth, Leander of Abydos, who swam the Hellespont nightly to reach the tower of Hero, a young priestess of Apollo at Sestus. Leander perished in a winter storm, and Hero in her grief flung herself from her lofty tower into the same sea. Ovid wrote of her in elegiac verse; Statius similarly told the legend. In the fifth century, Musaeus narrated the tale in full, in hexameter. The sixteenth-century English poet Marlowe retold it independently, in vigorous rhyming couplets. At his death his uncompleted poem was finished by George Chapman.

So much for the background of the legend. To cite an instance from fiction rather than tradition: the Creole heroine, Indiana, of George Sand's novel of that name (1832) and her sympathetic English cousin threw themselves into a waterfall on a desperate impulse, when Indiana found that her young lover had married another. Both were saved from death, however.

As implied earlier, legends of lovers' leaps have not been chronicled by folklorists in the same measure as legends of other types. Among the innumerable entries in Stith Thompson's monumental *Motif-Index of Folk-Literature* [1] there is a single brief reference to Leander's story (T 83), and none at all to Sappho, though Achilles, Perseus, Daedalus, Athena, Atalanta, and other personages of classical legend find place in it. The only other reference to lovers' leaps is a short entry under "Lovers" (A 985): "Lovers in despair throw themselves from a high place. This becomes a cliff." Thompson gives two bibliographical citations, both European, and adds: "Common among the North American Indians." Is this statement concerning the transformation of sites into cliffs in Indian lore one that can be supported by examples? Perhaps references to fatal lovers' leaps of the usual types were crowded out in the six-volume *Motif-Index*, which would be natural enough; or the stories may have seemed too literary for folklore; or they may not have interested the compiler. Dr. Alexander Krappe, in addition to the statement quoted initially, suggested a little farther on [2] that legends relating to the deadly leap might arise from general customs; for instance, from suicide or the punishment of grave crimes. Rites administering punishment might have been

---

[1] Stith Thompson, *Motif-Index of Folk-Literature* (6 vols.; Bloomington, Indiana: Indiana University Studies, Vols. XIX-XXIII, 1932-1936).

[2] Alexander Haggerty Krappe, *The Science of Folk-Lore* (London, 1930), p. 74.

held on some rocks, and the motive might easily have been extended to precipices elsewhere. The Leucadian rock of Sappho is supposed to have been used in the punishment of criminals. It may be added that Rome had its Tarpeian rock, and legal history seems to show that among German peoples the custom of throwing criminals from rocks existed.

2

> The North American Indian as a literary theme has had different phases in different periods: first, the Indian of the eighteenth-century revolutionists in Europe . . . "the noble savage"; second, the sentimentalized Indian of the new feminine school; third, the romanticized Indian of the Walter Scott era . . . ; and lastly, the melodramatic Indian of the mid-century dime novel.—FRED LEWIS PATTEE, *The First Century of American Literature, 1770-1870* (New York, 1935), p. 346.

In the Old World, legends of lovers' leaps are abundant. America also has its share. Although these pass as indigenous, much of their content is not. They are distinctive, however, in that their heroes and heroines purport to be Indians. In America we seem to specialize in fatal leaps of frustrated Indian lovers. This is to be expected, perhaps. Legends are supposed to descend from the past. In our country the past is not classical or feudal-chivalric but belongs to the aborigines. Tales of desperate lovers' taking refuge in suicide would be told less suitably of explorers, hunters, trappers, or soldiers. They would have less appeal than those told of Indians and colored by the preconceptions of the day, when the idea of the Noble Savage reigned and the Red Man was in the foreground of romantic interest. The history and traditions of the Indians seemed, in the earlier nineteenth century, to afford excellent material for American literary men, especially poets. Leading authors tried their hands at Indian themes. An instance is Whittier's early "Bridal of Pennacook." And the young Bryant, when at Williams College, began a narrative poem on an Indian subject. Longfellow's *Hiawatha* had, of course, tremendous popularity.

Surely, by this time, folklorists should discriminate, more definitely than they seem to do, between genuine Indian legends that have come from the Indians themselves and tales about Indians that were invented and circulated by persons of the white race. Stories of the latter type are always treated romantically and have stock characters and situations. With monotonous sameness the beautiful Indian maiden, daughter of a stern chief, leaps to death from some steep cliff. More rarely, her suitor leaps also. These legends of suicide purport to be of Indian derivation and Indian tradition; as a rule, they are vigorously championed as such. But skepticism is in order, I am convinced, when tales associated with definite local sites are told of Indian courtships with tragic outcome. If any of them have an indigenous basis, an assumption which is none too safe, it has been elaborated and furbished up beyond likelihood of authenticity. The characters are Indian in name only. Many customs of courtship and marriage of white folks are reflected. Little appears that comes plausibly from the red man.

Although Stith Thompson stated in his *Motif-Index* that lover's-leap legends in which a site is transformed into a cliff are common among the North American Indians, in his earlier *Tales of the North American Indians* (Cambridge, Mass., 1929) he included no Indian lover's-leap legends and made no mention of their existence. In his recent *The Folktale* (New York, 1946) he reiterates his statement of the *Motif-Index* that such legends are "common among the North American Indians." "There are," he says, "dozens of Indian tales of lover's leaps all over America." Again, he follows this by no expression of skepticism concerning their Indian derivation. Did he take stock in them as genuinely Indian? If so, why did he not reproduce one or more in his assemblages of 1929 and 1946? Whether he meant to do so or not, he leaves the impression that such tales abound among American Indians and that they came from Indians and were handed on by them. Exceptional is J. Frank Dobie, the collector and editor of *Legends of Texas*. He prints eight lover's-leap legends and has gathered a few more; but he terms this group "the least indigenous and least varied" of all his Texas legends.³ Each is a tragic story of thwarted Indian courtship, though in it sometimes appear other characters, such as a young Spanish caballero in one, and a beautiful Spanish maiden in another.

When I discussed "The Nebraska Legend of Weeping Water" a few years ago,⁴ the legend seemed to me to date from Professor O. C. Dake's ambitious poem of that title printed in 1871 in a small book of verse. Professor Dake, who was the first professor of English at the University of Nebraska, thought that the name of the little river flowing into the Missouri, Weeping Water, was of Indian origin, not knowing that it had been given by French explorers who called it *l'eau qui pleure*. To account for the naming he supplied a romantic story of an Otoe youth, Sananona, and an Omaha maiden, Nacoumah—a story ending in a double tribal massacre. Another instance of a romantic Indian story with a Nebraska setting—this author made no claim of a legendary Indian basis for it—is Elmer E. Blackman's *Niobrara's Love Story: An Indian Romance of Pre-Historic Nebraska* (Roca, Nebraska, 1900), composed in the measure of Longfellow's *Hiawatha*. This is a tale of the bold

---

3 J. Frank Dobie, *Legends of Texas* (Austin, Texas: Publications of the Texas Folk-Lore Society, No. III, 1924), p. 153.

Dorothy Scarborough was an earlier skeptic when she wrote of "Traditions of the Waco Indians," *Publications of the Texas Folk-Lore Society,* I, 1916, 50-51:

"There are legends in plenty concerning the Waco Indians but some of them bear the mark of the fiction factory. The most popular tradition is that of Lover's Leap. Of course, every self-respecting community boasts of its lover's leap and its tale of despair and devotion, and this recital differs in few respects from the conventional romance. The story goes that Wah-wah-tee, a beautiful maid of the Wacoes, became secretly acquainted with a young brave of a hostile tribe and fell in love with him. He was planning to steal her away to his camp and make her his wife, but they were discovered by the girl's relatives. Pursued by the angry braves, they fled, and in the effort to elude their would-be captors they came to the high bluff over the river. But the yells of the infuriated kinsmen behind them told them that escape was hopeless. In front was the face of the bluff, with the turbulent waters of the river on a sudden rise below them, while close behind came the Wacoes. Preferring death to the swift and terrible tribal vengeance, the lovers clasped their arms around each other and leaped into the river to perish."

4 See pp. 61-78.

young deer hunter, Keya Paha, and Niobrara, the beautiful daughter of King Tartarax of Quivera. The hunter is killed in Indian warfare; Niobrara dies of a fever; and the river Niobrara (*l'eau qui court,* the "running water" of French explorers) was named after her. Professor Dake's story lives in legend. That Blackman's ever will become legendary is unlikely. The relative lateness of its date and the Tartarax and Quivera features label it plainly as non-Indian. These are not lover's-leap legends, but they illustrate further the trend of their day toward romantic idealization of the Indian.

The factual recording of Indian tales began in the later years of the nineteenth century. With the development of the American Bureau of Ethnology and the recordings of individual ethnologists such as George A. Dorsey, Alice Fletcher, and Frances Densmore, working in the last decades of the nineteenth century and the first half of the twentieth, genuine Indian tales were first made available. Particularly desirable, of course, was the printing of the Indian texts and the English translations side by side—a practice sometimes followed. When phonographic recording came, accuracy was finally achieved.

In genuine Indian tales, women appear often, but they are far different from the charming, devoted maidens of the white man's romantic tales. A few titles will suggest the difference: "Woman Bewitched by a Fox," "The Spider Woman," "Buffalo Wife and Corn Wife," "The Dog Boy Who Married the Chief's Daughter," "The Woman Who Became a Horse," "The Poor Boy Marries the Chief's Daughter." Even the story of the poor boy is without the romantic slant supplied inevitably by white chroniclers. When I examined the numerous tales of the Pawnee collected from Nebraska by George A. Dorsey and G. B. Grinnell, those of the Omaha collected by Alice Fletcher and Francis La Fleche, and various tales coming from other tribes, I found no lover's-leap legend. In the contact of the white and red races there seems to be little assimilation by one race of the legend plots of the other. Not only do there seem to be no stories of transformations of sites of fatalities into cliffs, which the *Motif-Index* states are "common among the North American Indians," but there are no stories at all of suicidal leaps of despairing Indian lovers.

3

> The Nebraska legends indicate that the Indians' sense of romance was strongly developed, regardless of their apparent stoicism.—NEBRASKA FEDERAL WRITERS' PROJECT, Pamphlet No. 2, May, 1937, p. 11.

When I became interested in this theme, my primary purpose was to record the lover's-leap legends in Nebraska. I have found four: there may be others with which I am not acquainted. The four "leaps" are respectively in Banner County, Dawes County, Knox County, and Nance County—in the northern and western parts of the state, regions in which there are occasional bluffs and rocky precipices. Most of Nebraska is pretty flat.[5] Conjecturally, procedure in the emergence of the legends was something like this: Some eminence with a steep wall was conspicuous. In someone's imagination it became the site of a suicidal leap, and it was given a name that expressed this idea. Next, some local author accounted for the naming by attaching to it a romantic story of the past—the past of our region is Indian—and narrated it in verse or prose. The "legend" was thus preserved, and eventually it was generally accepted as of Indian tradition, despite its romantic features. The quotation cited

---

[5] The Dakotas, having many more precipices, probably have many more lover's-leap legends than Nebraska has. This is no doubt true of Minnesota also. A legend which has all the stock characteristics of this type is associated with Lake Pepin in Minnesota, which is about a hundred miles below the Falls of St. Anthony on the Mississippi. The heroine, a Sioux Indian girl, the noble-minded Oo-la-ita (in another version her name is Wenona), "the pride of the braves of the Dakotas," gave her heart to a young Indian, I-ta-tomah (White Eagle), of her own tribe. Her stern parents insisted that she marry an old chief. The hopeless lovers finally leaped from the limestone bluffs on the east shore of Lake Pepin and were dashed to pieces. Under the name "Oo-la-ita" this legend is narrated at length in unrhymed five-line stanzas in *Poems of Two Worlds*, by Willian Cotter Wilson (Kansas City, 1893), pp. 154-167. In the plot of the Lincoln, Nebraska, "Salt Basin Legend" of frustrated lovers, a legend to be traced unmistakably to a literary source, the maiden does not leap from a cliff; she is turned into a mound of salt—a fate reminiscent of that of Lot's wife.

above, from the Federal Writers' Project, Pamphlet No. 2, is an illustration.

Banner County.—In this county are Wildcat and Hogback mountains, the two highest peaks (5,038 and 5,082 feet above sea level) in the state. Near-by is Table Mountain. The Lover's Leap in Banner County is on this mountain, just south of Long Springs, near Harrisburg. The Federal Writers' Project, *Nebraska: A Guide to the Cornhusker State* (New York, 1939), p. 391, gives a short version of the legend: "Near here are two rocks called Lover's Leap. From one of these rocks, legend says, the daughter of a Sioux chief jumped to her death, rather than desert her own sweetheart for an Oglala brave to whom she had been betrothed by her parents."

Grant Lee Shumway's *History of Western Nebraska and Its People* (Lincoln, 1921) II, 37-38, gives a full account and prints a picture of the Banner County Lover's Leap, p. 515. Essentially the same in detail is the following legend, given me by Mrs. A. H. Rulkoetter.

Situated on a little table-land just south of a little creek, then unnamed, stood a Sioux Indian village. Thither had come an Oglala brave with his finest ponies to exchange for the chief's beautiful daughter. Tomorrow he would claim his bride.

The daughter loved a brave of her own tribe and was determined not to marry the Oglala. Secretly leaving her father's lodge, she found her sweetheart and persuaded him to run away with her when night came. They mounted two of the ponies tied before her father's lodge and rode away. They were seen leaving the village and were soon overtaken. The angry chief had his daughter whipped and the lover put to death.

The next morning the Indian maiden donned her wedding finery and went humming through the village, wending her way to the south. The people seeing her wondered at her taking her lover's death so lightly. The Sioux braves watched her with admiration and envied the Oglala his good fortune. He, too, looked on in admiration and anticipation and rated his prize the more highly since he had nearly lost her.

As she went up Table Mountain her song took a sadder strain. She paused at the eastern extremity where ages of weathering had made a perpendicular wall to the cliff. All the people were watching her now. She raised her arms to the sun and commenced to sing again. Her song, weird and sweet, was instantly recognized as her death song.

A dozen braves rushed after her, but before they could reach her she threw aside her blanket and stood for a moment as a statue of bronze in the morning sun. Then, with a cry to her dead lover, she leaped over the cliff and was crushed to death on the rocks below. Thus the cliff received its name.[6]

Dawes County.—Crow Butte, southeast of Crawford, is a conspicuous landmark with high, straight walls. Three miles north of the butte and facing it, slightly northwest of Crawford, is Lover's Leap. It is of light stone, with rougher rock at its base, and it, too, has high, straight walls. The legend of Crow Butte tells that a band of Crow Indians, hard pressed by the Sioux, retreated to the top of this butte and escaped by a ruse, leaving only a few old men there. Later, the Sioux and Crows made a lasting peace. This legend is cited in *Nebraska: A Guide to the Cornhusker State*, p. 321. The relation of the Crow Butte legend to that of the near-by Lover's Leap is a matter of conjecture.

A newspaper account, several columns long, of "The Legend of Lover's Leap," by Karl L. Spence, was printed in the *Northwest Nebraska News*, December 31, 1936. In summary it runs as follows:

> Long ago the region of the White Water and the Niobrara was the hunting ground of the Cheyenne Indians, who lived in peace with their neighbors the Crows. Then came Sioux warriors and drove them back in long-lasting warfare. The Sioux, led by a young chief, Eagle Feather, attacked the camps of the Cheyennes many times. Once, Eagle Feather visited the Cheyenne camp alone in the darkness to spy out the location for a next morning's attack. Drawing near the chief's tepee, he saw the chief's daughter, Crimson Cloud, and fell in love with her. He decided not to attack with his warriors but to come alone and try to capture the maiden. Luck favored him. He arrived with two horses, saw Crimson Cloud, followed her to a stream, grasped her, and, with her consent, carried her off. But he had been seen. The Cheyenne chief was told and gathered his fight-

---

6 "Lover's Leap," in Nebraska Writers' Project, *Nebraska Folklore*, Book II (Lincoln, 1940), pp. 3-4.

ing men to follow. They came closer and closer in pursuit of the fleeing pair. In the meantime, the Sioux had noted the absence of the chief's son. The lovers, caught between the two opposing forces, were driven to the highest point of the hills. Seeing no chance of escape, with their arms about each other they leaped from the high cliff and were crushed to death. And thus Lover's Leap received its name. The Sioux and Cheyenne did not continue their fight but became united against their common enemies and were henceforth as one people.

This version of the legend appeared again, in shortened form, in the Chadron *Record* for Wednesday, June 22, 1949, contributed by Dean Buckingham, a student at Chadron State Normal College.

Miss Bessie Fisher of Chadron and Lincoln has a slightly different version. According to her, the battle was not between the Cheyenne (a Siouan tribe) and the Sioux but was between the Crows and the Sioux. The Crows were victorious. Among the killed was a noble Sioux warrior who was affianced to the chief's daughter. She was brokenhearted at his death, could not become resigned to it, and slipped off to the butte to rejoin her lover in spirit land. When her crushed body was found at the foot of the cliff she was buried beside the slain warrior. Miss Fisher adds that, in June, 1949, as she was riding to Chadron in a bus, she questioned a Sioux squaw regarding the lover's-leap story. The squaw said that Miss Fisher's version was the right one, that her grandmother had told her the story many times. The battle on the buttes near Crawford was between Sioux and Crows, not the Sioux and the Cheyenne. The Crows were victorious and killed a noble Sioux warrior who was engaged to the chief's daughter. Miss Fisher has the probabilities on her side, for the customs of the Sioux and the Cheyenne are similar, and differ widely from those of the Crow.

Knox County.—The Maiden's Leap in Knox County is a chalk-colored cliff or mound of light stone, about a hundred feet high. It is said to have a profile like that of a human being. It is between the towns of Center and Niobrara, about four miles east of the latter, on the main highway. A crowd often gathers about the picturesque and romantic spot on pleasant days, especially Sundays. Names of visitors to the site are carved all over the surface of the light stone.

The legend associated with the place is supposed to be of Santee Indian origin. There is a Santee settlement, the Santee mission, on the bank of the Missouri River, beyond the town of Niobrara. It was named after the Sioux were transferred there from Minnesota and Dakota Territory after an uprising in 1862. In the legend, an Indian girl was betrothed by her stern father, not to the brave with whom she was in love but to another. When she could not marry the handsome warrior of her choice, she killed herself by riding one of her father's horses over the cliff. I have not found a poetic, or literary, or long journalistic serving up of the legend associated with this site.

Another legend connected with the cliff is that Jesse James, when pursued by Indians, leaped on horseback from the cliff and swam across the Missouri River to safety.

Nance County.—Two stories are associated with a site in Nance County, near Fullerton. One is that Indians hunting buffaloes in the vicinity killed many by driving them over the cliff. The other, the lover's-leap legend, is told in poetical form by Mrs. A. P. Jarvis, in the *Collection of Nebraska Pioneer Reminiscences,* published in Cedar Rapids in 1916 by the Nebraska Society of the Daughters of the American Revolution (pp. 196-197). A few selections from the poem's forty-four lines suggest the usual story:

LOVER'S LEAP
The hunting red men used to force
    The buffalo o'er this frightful steep;
They could not check their frantic course;
    By following herds pressed down they leap

. . . .

Yet a far more pathetic tale
    The Pawnees told the pioneer
Of dusky maid and stripling pale
    Who found in death a refuge here.

. . . .

She was the chieftain's only child,
    As gentle as the cooing dove.

Pure was this daughter of the wild;
    The pale-face lad had won her love.

Her father, angered at her choice
    Had bid'n her wed a chieftain brave;
She answered with a trembling voice,
    "I'd rather lie within my grave.

   • • • • • • • • • • • • • •

She led him to this dangerous place
    That on the streamlet's glee doth frown;
The sunlight, gleaming on her face,
    Her wild, dark beauty seemed to crown.

"Dear youth," exclaimed the dusky maid,
    "I've brought thee here thy faith to prove;
If thou of death art not afraid,
    We'll sacrifice our lives to love."

Hand linked in hand they looked below,
    Then, headlong plunged adown the steep.
The Pawnees from that hour of woe
    Have named the place The Lovers' Leap.

A University of Nebraska instructor whose childhood was spent in Fullerton gives the following testimony concerning the Nance County leap.

I talked with my uncle and my sister concerning the Fullerton leap. My uncle recalled that it was originally known as the Crazyman's Leap, and my sister and I recall that this was the name by which we always spoke of it. It was later called Buffalo Leap, and eventually Lover's Leap. My uncle seemed to remember that the latter name was applied at about the time that the Methodist Epworth Assembly began having meetings at Fullerton. A short account mentioning the leap appeared in a printed circular announcing the General Assembly at Fullerton Epworth Park, August 14-23, 1901. Part of it is as follows:

"One of the most beautiful spots in Nebraska is the natural park in which the Assembly will be held. . . . On the north flows the Cedar river, a beautiful stream excellent for boating and bathing. On the south rise the bluffs in all their beauty and grandeur, culminating just outside the grounds, on the west, in the 'Lover's Leap,' overlooking the valley. The ascent may be made by means of a winding path, and from the summit is a scene of transcendent beauty. . . ."

The leap is said to have been two hundred feet in height. My uncle is sure that the leap was a claybank. Sometime after 1901, the course of the river changed. It no longer winds beneath the bluff. Were any desperate lover or any buffalo to plunge over the bluff now, he, or she, or it would land in a clump of dry shrubbery.

In the long background of tales of the lover's-leap group, no doubt the Sappho legend and its affiliates, Addison's *Spectator* essays, and the cult of the Indian in romantic literature all had their influence. Today in the United States, lovers and other desperate persons do not leap over precipices but jump from the upper windows of hotels or other tall buildings. Mme. Kasenkina's leap to freedom from the Russian consulate, the leap of Masaryk in Czechoslovakia, and that of Lawrence Duggan in Washington, as well as James Forrestal's suicidal leap from a hospital, were from windows, and all were in 1948-1949.

Read at the Ninth Annual Western Folklore Conference, University of Denver, July 15, 1949. Reprinted from *Western Folklore*, Vol. VIII, No. 4 (October, 1949), 304-313, published by the University of California Press.

The Legend of
the Lincoln Salt Basin

Lincoln, Nebraska, my home town, was selected in the mid-nine-teenth century as the capital of the state chiefly because of the now-vanished salt basin a few miles to the west. In my youth, the basin proper, the "big basin," was about a mile long and half a mile wide. It was early a salt lick for Indians and buffalo. When my parents came to Lincoln, its large white expanse was the leading feature of Lancaster County. It attracted visitors of all types. In pioneer times settlers came from near and far to scrape up salt crystals or to trade with others for them if recent rains had flooded the basin.

The area was discovered by government officials in 1856 and it must have been much larger then, perhaps very large in still earlier times. In the 1890's there were salt basins extending six miles north of Lincoln along the west bank of Salt Creek, a stream flowing northeast into the Platte. The "big basin" was the southwestern one. It was thought that millions would be made from it. Horace Wesson of the Smith and Wesson firearm manufacturing firm expended some $50,000 in all, a large sum for that day, for the improvement of the basin. But the project was not successful: not a cent was realized by his or any other serious attempts to develop the basin. The salt springs in the southern part were active in producing brine; but the overflow of the near-by Salt Creek bottoms after the rains carried down the creek the vats damming the salt. Work was stopped, too, by disputes over the title to the region. Investigators finally reported that the production of salt from the brine, found at the depth of several hundred feet, could not be made profitable. When the railroads came, cheaper salt could be brought from Utah and Kansas and soon salt could also be had from Michigan. The optimistic dreams of vast wealth to be derived from the location of the capital city near the salt basin were not realized.

Salt Creek, which so hampered the development of the basin, has been straightened at various times in later years and some of it has been drawn off. It is now a far from impressive stream, whatever it may have been once. Apparently it was large enough in earlier times not to be overlooked. The first mention of the stream by a white explorer (he seems also to be the first recorder of the name, Nebraska) is to be found in *La Découverte du Missouri et L'Histoire du Fort Orléans, 1673-1728,* edited and published by Baron Marc Du Villiers in 1925. The first part of this book is entitled "L'Exploration du Missouri, 1673-1719," with page headings "Les Voyages de Véniard Du Bourgmond." Etienne Véniard Du Bourgmond, a *coureur de bois* and commissioned commander and explorer in the Missouri region, kept a diary of the route of his explorations. His diary, which stops with June 16, 1714, was not published complete until by Du Villiers. The latter adds that the explorer did not pass the Platte in 1714 but went up the Missouri again, going beyond the mouth of the Kansas this time and noting the different tribes of Indians, the Missouri, the Osage, the Kansas, to be found along its banks. Then follows (page 61) this passage, which I translate:

> Higher is the *Rivière Large* [Platte] called by the French and the savages [Indians] *Nibraskier* [Nebraska] which runs to the north and to the west-northwest. At ten leagues are the Maguatantala [Otoe], an Indian nation allied with and friendly to the French. They are on the banks of a little river the water of which is salt [Saline] and from which they make salt. . . .

Following the Saline River twenty-five leagues higher are the
Panis [Skidi Pawnee], numerous, alert, and good horsemen.
The French know them and see them sometimes. . . . Twenty
leagues higher are the Panimahas [Omaha] that the French
also see sometimes.

The *Mémoires et Documents* (1614-1764) of Pièrre Margry [1]
include much material concerning the activities of Du Bourgmond along the Missouri.

Here, then, in the second decade of the eighteenth century
is the first mention of the Platte and Salt Creek region, its
supply of salt and the Indians' knowledge of it. The narrative
of Lewis and Clark, early in the nineteenth century, notes that
they reached the Saline River on July 21, 1804. On the river
were Otoe and other villages. Lewis and Clark did not ascend
the stream as far as the salt basin.

Late in the nineteenth century the water from Oak Creek, a
stream from the northwest, was turned into the salt basin and
a small "lake," so called, was formed making mild boating
possible for a time. The picturesque and historic white expanse
of basin disappeared for good. Newcomers to Lincoln know
nothing of it. "Capitol Beach," which succeeded it, became an
amusement park and its salt-water swimming pool formed a
chief attraction. By this time, the mid-twentieth century, the
main body of water from Oak Creek has been diverted to form
Oak Park Lake some distance northeast.

Though no traces of Indian villages or burial grounds have
been found in the salt basin area to indicate that Indian tribes
ever stayed permanently in the vicinity, their knowledge of it
is unmistakable. W. W. Cox, historian of Seward County, says
that as late as 1862 a vast throng of Omaha Indians camped
at the head of the basin, adding that Indians often came there
on their way to their summer hunting grounds on the Republican River.[2] The Omaha Indian word or name for the salt
basin is said to have been *niskithki.*

---

[1] (Paris, 1886), VI, 382-483.
[2] "The Beginnings of Lincoln and Lancaster County," *Transactions and
Reports* of the State Historical Society of Nebraska, III (1888), 85 ff.

Apparently all over Nebraska in pioneer days names were given to conspicuous natural features by Indians and whites. Then the whites created some legend, often originated or written up in a poem, to account for the name, and the legend came to be ascribed to the Indians. That a legend should be associated with so striking a natural feature as the Lincoln salt basin was inevitable. The legend is now all but forgotten by Lincoln people, like the basin itself, and its origin is nearly forgotten too, though it is preserved in an accessible printed source. There are, of course, genuine Indian tales associated with striking topographic features in Nebraska. These and numerous other Indian legends have, however, been pretty well assembled by ethnologists versed in the languages of the Nebraska Indian tribes; they are preserved in government and other assemblages. But these genuine Indian tales are of quite a different type. A few years ago I discussed the origin of the Nebraska legend of weeping water, apparently from a poem written by the first professor of English literature at the University of Nebraska; and last year I discussed four lover's leap legends in the state, all, with the possible exception of one, demonstrably of white origin and all ascribed to the Indians. Similarly, the legend of the salt basin had, I believe, a literary derivation. It seems to me doubtful that it antedated 1833-1835, when John Treat Irving, Jr. (1812-1906), nephew of Washington Irving, gave it a special short chapter in his *Indian Sketches* (1835), published in Philadelphia on his return from his excursion to the Nebraska Pawnee of two years before. Thus the salt basin legend can be taken back for more than a hundred years—a pretty long time for Nebraska, which did not become a state until 1867.

Young Irving accompanied Henry L. Ellsworth (1791-1858) when, in the summer of 1833, the latter was sent as government commissioner to the Indians with a small military escort from Fort Leavenworth. Certain Indian tribes, transplanted from other regions to the Midwest, encountered fierce opposition from those already on the prairies. Only by constant fighting could they exist, since they had no place to which they could retreat. Ellsworth was sent to purchase **the** contested lands and to make treaties with the Pawnee. This tribe, living along the banks of the Platte, and their allies in the region, the Otoe, laid claim to all the land lying between the Platte and the Kansas rivers, a tract granted by the government to the Delaware. The Pawnee were to be induced by Ellsworth to move north of the Platte. Young Irving, then a youth of twenty-one, went with Ellsworth for the adventure, as he states in his two-volume *Indian Sketches*. He describes his experience with Ellsworth as "an excursion fraught with novelty and pleasurable excitement" conveying "an idea of the habits and customs of Indian tribes . . . who at that time lived in their pristine simplicity uncontaminated by the vices of the lawless white man." The "Legend of the Saline River" is to be found in the twelfth chapter of the first volume. It is the earliest specific mention of the Lincoln salt basin that I have been able to find in the reports of travelers and the writings of historians. De Bourgmond and Lewis and Clark mentioned Salt River, or Creek, but not the basin, nor do other Western explorers mention it so far as I have been able to learn. The Irving legend is reprinted without comment by A. J. Sawyer.[3] He seems to have accepted it as traditional and to have believed, perhaps, that Irving reached the basin himself. To a present-day reader familiar with the early nineteenth-century cult of the "noble red man," it seems practically certain that Irving himself created the legend, with its reflection of the literary tastes of the period and its echoing, in one version, of the Scriptural story of Lot's wife. It seems certain, too, that although Irving came close to the Lincoln region and camped along Salt River, probably somewhere near Ashland, he did not reach the "big basin." His account does not suggest to me firsthand presence at the site.

Irving's legend has all the marks of an early eighteenth-century romantic tale. It is represented as being told by a guide of the party. Nothing identifying is said of the guide; perhaps he is supposed to be one of the escorting soldiers. Assumedly he knew Indian speech and he knew of the salt basin. The

---

3 *Lincoln and Lancaster County* (1916), pp. 57-58.

intercalation of tales in longer narratives was then a favorite literary device. It is used by Sir Walter Scott, by Washington Irving in his Spanish works, and by Dickens. In J. T. Irving's *Indian Sketches* there are other fairly complete short narratives of Indian incidents or episodes. Examples in his first volume are "The Iotan and His Brother—or Indian Revenge" in the fourth chapter, and "Indian Habits—the Escape" in the seventh, and "The Chase" in the eighteenth. But these are not told romantically nor have they the completeness and the finish of the salt basin legend. What they narrate seems incidental chronicling, not tradition.

Irving's central figure, the Indian chief, is Byronic. He is as proud and lone and bitter as are Manfred and Childe Harold. Of similar stripe are Charlotte Brontë's Rochester or Emily Brontë's Heathcliffe, or Augusta Evans Wilson's St. Elmo, those post-Byronic fictional heroes that were to have their day of literary vogue. The Nebraska Indian tribes involved are not identified. The party of white men have passed the Sacs and Foxes, but have not yet reached the Pawnee. They came to the Missouri, then went up the Platte. They camped the first night on the bank of the Saline River "which flows through the prairies until it empties into the Platte." In the spring of every year, writes the author, "moisture exudes from the soil near its source, covering the prairie for the distance of many miles. This is dried up by the heat of the summer, and leaves in its place a thick incrustation of salt. This is in turn dissolved by every successive rain, and carried off into the Saline river, giving its water its brackish taste from which it derives its name. There is a barrenness around the stream contrasting strongly with the other rivers that grace the prairies. Around *them* is always a rich forest of the deepest, rankest green—but the Saline is far different. There are no groves to fringe its banks, only a few trees here and there." The party, he continues, "had supper of roasted deer on the banks," and, that finished, "collected round the large fire of blazing logs." Query: where did the large logs come from in so treeless a region, and was a fire likely to be needed in a Nebraska summer? But this is the conventional setting for legend telling. Then "our guide having lighted his Indian pipe, related to us an Indian tale, of which the following is the purport." The chapter narrating "The Legend of the Saline River" begins:

About 40 miles above the spot where we are now encamped, lie the great salt plains, which cause the brackish taste of the Saline river. In one part of these plains is a large rock of pure salt of dazzling whiteness, which is highly prized by the Indians, and to which is attached the following story.

∽ ∽ ∽

Many years since, long before the whites had extended their march beyond the banks of the Mississippi river, a tribe of Indians resided upon the Platte, near its junction with the Saline. Among these was one, the chief warrior of the nation, celebrated throughout all the neighbouring country, for his fierce and unsparing disposition. Not a hostile village within several hundred miles, but wailed for those who had fallen beneath his arm; not a brook, but had run red with blood of his victims. He was forever engaged in plotting destruction to his enemies. He led his warriors from one village to another, carrying death to the inhabitants, and desolation to their homes. He was a terror to old and young.

Often alone and unattended, would he steal off, to bathe his hands in blood, and add new victims to the countless numbers of those whom he had already slain. But fearful as he was to the hostile tribes, he was equally dreaded by his own people. They gloried in him as their leader, but shrank from fellowship with him. His lodge was deserted, and even in the midst of his own nation he was alone. Yet there was one being that clung to him, and loved him in defiance of the sternness of his rugged nature. It was the daughter of the chief of the village; a beautiful girl, and graceful as one of the fawns of her own prairie.

Though she had many admirers, yet when the warrior declared his intention of asking her of her father, none dared come in competition with so formidable a rival. She became his wife, and he loved her with all the fierce energy of his nature. It was a new feeling to him. It stole like a sunbeam, over the dark passions of his heart. His feelings gushed forth, to meet the warm affection of the only being that had ever loved him.

Her sway over him was unbounded. He was as a tiger tamed. But this did not last long. She died; he buried her; he uttered no wail, he shed no tear. He returned to his lonely lodge, and forbade all entrance. No sound of grief was heard from it—all was silent as the tomb. The morning came, and with its earliest dawn he left the lodge. His body was covered with war paint, and he was fully armed as if for some expedition. His eye was the same, there was the same sullen fire that had ever shot from its deep sunken socket. There was no wavering of a single feature; there was not the shrinking of a single muscle. He took no notice of those around him; but walked gloomily to the spot where his wife was buried. He paused for a moment over the grave—plucked a wild flower from among the grass, and cast it upon the upturned sod. Then turning on his heel, strode across the prairie.

After the lapse of a month he returned to his village, laden with the scalps of men, women, and children, which he hung in the smoke of his lodge. He tarried but a day among the tribe, and again set off, lonely as ever. A week elapsed, and he returned, bringing with him a large lump of white salt. In a few words he told his tale. He had traveled many miles over the prairies. The sun had set in the west, and the moon was just rising above the verge of the horizon. The Indian was weary, and threw himself on the grass. He had not slept long, when he was awakened by the low wailing of a female. He started up, and at a little distance, by the light of the moon, beheld an old decrepit hag, brandishing a tomahawk over the head of a young female, who was kneeling, imploring mercy.

The warrior wondered how two females could be at this spot, alone, and at that hour of the night; for there was no village within forty miles of the place. There could be no hunting party near, or he would have discovered it. He approached them; but they seemed unconscious of his presence. The young female finding her prayers unheeded, sprang up, and made a desperate attempt to get possession of the tomahawk. A furious struggle ensued, but the old woman was victorious. Twisting one hand in the long black hair of her victim, she raised the weapon in her other, and prepared to strike. The face of the young female was turned to the light, and the warrior beheld with horror the features of his deceased wife. In an instant he sprang forward, and his tomahawk was buried in the skull of the old squaw. But ere he had time to clasp the form of his wife, the ground opened, both sank from his sight, and on the spot appeared a rock of white salt. He had broken a piece from it, and brought it to his tribe.

This tradition is still current among the different tribes of Indians frequenting that portion of the country. They also imagine, that the rock is still under custody of the old squaw, and that the only way to obtain a portion of it, is to attack her. For this reason, before attempting to collect salt, they beat the ground with clubs and tomahawks, and each blow is considered as inflicted upon the person of the hag. The ceremony is continued, until they imagine that she has been sufficiently be-laboured, to resign her treasure without opposition. This superstition, though privately ridiculed by the chiefs of the different tribes, is still practiced by them, and most devoutly credited by the rabble.

Here is a version of the legend from the 1930's, a hundred years later. It was obtained from Irene Courtenay Johnson of Atkinson, Nebraska, the granddaughter of a Lincoln pioneer. The "females" have become women, and a reason different from his—*Indian Sketches* was his first literary venture—is supplied for young Irving's Western adventuring. In Mrs. Johnson's version occurs the transformation into a block of salt that suggests the Scriptural transformation of Lot's wife. With Irving, a rock of salt appeared on the spot where the ground opened to swallow the struggling figures. Mrs. Johnson entitles her account "The Otoe Legend."

When John Irving, who was searching for material for a new book, came to the unsettled land of Nebraska in 1833, he heard of the salt basin which was located near the present site of Lincoln. In answer to Mr. Irving's inquiries about the fertile source of the salt the Indians related an old legend of the tribe.

The Otoe Indian tribe was living about thirty miles west of Omaha on the present location of Ashland. A strong young chief of the tribe had taken for his bride a beautiful Indian maiden whom he loved. They had not lived together many moons when the dark-eyed girl became ill and died. Sorrow and grief overtook the young chief, and he became so sad and restless that he determined to leave the tribe.

From that time onward the brave was a wanderer; he often went on trips by himself from which he would not return for many weeks. It was while he was on such a trip down the Saline river that the unhappy Indian saw a vision—or was it a reality? As he was paddling down the stream by night the chief heard a cry from the shore. When he looked up he saw an old squaw with a club beating a younger woman. The brave went to the rescue but as he neared the two the hag pulled the maiden's hair so that her face was lighted by the moon. To the chief's horror he recognized the features as those of his buried bride. He raised his hand to strike the squaw but as he lowered it the two figures turned into a block of salt.

Thus the salt basin came into being.

A second and still shorter version from the 1930's is from Margaret Theobald Elliott of Lincoln, who says she does not know how she got it. In her version a large cake of salt appears in the morning, after the ground opened and swallowed up the girl. Like Mrs. Johnson she credits the legend to the Otoe.

A fierce tribe governed by a bloodthirsty chief lived on the banks of Salt Creek. Only the beautiful daughter of the chief had no fear of the greatest warrior of the tribe and was his constant companion. Other braves dared not woo her. They were married and henceforth the warrior was subdued and completely ruled by his beautiful wife. She died and he made her grave on the highest hill. He did not weep at her death. After mourning awhile by her grave he plunged into a thicket and strode away along the banks of the stream. He slept in a lonely spot when night came. Suddenly he was awakened by a wailing of a woman's voice. In the light of the moon he saw an old hag with a tomahawk raised above the girl. He recognized the girl as his wife. He sprang forward, killed the hag, and reached to clasp his wife, but the ground opened and she was swallowed up. In the morning he found a large cake of white salt where the struggle had occurred. He broke off a piece and returned with it to his people. Afterwards Indians when they came to the salt basin at the head of the creek always beat on the ground with clubs to frighten the old witch who guarded her treasure of salt at the place.

Additional lore of the Lincoln salt basin has been given me

by Mari Sandoz, who is exceptionally well versed in the history of the Indians of the state. She has known and talked with many, especially those near-by her home in the Upper Niobrara region. Brule Sioux from the Rosebud Agency in South Dakota and also an old Pawnee told her, she says, that both Sioux and Cheyenne frequented the salt basin area partly for salt and partly to prey on other Indians who went there. One of the tales was of the massacre by the Pawnee of a small hunting party of Brule Sioux who came to the great salt lick. Another of their tales was of a great sickness that struck the animals around the lick; so many died that the stench reached the Platte. It was something like the historic murrain (rinderpest) that struck the buffalo and antelope herds up the Missouri in the 1820's or thereabouts. Hundreds of animals are said to have died there. In any case, a story arose of the complete isolation of the basin after the wholesale demise. Sir Charles Augustus Murray, in his book about his travels in America during 1834, 1835, and 1836,[4] tells of reaching the Saline River, and he leaves the impression that the region was pretty dead. His report comes from the same period as Irving's.

I do not wish to assume that some Indian legend associated with the Lincoln salt basin, perhaps one of a chief and a doomed maiden, did not exist before Irving wrote his *Sketches* of 1835. If it did, he may have heard of it and elaborated it. But I am sure that, as he served it up, the Indians could not have felt that it was theirs. As it comes down to us, it must be credited to him rather than to the Indians. On the whole, the record of the Lincoln salt basin, gone now and forgotten like the Indians and buffalo that haunted it, seems to me a melancholy one. The legend is all that remains, and I do not see how it can outlast much longer the historic expanse of salt that it purported to explain.

Read at the Western Folklore Conference, University of Denver, July 14, 1950. Reprinted from *Western Folklore*, Vol. X, No. 2 (April, 1951), 109-116, published by the University of California Press.

---

[4] *Travels in America* (2 vols.; London, 1839).

The John G. Maher Hoaxes

---------------------------------- 🐾 ----------------

John G. Maher, in later life usually known as Colonel Maher, should not be recalled primarily for his flair for tall tales and hoaxes. He was a prominent figure in Nebraska newspaper, business, and political circles and was in general a helpful citizen. He volunteered in the Spanish-American war and he was an important figure in the military world of the first European war. He deserves and should be given space in the annals of Nebraska history. The following paper will be selective, however. By invitation it will attempt to record his folkloristic and related exploits while they can yet be recalled.

Maher's father took up a homestead claim in Platte County, Nebraska. He was a member of the state senate, 1888-89, and he is credited with being the first to bring winter wheat to Nebraska. Young Maher was educated in pioneer schools and at the Columbus high school and he attended the Fremont Normal school. He taught in Platte County a few years, went into government mail service between Columbus and Atchison, Kansas, and in 1887 opened a government land office at Chadron in Dawes County in northwest Nebraska. He was to spend much of his young manhood at Chadron. Most of his hoaxes were associated with that area, which is adjacent to the sandhill region and is near to the Sioux Indian reservation on the South Dakota border. For several years he was a court reporter in Dawes County under Judge Moses P. Kinkaid of the Kinkaid

Homestead Law fame. He was clerk and registrar of deeds in Dawes County for a few terms. Meantime he studied law with his deputy, Andrew D. Morrissey, later chief justice of the supreme court. He was admitted to the bar and to practice before the supreme court. Maher went with the U.S. troops as a special correspondent of the New York *Herald* during the Indian Ghost Dance excitement in northwest Nebraska. He volunteered and served as a private during the Spanish-American war of 1898. Some persons recall interesting controversial publicity, mostly humorous, concerning his use of his typewriter in his work as a stenographic clerk. Maher served on the Mexican border under General Pershing when U.S. troops were sent in 1916 to search out Pancho Villa, the revolutionary general who crossed the border, raided and partly burned a town, and killed a number of citizens.

Maher volunteered again in World War I, 1917, and was at once commissioned a major and assigned as chief officer for fourteen states of the Middle West with headquarters at the quartermaster's office at Omaha. Next he was sent to France where he became the chief disbursing officer of the American Expeditionary Force in charge of finance. His office was in Paris and he had responsibility for the handling of more than $500,000,000. During the war period he served in Germany, Rumania, Italy, and Belgium. In 1919 he was promoted to the rank of lieutenant colonel and given honorable discharge. In the United States again, he was appointed Nebraska delegate to the national advisory committee of the Secretary of War, organized to assist soldiers returning from overseas. In 1933 President Franklin Roosevelt appointed him state adviser to the board of Public Works Administration. He with others recommended useful projects to be carried out. Maher was always active in party politics. He was a good speaker. According to A. E. Sheldon, former secretary of the State Historical Society, some termed him "Nebraska's ablest and most elegant orator," a characterization usually reserved for W. J. Bryan. Maher was a close associate of U.S. Senator George Norris.

Prior to his service on the Mexican border Maher engaged in the real estate business in Lincoln. He helped found the

Old Line Insurance Company in Lincoln in 1913 and he became its first president in 1916, the year before he volunteered in the European war. After the war he spent much time abroad and from the early '30's onward he lived with his wife and daughter in Rome, returning to Lincoln for several months each year. In 1938 he was on a Mediterranean cruise with the former King Alfonso of Spain. He died of heart failure June 10, 1939, at the age of 70. His body was brought to America and buried at Arlington. One of his last newspaper contributions was to the Omaha *World-Herald* advising this country to stay aloof if war broke out.

Maher was the leader and past president of the Friends of the Irish Republic, a local branch of the American Association for the Recognition of the Irish Republic. He served as president of the Nebraska Progressive League, was one of the organizers of the American Legion and its first department commander and he was a past commander of the Spanish-American Veterans and acted as aide-de-camp on the staff of the commander-in-chief.

Many of Maher's ingenious ventures gained wide currency through their appearance in the New York *Herald,* for which he was a western correspondent. The newspaper was not so reliable historically then as it is now. Under the editorship of James Gordon Bennett it opened its columns to the sensational. It seems to have encouraged highly colored western contributions such as those sent in by Maher. Eastern newspapers in general were interested in the plains region, in Indian fighting, natural phenomena, newly explored areas and bad lands and unusual happenings. To meet this demand Maher often supplied fabricated occurrences to help out the real happenings he reported.

Following are some of his leading exploits. How many more there were I do not know.

The Petrified Man

My best account of the petrified man found near Chadron comes from Mrs. J. G. (Florence Tierney) Maher. It was sent me from Lausanne, Switzerland, in April, 1949, in response to an inquiry from me regarding it. In men's minds in those days were the striking discoveries of dinosaur eggs and skeletons in the Gobi Desert of central Asia. Mrs. Maher said, "The story of the petrified man as I remember it from dinner table conversation and an incident or two during my time in Lincoln runs about thus:"

An eastern archaeologist, Dr. Hatcher [1] had found dinosaur material near Washington in 1887. The American Press gave it great publicity. Mr. Maher thought of it as a great overstatement, especially when the New York press referred to the dinosaur remains as being "a million years old," and he and some others wondered why they never found any "million year old" human skeletons. From these remarks came the idea of creating an ossified man, and as Dr. Hatcher had come out to the bad lands to dig for fossils the temptation to "plant" an ossified man in the path of archaeologists finally became a reality.

They selected a gigantic young colored man from the Ninth Cavalry at Fort Robinson as a perfect specimen and made a plaster cast of him from which they did in solid cement or concrete the figure of a man. His feet were made flat by the use of shingles, as flat feet were supposed to be the mark of prehistoric man. After he was completed in secrecy he was hauled by a dray wagon to the bad lands and planted not far from where the archaeologist and his men were digging. One rainy Sunday morning he was found half uncovered in the clay and an astounded group of onlookers pronounced him an ossified man and classified him in a prehistoric century.

After the tests had shown the calcium content and structural arrangement to be correct the "man" was pronounced genuine and was exhibited in a sort of carnival way in towns in Nebraska and in large areas of the United States. After a while Mr. Maher's lawyer, D. W. Sperling of Chadron, who had taken the "man" on tour, wrote that the enterprise was getting out of hand and the exhibitions should be stopped. So the

---

[1] John Bell Hatcher (1861-1904) made extensive collections of fossils in western states for Yale University. After his finding of dinosaur material in 1887 he discovered, 1889-92, important fossil remains in Wyoming and, 1893-95, made explorations in Utah, Wyoming, and South Dakota. Later Dr. Hatcher led three expeditions to Patagonia, which had never before been entered by white men. He became known as "the foremost collector of the remains of prehistoric animals in America."

petrified man was laid away respectfully in a vault in Champaign, Illinois. In the later '30's Secretary A. E. Sheldon asked Maher to find out what it would cost to bring him to Lincoln for the Historical Society. The expenditure would have been too great for something of no historical or educational value and the matter was dropped.

A few newspaper notices may be cited.

The Dawes County *Journal,* October 14, 1892, tells of "Chadron's Petrified Man," discovered October 10.

Ed Rossiter and his father and brother have collected many valuable petrifications and fossils from the bad lands in this vicinity, but the former stumbled onto the greatest curiosity ever found last summer—it being nothing less than the petrified corpse of a man. . . . The two Rossiter Bros were collecting fossils about 3 miles from town in a strip of bad lands at the Natural Wall when Ed discovered what he at first thought to be a bone projecting from a bank of clay. A little digging brought him to what he found to be the hand of a man. He called his brother Clyde to watch the treasure while he came to the city for help. That evening the valuable find was safe at the Rossiter hotel and after the clay was partially removed from the body it was placed on exhibition.

A minute description of the body follows.

The face resembles that of a Negro . . . but his shapely heels indicate caucassian blood. . . . The medical fraternity and all others who have seen the specimen laugh at the idea that it is not genuine. It is undoubtedly the most perfect specimen of the kind ever discovered and is worth many thousands of dollars. Mr. Rossiter intends taking it to the Chicago World Fair.

Then follows a learned account of the geology of the region.

No relic of the human family has ever been found in so early a geological formation as this. It lay solidly imbedded in a greenish stratum of butte clay, with the remains of creadons, retotheriums and turtles. The stratum belongs at the beginning of the Miocene age, in the tertiary period. Originally the body must have been 200 feet below the surface. The face of the cliff above the greenish stratum where it lay shows twenty-four distinct strata, and as all are composed of sedimentary deposit there can be no doubt of the immense antiquity of the find.

... There are also three layers of rock above the stratum in the butte clay cliff in which the man was found, one a thin layer of agate, the others sandstone. Local geologists believe the stratum of green butte clay must have been deposited at least a million years ago. There seems to be no escape from the belief that the man was in some way buried in that deposit when it was soft and yielding. There were no signs of a disturbance such as volcanic action would produce. Neither is it possible that the caving in of the cliff in modern times could have buried its victim, as such a landslide would certainly have disturbed the well marked geological formation, and the greenish stratum is only two and a half or three feet in thickness. Scientific men will certainly be interested not only in the specimen itself, but also in the location in which it had been found.

The West Point *Republican,* November 4, 1943, under the heading "50 Years Ago" had:

The petrified man discovered recently at Chadron, Nebraska, is on exhibition in this city today. It is an object worth seeing. ... By the head one would judge it to be the body of an Indian. The form is about 6 ft 4 in. long and is solid stone weighing several hundred pounds. The finder has been offered $10,000 for the curiosity.

Soda Springs Near Chadron

One of Maher's minor hoaxes was his "soda springs" venture. Many people about the Chadron region were going to Hot Springs, South Dakota, or to Thermopolis, Wyoming, and drinking "bad water." Why should not Chadron capitalize on this? There are two boiling springs near Chadron. Maher and his cronies sank sacks of soda in the bottom of the springs. On Sundays people came to try the water. Evidence of persons who drank it and "threw away their crutches" and similar testimonies had been prepared. Stories about the springs were told for some years.

Threat of British Reprisals Up the Niobrara

O'Neill, the largest town in Holt County and its county seat, was named for its first settler, John O'Neill (1834-1878), a soldier and Fenian leader who came from Ireland to America in 1848. He became currently known as General O'Neill. The Fenian or Irish-Republican Brotherhood had for its purpose the overthrow of British rule in Ireland. O'Neill, a cavalry lieutenant in the Civil War, interested himself in a plan to invade Canada and acted as a Fenian organizer. He led a raiding party across the Niagara, seized a Canadian village, then escaped before British troops could capture him and his men. In the United States again, O'Neill and his raiders were charged with breach of neutrality and arrested but they were soon released by the courts. Shortly afterward he was appointed "inspector general of the Irish republican army." He prepared another attack on Canada. It was abortive and he was again arrested and again released, this time pardoned by President U. S. Grant. He made two other vain attempts at invading Canada, meantime quarreling with his associates.

There were Fenian groups in Denver at this time. One of the things the Fenian movement needed most, O'Neill thought, was some western outposts, these for the invasion of Canada all along its border. After his last release from jail he served as agent for land speculators who wished to settle Irish in Holt County, Nebraska. He himself was the first settler in the town of O'Neill, May 12, 1874, when the town site was platted. In 1875 he platted an addition to the town site and brought there a colony of Irish from Scranton, Pennsylvania. The town was named O'Neill perhaps by himself, perhaps by others. He was successful in establishing two other colonies, one at Atkinson in the same county and the other in adjacent Greeley County. All this is history, not hoax, strange and futile as the idea may seem of winning freedom for Ireland from Britain by the invasion of Canada. The Fenian cause lost in Ireland and lost sympathy in this country. O'Neill's prestige failed. Drought and grasshoppers and hard times came to the Nebraska region. The

O'Neill and Atkinson colonists, too poor to get away, stayed and from them came the numerous Irish in Holt County today.

I have vague memories myself of the Fenian movement. Patrick Egan, a prominent Irish expatriate, lived in my juvenile days not far from the Pound home, with his family of twelve children. He was deeply committed to the cause of Irish freedom. And John Fitzgerald, at that time a wealthy railroad contractor, lived more than a mile away in the opposite direction from the Egans. Whether there were military supplies at the Egan home seems doubtful. At Fitzgerald's death several hundred guns were found stacked away on his premises and were confiscated.

With this background to build on after the petrified man and the soda springs ventures had run their course, the Nebraska Fenian doings seemed to Maher and his cronies fine material for launching new tales. Nebraskans were warned through the newspapers that the British would surely exact reprisals for the invasion of Canada and would seek out Valentine and O'Neill. Their plan was, said Maher, to send the British navy up the Mississippi and up the Missouri, then to steam up the Niobrara to Valentine. Valentine would be taken easily and the Irish there "made to cry uncle." A landing party would be sent to capture O'Neill, the former center of preparations for Canadian invasion. The story of the imminent coming of the British navy up the Niobrara for reprisals went to the New York *Herald* and down the Nebraska newspaper line along the Northwestern railroad from Valentine to Ainsworth and O'Neill. It was kept up jocularly for the next ten or fifteen years.

Mari Sandoz recalls hearing, as one feature of the tale, that "Maher sent a big box apparently containing rifles to the Irish in Valentine. The box was one such as government arms came in and it was well labeled. But inside were a lot of Irish clubs cut, I hear, along the brush of Bordeaux creek in Northwestern Nebraska."

The Spanish Prisoner Hoax

This tale is also known as "The Man Who Blew Up the Maine." Presumably it was perpetrated sometime between 1902 and 1913, the period of much interest in the Maine incident and the raising of the sunken ship. In most versions the man involved was a Spaniard. In some he was an American. A few persons, among them Herbert Kelly, formerly of Lincoln, now of the Des Moines *Register and Tribune,* recall Maher's telling of the story informally following a dinner of newspaper men held probably in honor of Charles Ryckman who had won a Pulitzer award for an editorial in the Fremont, Nebraska, *Tribune,* November 7, 1930. Possibly, Mr. Kelly says, the occasion may have been another one that year. This time, in the traditional version of the tale, Maher became involved with the government.

Maher sent a short item to the New York *Herald* about the discovery of the man who sank the Maine. He followed it with running wire reports about falling in with the man by chance, the chase, how the man was found in Louisiana, his confession, details of how the destructive bomb was attached and the like. As the reports continued great excitement arose. Other newspapers suspected a hoax and sent a man down to find the Spaniard. Accounts ran on for about a year and finally aroused the government. It thought that if the man was found who caused the Spanish war the matter should be inquired into. Maher went to Louisiana, got a cadaver and put it in an old ruined Spanish prison outside a town, then set fire to it and produced the burned corpse. "He had been walled up to hold for the government and some one had set the place afire." The government proved that the remains had been dead a long time and the matter was dropped. In another account the finale may have taken place not in Louisiana but in the Southwest.

This is the story as it reached me in tradition. The authentic story of the hoax as remembered by Florence Tierney Maher is briefly as follows. It is no less interesting than the folklore version.

John was employed at his daily work, which was clerical, and the New York *Herald* from time to time wired him to ask for news of some sensational rumor. He used his evenings to originate hair-raising replies for which he received space-rate pay and usually a request for "more." One day there appeared in Chadron a Spanish-speaking man who was arrested as a vagrant and requested to leave town instead of being sent to jail. He said he was a Cuban soldier and wanted to stay in the United States, but he was forced to leave anyhow. It came to John's imaginative mind that this Cuban must have been a fugitive from justice, and the idea of a "man who blew up the Maine" emerged forthwith. John made up a name for him, Captain Manuel de Silva Braga, an officer in the Cuban army; and he manufactured a story of a shady record, a reprimand from a superior officer, a dismissal from the army, and an urge for revenge against those who had wronged him. Next John pictured him as deciding to blow up the Maine lying at anchor in the harbor at Havana, as doing so, then escaping to the United States and fleeing to the mountainous northwest for safety. With that sequence in mind he wired the editor of the *Herald* to say that Captain Manuel de Silva Braga, late of the Cuban army, supposedly the perpetrator of the bombing of the Maine, had passed through northwest Nebraska seeking refuge. He asked if a full account was desired.

The reply came back at once, "Send all you can get." So each evening John sent off a story, rather short but full of suspense, to the effect that a posse was hot in pursuit of the criminal, that one night he was practically surrounded, and that the next day he was still at large. To add to the interest John implied that the renegade Captain had on his person documents to show that he had intimate knowledge of the structure of the Maine and other related details. Finally the *Herald* wired "Spare no expense, ask whatever assistance is necessary, surround and capture the criminal." As the story had gone on long enough John was strictly on the spot to bring it to an end. So under the date line of a small place in the Black Hills he wired that the man had taken refuge at night in an abandoned cabin of gold prospecting days; that the posse, of which John, according to his account had become a party, covered the ground rapidly, surrounded the cabin and determined to wait till morning to close in to force a surrender. But just before dawn the Spaniard decided that escape was impossible for him and he simply burned the cabin, his papers and himself, to ashes. When the imaginary posse reached the spot there was nothing there at all. The government entered into John's story only as investigating and verifying the existence of Captain Manuel de Silva Braga (purely a fabrication) and admitting that there had been such a man in the Cuban army and that his "present whereabouts were unknown."

An examination of the files of the New York *Herald* would be of especial interest for this yarn. But they are far from Nebraska, are not indexed for the older periods, and to see them has been impracticable.

The Alkali Lake Monster

Tales of water monsters seem to have existed at all times and in many places. Yet to find them associated with our mild Nebraska lakes and rivers is unexpected. There have been several, however. That most widely circulated and still recurrent has for its locus the Alkali Lake at the far end of Mirage Flats near Hay Springs in Sheridan County. It was from 1885 onward that pioneers came to the region. The lake now goes by the name of Lake Walgren after a family of landowners who settled there in 1886. It is now reached by a graveled highway. Mari Sandoz states that she has known all her life gossipy stories of a "big sea monster" inhabiting it. There is a reference to the monster at the end of her book about Old Jules, her father. There were, then, early stories of a creature suggesting a prehistoric dinosaur. Their heyday, however, came in the 1920's. Mary M. Mielenz of Stanton, for instance, states that "In the '30's Nebraskans were interested in newspaper tales of the lake emanating from Hay Springs. Several persons of the little western community testified to seeing in the waters of the lake there a strange monster of pre-historic kind. Most hearers were highly skeptical. Though they scoffed, many of them drove for miles to view the lake to try to glimpse the monster, were there one. Some talked of draining the lake. In time the story quieted."

The Nebraska folklore pamphlet of the Federal Writers' Project (No. 13, July, 1938) recounts some of the reports of the gigantic creature, giving as a rule no dates or sources. "Its head was like an oil barrel shiny black in the moonlight." "Its flashing green eyes spit fire." "When it roars and flips its powerful tail the farmers are made seasick." "It eats a dozen calves when it comes ashore." "It flattens the cornfields." "The gnashing of its teeth sounds like a clap of thunder." "Once an unbelieving man from Omaha went alone to spend the night at Walgren lake. When he returned his hair was white and he looked haggard and worn. Three days later when he recovered his voice he said that the monster was 300 feet long and its mouth large enough to hold the Woodmen of the World building."

The exaggerated whoopla about the monster in the '20's was undoubtedly really started by Maher. Accounts from his hand of its fearful doings and depredations got into the New York papers, the *Herald* especially. The *Pathfinder* ran a series of letters about it and the Minneapolis *Journal* had an article on it (1923) but mistakenly gave it the wrong location. Even the Boston *Transcript* took up the story. The testimony of E. W. Bowman and J. G. Gilmore of Hay Springs who kept a scrapbook of clippings is that letters about the monster came from all over the world. From Maher surely came the account and the picture of the monster printed in the London *Times* (1923):

> By far the most vivid picture of the actions and features of a mediaeval monster which for three years has been terrifying the natives of the vicinity of Alkali Lake near the small town of Hay Springs, Nebraska, U S A, was received from our Omaha correspondent today.

The London picture, a curious one, was reproduced in the Nebraska folklore pamphlet, probably from the scrapbook of Messrs Bowman and Gilmore.

The Alkali Lake must have been fairly large at one time. One statement is that it covered 120 acres. Drought years such as the early '90's and the 1930's left it only a small puddle. After the rains came again it looked like a large body of water. By the present time a small stream has been turned into it to help it out.

In the 1920's an investigation of the lake was ordered at Hay Springs, apparently planned as a money-making adventure. It was proposed to drag the lake and to charge admission for watching the process. The project was not carried out since nearby land owners asked too high a price for leasing the ground. The cost of dragging the lake would have been about $1,000, and $4,000 was asked for a three-months' lease of the ground.

Following are a few newspaper testimonies:

If the land owners consent and it is possible for the towns-people to finance the undertaking—which will take from $800 to $1,000, the work of capturing the monster will proceed . . . it is a big undertaking to drag a lake ¾ of a mile wide and nearly a mile long . . . 4½ miles in circumference.[2]

Hay Springs Investigating Association has, after due consideration, practically given up the idea of dragging Alkali Lake in an effort to locate the sea monster which has been seen by several of our citizens on various occasions. Land owners want $4,000 for three months lease and certain per cent of exhibition money of animal if found. Considered excessive and Investigation Association concluded to go no farther.[3]

Have a tip that Bruce Hewitt and J. Mayes of Rushville solved the Hay Springs Lake mystery by finding a mermaid frozen in ice of the lake. Wire 300 word story if above is correct, also rush photo of mermaid. Editor Hays wonders "if John has been playing jokes on us again." [4]

A letter from Lincoln, Nebraska, November 19, 1925, apparently to a Norfolk paper, runs, "I note by an article in today's *News* [that a mermaid has been caught in Alkali Lake]. I am much pleased to learn this since we recently delivered a large consignment of fish to be planted in this lake and it is a well known fact among fish culturists that fish will not thrive or propagate in waters infested with mermaids."

The Rushville *Recorder,* September 2, 1937, printed a "Historie of Ye Lake or Adventures of Ye Sea Monster" by Mary Jane Barnes. It tells much about the lake, using archaic spelling only in the title.

---

2 Hay Springs *News,* March 23, 1923.

3 *Ibid.,* July 6, 1925.

4 Rushville *Standard* quoting from a telegram from Omaha *World-Herald,* November 20, 1925.

Indian Ghost Dances and Government Troops

In her prize-winning biography of Jules Sandoz (1935), his daughter has, "On Pine Ridge in 1890 the Messiah craze was spread among agency-starved Sioux. An holy man had risen far to the west, one who promised the old buffalo days again with the white man swept from the earth as the chinook clears the snow from the red grass. John Maher of Chadron kept the New York papers full of stories of depredations and atrocities. Jules complained, 'Eastern people don't know better. They believe them.'" Old Jules, whose attitude toward the Indians was in general a sound one, seemed to think that it was Maher's tales that brought on the killing—some called it the "assassination"—of Sitting Bull, the famous chief at Standing Rock Reservation in North Dakota, which was followed by the wholesale massacre at Wounded Knee Creek of the Sioux of the Pine Ridge Reservation near the Nebraska border. Old Jules lived near Pine Ridge and knew Maher's flair for exciting newspaper reports. It was not, however, manufactured newspaper tales that brought on the death of Sitting Bull and the massacre. The troops came at the request of the United States agents at the reservation. Local civil authorities, not the government under pressure from newspapers, were responsible. The government was, indeed, reluctant to send troops. The whole tragic story is no credit to the white race. Far from it. It contributes another chapter in the story of our stupid and often brutal treatment of our Indian wards.

Examination of sources such as James Mooney's exhaustive investigation of "The Ghost-Dancing Religion and the Sioux Outbreak of 1890" (Fourteenth Annual Report of the U. S. Bureau of Ethnology to the Smithsonian Institution, Part II, chapter III, Washington, 1896) and Stanley Vestal's sympathetic life of Sitting Bull (1932) makes clear that there was little or no connection between Maher's highly colored newspaper reports and the bringing on of the tragedies. Apparently they would have taken place had Maher not existed, although his lurid reports as correspondent for the New York *Herald* could have done nothing to allay excitement, rather the contrary.

The ghost dances of the Indian tribes everywhere in the west and northwest were peaceful, were indeed religious. The Indians had no hostile intentions, rather taught non-resistance, as they danced within their reservations to bring on the messiah they awaited. Only from Standing Rock and Pine Ridge were troops asked for. Sitting Bull, says his biographer, had nothing to do with instituting the dancing. His arrest and slaying came from other causes.

The Indian agent at Standing Rock, Major James McLaughlin, was a man of above the average ability as an agent but he was not always infallible. Sitting Bull was a conspicuous and influential figure among the Sioux and McLaughlin tired of his "domination." Among other things the chief had opposed the further cession of Indian lands. Like most outstanding personages he had devoted friends and bitter rivals. He came to be looked on as a leader in incitement on the reservation. McLaughlin complained of his influence and was backed more or less by settlers, missionaries, and traders. His name was forwarded to the government with that of other "disturbers." It seemed wise to McLaughlin to remove the chief elsewhere. Mooney reprints McLaughlin's order for Sitting Bull's arrest. The agency's Sioux Indian police force, no white man among them, was sent to carry out the arrest. Midnight was the time fixed for it. In an ensuing melée between the chief's friends and the Indian police one of the latter shot and killed Sitting Bull and an Indian panic followed.

The Pine Ridge reservation on the Nebraska border was the largest of the Sioux reservations, numbering 6,000 Indians. Dr. V. T. McGillicuddy, a man of unusual ability, had managed the Indians for seven years without a soldier on the reservation. After a political change of administration he was succeeded by an agent named Gallagher and then in 1890 by G. F. Royer, whom Mooney describes as a man "without experience, force of character, courage, and sound judgment." Royer was frightened at the ghost dancing, although it was really harmless enough, and always confined to the reservation. He reported to the government that more than half of his 6,000 Indians were dancing and that they were beyond control and suggested that it would be necessary to call out the military. On October 30, thoroughly alarmed, he wrote a long letter to the department at Washington stating that the one remedy was the use of soldiers and that about 600 troops would be needed. Also many telegraphic reports were sent. On November 15, Royer was finally instructed by the government to report the condition of affairs to the commander at Fort Robinson, Nebraska. That same day Royer telegraphed that the Indians were wild and crazy and that 1,000 troops were needed. So at last troops were ordered to the reservation and nearly 3,000 were soon in the area. The flight of the Indians became a stampede and an inexcusable massacre by an uninhibited soldiery not only of Indian braves but of women and children followed.

"Watch Stuffing"

In earlier days in Nebraska and other states "watch stuffing" was listed in law books alongside stealing, picking pockets, swindling, assault, and numerous other punishable offenses. Sometime in the '30's when the Laws of Nebraska were being revised at the State Capitol, a letter was sent me asking whether I knew what was meant by the unfamiliar term "watch stuffing," not to be found in dictionaries. I did not know and neither did my brother Roscoe nor anyone else I consulted. I learned at last what "watch stuffing" meant from a philologically inclined convict in the state penitentiary at Richmond, Virginia. "Watch stuffing" is now entered in the *Dictionary of American English* (Vol. IV) of 1944 and is mentioned briefly under "stuffer" in the *Dictionary of Americanisms* of 1951.

Whether or not John Maher knew the name, he knew the practice and made use of it in the last of his hoaxes that I shall mention here. Again Mari Sandoz is my authority. She once heard, she told me, that Maher on a certain special occasion formally presented a handsome watch at a dinner to a dignitary being honored. The watch was of beautifully shiny brass outside and looked like gold. Inside was an old Ingersoll watch that would not run.

Interview with Colonel Maher

The following is an informal account by Mari Sandoz of an interview with John G. Maher.

Along about 1930 I went up to John Maher's office in Lincoln to ask him about the Old Jules trial for leading a vigilante group that hung a man. Maher was court reporter at that trial and was in a particularly good position to give me a good version of the day if he would, and to certify or discount what I had accumulated.

But Mr. Maher never seemed to listen to anyone, and although I said who I was, he paid no attention to anything beyond the one name that he somehow recalled, Jules Sandoz. He was off into a fantastic version of the snake bite incident, stating how the rugged old pioneer had been bitten by a rattler. "In the midst of his numerous family and before the white horrified faces of his wife and small children about to be robbed of their father by a dastardly snake, he grabbed up his thirty-thirty Winchester and shot off his hand—"

All this time I was trying hard to interrupt because he did have so much important information if I could get him down to facts, and I didn't want to embarrass him when he finally understood that I was one of the daughters of the Old Jules he was talking about and had to admit that he was caught in a fantastic fabrication.

But I didn't need to worry. When I finally did get John Maher stopped and made to understand who I was he looked at me.

"You're the girl, the daughter who was with him when he was bitten." Yes, I was.

He laughed, his fine eyes merry and unabashed. "Well, it was a damn good story the way I was telling it, wasn't it?"

Fortunately he settled down then and gave me at least two hours of time, going over what I had on the court scene word for word, checking, adding, etc., and all without any more of his exaggeration. I had the complete scene from a dozen others and from the court records, and he was very helpful.

This account is of interest as showing the two sides of Colonel Maher, his love of the tall tale and his spontaneity in creating one, and his ready helpfulness when he turned serious. Miss Sandoz added when she read this article, which she prompted me to write, and let me have her story of the interview, "I am happy this much of the fabulous man is to be set down before any more is forgotten. He is so distinctly a man of the later frontier."

Read at the Western Folklore Conference, University of Denver, July 17, 1952. Reprinted from *Nebraska History*, XXXIII (December, 1952), 203-219.

Nebraska Strong Men

Legends of strong men are, of course, no new or rare or purely American phenomena. The literature and lore of many races exhibit tales of the supernormally mighty. There are stories of their birth, rearing, precocity, and their marvellous achievements, such as their feats of lifting, uprooting trees, victories over antagonists, or rescues of victims.[1] Ajax of Homer's *Iliad* is a man of brute strength and courage. So is the mythical Hercules, of whose superhuman power tall tales are told, one of which was that on occasion he relieved Atlas by supporting the world. Another strong man was Samson, the Hebrew judge whose strength was liquidated by Delilah. Another was Beowulf who "had the strength of thirty men in his hand-grip." In American lore there are Kwasind, the strong man of Longfellow's *Hiawatha,* John Henry, the Negro steel driver who "died with his hammer in his hand," Paul Bunyan of the Northern woods, and there are those two up-to-date muscle men, Tarzan the "giant," who springs from tree to tree—these always miraculously at hand and the branches unfailingly holding and concealing him—and there is Superman.

Febold Feboldson

Nebraska, too, has its offering of strong men. There are at least three of whom stories have been current: Febold Feboldson,

[1] See Stith Thompson's *Motif-Index of Folk-Literature* (III, 142-150), 1934, for instances of legendary strong men among the Celts, Norse, Dutch, Italians, Hindus, American Indians, etc.

Antoine Barada, and Moses Stocking. Of these Febold looms largest. He has achieved by this time something of a bibliography as a folk hero. Originally the protagonist of a number of yarns, by known authors, in Gothenburg, Nebraska, newspapers, Febold made his début before the general public in an article "Paul Bunyan and Febold" published by Paul Robert Beath in the *Prairie Schooner* (VI, 59-61) in 1932. Mr. Beath's yarn narrates "How Paul Bunyan and Febold Became Acquainted." It is supposed to be told by Bergstrom Stromberg, who is "over 90" and who is a "grand-nephew of Febold"; "Bergstrom remembers both men well." Febold's deeds were selected and written up or edited by Mr. Beath for the Nebraska Folklore pamphlets of the Writers' Project of 1937. Next a story, "How Febold Cured the Coyote Plague with Whimpering Whingdings," was included in Carl Carmer's *Hurricane's Children* (1937). Then came Anne Malcomson's *Yankee Doodle's Cousins* (1941) giving Febold added recognition. A Febold story is to be included in B. A. Botkin's *Treasury of American Folklore,* announced as in preparation. There is an unpublished volume, a compilation of Febold tales with a foreword by Frederick Christensen, which I have seen but which is not yet available to the public [*Febold Feboldson: Tall Tales from the Great Plains,* compiled by Paul R. Beath, Lincoln: University of Nebraska Press, 1948].

Mr. Carmer's headnote to the Febold tale he includes in *Hurricane's Children* reads:

Febold Feboldson is a bit younger than most of the giants in this book but he is just as strong and just as smart. News of him and his adventures has been traveling about Nebraska from Lincoln and Gothenburg to David City and Red Cloud, Wahoo, and Prairie Home, North Star and Horsefoot. Perhaps he is one of Paul Bunyan's Swedish lumberjacks who has started out on his own in Nebraska.

The "Paul Bunyan Twenty-Five Years After" of Gladys J. Haney [2] cites Febold as "among the best known folk heroes."

2 *JAFL,* LV, July-September, 1942.

In view of his rapid rise to celebrity, it seems in place to record Febold's history before it is forgotten. I have been interested for years in Nebraska lore. Masses of materials have been sent me or gathered for me. Various studies made by graduate students are available in printed form: for example, *Proverbial Lore in Nebraska* by Louise Snapp and *Signs, Omens and Portents in Nebraska Folklore* by Margaret Cannell,[3] *Nebraska Folk Cures* by Pauline Black,[4] and Florence Maryott treated "Nebraska Counting Out Rhymes" in the *Southern Folklore Quarterly*.[5] B. A. Botkin's notable *American Play-Party Song* took final form and was printed in Nebraska.[6] And considerable folklore and folksong material is at hand which has not yet been published. But never, in more than a quarter of a century, has anything been contributed to me about Febold. Those persons I have questioned who come from Gothenburg, Wahoo, North Platte, and Lincoln testified promptly that they had never heard of him. The stories of Febold published in the Writers' Project pamphlet do not name the tellers or give place and date. They are not "documented" in scholarly fashion. The fact is that Febold, the prairie hero, originated as a flight of fancy, patterned after Paul Bunyan, and he owes most of his fame, I think, to Mr. Paul R. Beath, who, though not his creator, has spun many stories about him and floated him into fame. Those who have been most closely associated with the Febold stories, men such as L. C. Wimberly of the *Prairie Schooner*, Frederick Christensen, J. Harris Gable, and Paul Beath himself readily admit the success of the venture and that Febold gained national prominence as a folk hero with surprising quickness.

The character Febold, the strong man, and his name seem to have been created by Wayne Carroll, a local lumber dealer, who wrote a column under the name of Watt Tell in the now defunct Gothenburg, Nebraska, *Independent*.[7] This series began

---

3 *University of Nebraska Studies in Language, Literature and Criticism*, 1933.

4 *Ibid.*, 1935.

5 December, 1937.

6 Lincoln: *University of Nebraska Studies*, 1937.

7 This is the testimony of Don Holmes to Paul R. Beath.

about 1923. Later Carroll used Febold in advertising that he wrote for his lumber company. Febold could never have been made a lumber hero like Paul Bunyan, for there are no trees on the great plains. So he became a hero wrestling with the adversities of the prairie region, tornadoes, droughts, extreme heat and cold, Indians, politicians, and disease. Later matter, concerning Febold, from the pens of Carroll and Don Holmes and other contributors, appeared in the Gothenburg *Times,* 1928-33, and sporadically since.

Carroll may have had in mind for his creation of Bergstrom Stromburg, the fabulous person usually cited as relating the Febold tales, a real person, Olof Bergstrom, who founded Gothenburg, Nebraska. He is sometimes said to have founded Stromsburg also, probably through confusion with his brother who located there. Olof Bergstrom was a pioneer leader of immigrant Swedes into Nebraska, who had a somewhat hectic career and stories of whom, Mr. Beath says, were current when he was a boy.

The Febold stories "caught on" about 1928. After Wayne Carroll, not only did Don Holmes write them but contributions began to come in from readers of the *Times.* From this mass Mr. Beath gleaned the stories which he wove into his version of Febold's exploits which appeared in the Nebraska folklore pamphlet and earlier in the Omaha *World-Herald* and the *Prairie Schooner* (1932). All the material has now been turned over to B. A. Botkin, who is in charge of the Archive of American Folksong in the Library of Congress at Washington.

But for Paul R. Beath I fear that Febold might have died with the early newspaper yarns about him, yarns of the extravagant type liked by newspaper writers and readers in the later nineteenth and early twentieth century, and usually pretty ephemeral. Mr. Beath was educated at the University of Illinois and at Columbia. Formerly of Gothenburg, he is now an attorney for the government at Washington. I first knew of him as a contributor of interesting matter concerning the living language to *American Speech.* He writes on folk topics and is a lover of folklore. In answer to inquiries from me he wrote:

I first became aware of Febold when stories of him were appearing in the Gothenburg *Times*. About this time I read James Stevens' *Paul Bunyan* (1925). I recognized the resemblance of Febold to Paul. . . . It was during this period that I started contributing an occasional story to the *Times*. . . . My stories were mostly adaptations of those I heard about town, yarns of various types, not however Febold yarns. These I elaborated and embellished to fit Febold and what I conceived to be his character, i.e., an indomitable Swedish pioneer who could surmount any difficulty. As a boy and young man I worked my way as a night clerk in a hotel in Gothenburg where I heard literally thousands of stories told by traveling salesmen and other garrulous wayfarers. I suppose I received clues to many of the stories from this ever-flowing stream.

As a contemporary instance of the type of yarning to which he refers, Mr. Beath tells that when he was traveling by bus from Schuyler to Grand Island, Nebraska, recently, a passenger exclaimed that he saw a rabbit. Another passenger promptly said, "That is no rabbit but a Kansas grasshopper." Asked how he knew, he answered that rabbits are as big as coyotes in the Nebraska region. This bantering and yarning was continuing when Mr. Beath left the bus at Grand Island. His testimony concerning Febold ended with the remarks:

I cannot let this opportunity go by without having my say about that school of folklorists who try to find the origins of stories in the race or in some mythical super-personality, some "geist" lurking in the twilight. This seems to me all poppycock. Stories are told, even concocted, by individuals for the entertainment of individuals. Every story that was ever told was told by an individual and his individual artistry or lack of it is apparent. Every Febold story has been told or written by an individual and I know at least six of these tellers personally— and it has been put together out of the narrative material already in the teller's head.

So much for Febold, the folk hero. Folklore is folklore, whatever its origin, and Febold now belongs to folklore. But it is the lore of the literary class, the lore of educated lovers of lore, rather than of the sub-literary, the less educated strata usually thought of as the "folk" of "folklore." The same may be true, or is true, of Paul Bunyan. Lore of Paul is now folklore, but it is the folklore of the reading class. There may have been an *ur*-Paul Bunyan, possibly a real person about whom stories centered; but the legendary Paul neither seems to have emerged from the woodsmen nor to be very current among them, except as handed down from above.

Since Paul Bunyan is so obviously the progenitor of Febold, it may be in place to digress a little concerning him here. Tales of him are said by Esther Shephard (1924) to have originated even earlier than the 1860's and to have been at their height in the 1880's and '90's, though some of her tales involve materials and inventions (as a parachute and pipelines) that did not exist in those decades.

Mr. Carleton C. Ames of the River Falls State College, Minnesota, writing on "Paul Bunyan—Myth or Hoax?" in the *Minnesota History Magazine*,[8] does not accept the tales of Paul Bunyan as indigenous folklore, i.e., as yarns actually spun by the shanty boys of logger camps in Wisconsin, Minnesota, and Michigan. His father, he says, was raised in an atmosphere of logging camps and his grandfather spent most of his active life in the logging industry. They had never heard of Paul Bunyan nor did those old-timers with whom Mr. Ames had informal conversations, men from camps representing Minnesota, Wisconsin, Maine, also some from Canada, including Scandinavians. Not one had ever heard Paul Bunyan mentioned. Nor does his name appear in Franz Rickaby's authentic *Ballads and Songs of the Shanty Boy* (1926), gathered at first hand from loggers, nor, I may add, is there a single reference to Paul Bunyan among the songs, older, later, and contemporary, of Maine woodsmen, gathered at first hand by Mrs. Eckstorm and Miss Smyth in their *Minstrelsy of Maine* (1927). Moreover (this too was pointed out by Mr. Ames), Stewart H. Holbrook in *Holy Old Mackinaw* (1938), a history of the logging industry, in a chapter headed "Around the Barrel Staves," states, "legends grew out of these bunkhouse discourses—not the made-up tales of Paul Bunyan

8 XXI, 55-58. 1940.

but tales of actual men." Apparently, Esther Shephard and many others since accepted the tales at face value as emerging from the mid-nineteenth century loggers themselves. Another researcher who, like Carleton Ames, believes that the Paul Bunyan legends did not come up out of the woods and logging camps but were superimposed upon them, is Dr. M. M. Quaife of Wayne University, Detroit, Michigan, who testifies [9] that "after tackling the subject" he came to the same conclusion as Mr. Ames.

The real impetus given the Paul Bunyan legends seems to have been commercial. They first gained currency in the publications of the Red River Lumber Company of Minnesota, which started giving Paul Bunyan stories in 1914. At that date Paul was unknown to the general public and to the distributors and sawmill people. Whether Paul was an earlier or a new creation (an unsigned note in the *Minnesota History Magazine* cites a solitary instance of an individual over 80 who thought he remembered the existence of Paul Bunyan stories as far back as the 1870's), it seems certain that America in general would not have heard of him but for W. B. Laughead, who may be termed the real promoter of the yarns and who was no doubt the creator of many of them. Mr. Laughead was the author of a booklet on the marvellous exploits of Paul Bunyan, published by the Red River Lumber Company in 1922. Laughead said he first heard of Paul Bunyan in the region about Bemidji, Minnesota, in 1900. Whether he found earlier tall tales (an *ur*-Paul) and elaborated and added to them and created others, or was in most respects Paul's sponsor, I do not know. In any case Paul, floated commercially, now belongs to folklore. Witness writers like Stuart Chase who stated in 1925 that the Paul Bunyan stories are "a golden chunk of almost pure primitive literature." Lucy L. Hazard said Paul Bunyan is now "of the stature of the nation," this in 1927. James Cloyd Bowman in 1941 termed the Paul Bunyan tales "the most fundamentally American of all our folklore." No, there is no doubt that Paul won wide accep-

---

[9] *Minnesota History Magazine*, XXI, 176-178. 1940.

tance as a folk hero genuinely of folk emergence.[10] By the middle of this century, however, theories of his origin and the origin of the tales attributed to him have been given up.[11]

For later Febold matter see my review in *Nebraska History*, XXX, 77-80, of Beath's *Tall Tales of the Great Plains* (University of Nebraska Press, 1948), and especially the dependable summary "The Febold Feboldson Legends" by Robert F. Chamberlain, in *Nebraska History*, XXXIII (June, 1952), 95-102.

I have omitted account of the nature and content of the Febold tales, offspring of the Paul Bunyan tales, for they are available in print in various places. They are of much the same extravagant character as the Bunyan stories. For example, one

---

[10] See Gladys J. Haney's bibliography, *JAFL*, LV, July-September, 1942. J. Frank Dobie, 1925, seems to have been skeptical concerning Paul Bunyan.

[11] Since this article was written I have heard from Mr. W. R. Laughead, who now represents the California Plant of the Red River Lumber Company at Westwood, Lassen County, in that State. His tall tales of Paul Bunyan seem to have been the first to appear in print. I have a copy from him of the first booklet of the Company on Paul Bunyan, issued in 1914. Newspaper contributions concerning Paul seem to have followed, much as for Febold. Esther Shephard's book came in 1924 and James Steven's in 1925. The part of Mr. Laughead's letter responding to my inquiries concerning Paul Bunyan is of especial interest to folklorists:

"Where and how Paul Bunyan started no one seems to know, although there is evidence that he was known in Eastern States, where logging was at its height before the Great Lakes period of the industry. The material in the 1922 Red River book *Paul Bunyan and His Blue Ox* was gathered from many sources. It started with what I remembered from Minnesota logging camps (1900-1908). I then picked up odds and ends from letters we received and from columns that ran in various newspapers, in the Seattle *Star* by Lee J. Smits, the Portland *Oregonian* by DeWitt L. Hardy, and others. Correspondence to the *American Lumberman* also provided clues. Most of this had appeared between the publication of our first booklet in 1914 and the trade journal advertisements we ran 1914-1916, and the compilation of *Paul Bunyan and His Big Blue Ox*, 1922.

"At original sources (conversation of loggers and other workers) I never heard the narrative form. Even the extemporaneous additions came as offhand mention of events and Paul's inventions, as if referring to well-known facts. My own 'invention' included names of characters, 'Babe,' 'Brimstone Bill,' 'Johnny Inslinger,' 'Sourdough Sam,' etc. . . . My writing has been almost entirely advertisements."

On the whole, the testimony of Mr. Laughead tends to strengthen the assumption that the floating of Paul Bunyan stories was commercial and that Mr. Laughead played much the same role for Paul that P. R. Beath was to play for Febold.

tale mentions that strange animal the "hodag," which is taken directly from the Paul Bunyan stories. And I shall treat the other two Nebraska strong men more briefly.

Antoine Barada

The Writers' Project pamphlet of the Nebraska W.P.A., 1937, characterized Antoine Barada as "the strongest man who ever roamed the shores of the Missouri River." The headnote prefixed to stories of him in the pamphlet ranks him as "second only to Febold as a legendary or mythical character." Antoine has a very different history from Febold. There is evidence that a person of that name really lived, though the stories of his parentage do not agree. The account in the pamphlet states that Antoine Barada "was the son of Count Michael Barada, a gay Parisian, and Laughing Water, a pretty Omaha maiden. Since she was of the Omaha tribe, the Count and his wife resided in Thurston County, Nebraska. Antoine spent his later years on the reservation with them. He died in 1866 and was buried beside his wife in Richardson County at the little village of Barada, which was named in his honor." This was the parentage ascribed to Antoine by Robert Maher, who wrote of his remarkable deeds in the *Sunday Journal and Star* of Lincoln, Nebraska, June 14, 1936. Maher's account may have been used by the Writers' Project authors, or the two accounts may have been derived from the same source.

Mari Sandoz, best known as the author of *Old Jules* (1935) and *Crazy Horse* (1942), who was employed for some time in the office of the Secretary of the Nebraska State Historical Society and who served as Assistant Editor of the *Nebraska History* magazine, is my chief informant concerning Antoine. She testifies that she knew stories of him when she was a child. He was a half-breed, she says, the son of Michael Barada, who "was supposed to be of royal connections in Spain. . . . The town of Barada in Richardson County was named after Michael. . . . Around 1934, while I was working at the State Historical Society, a letter came in seeking information on the Barada family, to settle as I recall now, an estate. Whether this was another of the recurring Spanish inheritance hoaxes I don't know now. . . . There was also a Michael Barada in the Custer County region for a while, I'm told."

Still another statement, this the earliest printed statement I have, appears in *Nebraska Place-Names,* compiled in 1924 and published in the *University of Nebraska Studies in Language, Literature, and Criticism* (1925). This account of leading town-names in the state was made by Lilian Fitzpatrick, A.M., with some assistance from her father, Professor T. J. Fitzpatrick of the Botanical Department, an experienced place-name researcher. The entry reads: "Barada. This place is situated in Barada precinct and it and the precinct were named after one of the first settlers, Antoine Barada (1807-1887), a French-Omaha half-breed whose wife was a French woman. He named the village after himself. His descendants still live in the vicinity."

The name Barada is on the certified copy of the census of half-breeds listed in volume XVI, p. 40, of the *Nebraska History* magazine. In volume I, page 2, a Michael Barada is said to have been elected a "sentinel of the Union Club" in 1863, the Civil War period.

All in all, whether Antoine Barada the half-breed was Spanish-Indian as suggested by the name Barada which sounds Spanish, or French-Indian as suggested by Antoine, and whether the town was named after him or after Michael Barada, he seems to have been a real person, perhaps some one of unusual strength and of various adventures. In the legends about him he pulls out a big boat stranded in the sandbars, picks up a 400 pound boulder, and does similar feats. Miss Sandoz recalls of him:

> Antoine Barada was a hurry-up man, always rushing, rushing, can't wait for anything. One time he got tired of watching a pile driver working along the Missouri with the hammer making the up-down, up-down, the driver yelling "Git up! Git up! Whoa! Back! Back! Whoa!" and then all of it over again and the piling going down maybe a half inch. So Antoine he picked up the damned thing in his bare hand, throws it high

and far so it lights clear over the Missouri where it bounce and bounce leaving ground tore up for miles and miles and making what the greenhorns call "Breaks of the Missouri." But at last it stop and if you dig down in them high ridges you find it is the damned pile driver with grass growing over him, a little poor soil, you understand, but it seems to satisfy them that ain't never crossed the Missouri and don't know better. When Antoine had disposed of the Johny Jumper hammer he sees that the piling that is left stands a mile higher than the rest, so he gives it a lick with his fist and it pop down into ground so deep it strike buried lake, the water flying out like from bung hole fifty feet high and like to drown out the whole country if Antoine he did not sit on the hole first.

Miss Sandoz says that she "grew up on the Barada stories as told by half-breeds around Pine Ridge." They were brought there, she suspects, by the Ruleaus and other families who used to live on what is called the Breed Strip in southeast Nebraska, and in the early 1900's still had relatives to visit there.

Moses Stocking

Concerning the stories of my third and last Strong Man figuring in Nebraska legend, Moses Stocking, my only informant so far is Miss Sandoz. She reports:

A rather neglected group of strong man stories in which mind rules over mere brawn are the Moses Stocking stories. These were floating around Western Nebraska in my childhood, always about a man in Eastern Nebraska who ran sheep. I don't remember many of these and know of no place where they reached print. All the great plant and animal stories were fastened to him, such as the squash vines that grew so fast they wore the squashes out dragging them over the ground. Or the corn that grew so tall a boy was sent up the stalk to measure it and was never heard from again except that they know he's still alive because they sell a trainload of corn cobs every year from around the foot of the Stocking corn stalk, thrown down by the boy, who must be a gray-haired man now because the bird nests found in the corn leaves are made with grey hair.

There was also a story of how Stocking went into sheep:

He had an acre of bottom land broke (Stocking never did any of the work himself, you understand), and because it was late he couldn't sow anything himself except a few turnips. The seed was bad and only five plants came up, one in each corner and one in the middle; but they grew pretty well. The corner ones squashed and flattened of course, being so close together, and too puny for any real use, although they hauled one of them to the top of a hill somewhere along the Platte and when it was hollowed out and the wind dried it, it was used as a military academy and did very well for years to house the boys. Another one from the corners was used for the railroad depot at Omaha, since there would be only temporary use for a depot there. The other two corner turnips were wasted, as I recall, but the center one was worth saving and from it grew the Stocking fortune. After walking around it once and coming back footsore and with cockleburrs in his beard, old Moses took the train for Chicago and bought up all the sheep at the stock-market and for the next month there was a stream wide as the Missouri of sheep coming across Iowa to the Stocking place. They started eating at the turnip where Moses blasted a hole and they lived there fat and sung all winter, not having to go into the blizzard cold at all, just eating the pulp out, the shell making a shelter for the sheep that were worth enough to keep Jay Cook afloat for a whole year after he really was broke, only the public didn't know it.

These yarns testify to the intellectual rather than to the physical strength of Moses Stocking, but Miss Sandoz recalled that old timers told also how the old fellow lifted wagons out of the mud and did similar strong-man feats.

Miss Sandoz added, when recounting Moses Stocking stories, that she believes there really was a Moses Stocking who lived in eastern Nebraska, although the stories she knew of him floated about western Nebraska. She is right in her belief. A Moses Stocking existed. He was a pioneer of ability and considerable distinction who lived on a farm in Saunders County, Nebraska, in the Ashland-Wahoo region. He was a charter member of the Nebraska Historical Society. His Autobiography, telling of his difficult and venturesome life, was printed in the first volume of the *Transactions and Reports* of the Nebraska Historical Society, pp. 128-137, 1885. He was a member of the Fine Stock Breeders' Association and of the State Board of Agriculture. In the column reprinting, day by day, news from old files of the Nebraska *State Journal,* I found in the *Evening Journal* for July 22, 1943, under the heading "Sixty Years Ago Today," the entry "Moses Stocking of Eldred, Saunders County, was the most extensive wool grower in the state. He had 1,500 sheep."

This exhausts my knowledge to date of Nebraska Strong Men in legend. The Nebraska heroes, surviving into the present in print or orally, are obviously not "sissies," or "cream puffs," or in contemporary jargon, "panty-waists." They are genuine strong men. Two of the sets of tales seem to have become attached to or centered about real persons. In this there is no novelty. To recall but a few prototypes of Antoine Barada and Moses Stocking, the emperors Alexander the Great, Charlemagne, and Friedrich Barbarossa were historic personages about whom tall tales gathered and were handed on.

Read before the Western Folklore Conference at the University of Denver, July 16, 1943. Reprinted from the *Southern Folklore Quarterly,* VII (September, 1943), 133-143.

Nebraska's Antoine Barada Again

—— 🐾 ——

Antoine Barada of Richardson County, Nebraska, was a real person, notable among our nineteenth-century pioneers. He was a man of fabulous strength who had an adventurous life and who developed into a prominent figure in Nebraska folklore. The Federal Writers' Project, Pamphlet 8 (1937), characterized him as "the strongest man who ever roamed the shores of the Missouri river." The headnote prefixed to mention of some of the tall tales concerning him ranks him as "second only to Febold as a legendary or mythical character of Nebraska." In an article on "Nebraska Strong Men" in the *Southern Folklore Quarterly* (VII, September, 1943, pp. 133-143) I referred to some of the stories of his prowess and quoted in full one known to Mari Sandoz. By our own time, folklore seems to have arisen concerning his ancestry as well as concerning his feats of strength. I bring up the matter now because of recurrent press items such as the following from the Lincoln, Nebraska, *Evening Journal* of January 23, 1949:

> A.P. Falls City, Nebraska. An 84-year-old descendant of Count Barada, a French nobleman, will be buried here. William Barada died at Hiawatha, Kansas. He was a grandson of

the Count who married an Indian girl and became a legendary figure. Survivors include seven daughters and four sons.

For one thing, this statement does not differentiate Antoine Barada, primarily the legendary figure, and his father Michael who is customarily described as a French nobleman, a Count. Another story is that Michael was a Spanish grandee. The Federal Writers' pamphlet serves as a chief source, no doubt, of the now stock story of Antoine's romantic parentage, which it seems to accept without question:

Antoine Barada was the son of Count Michael Barada, a gay Parisian, and Laughing Water, a pretty Omaha maiden, whose romance is said to be one of the most beautiful in history . . . . He died in 1866 and was buried beside his wife in Richardson County at the little village of Barada which was named in his honor.

Robert Maher, who wrote of Antoine's deeds the year before in the Lincoln, Nebraska, *Sunday Journal and Star* (June 14, 1936), gave him the same parents, Count Michael and Laughing Water. He commented:

Accounts of their romance and marriage comprise one of the tender chapters of the history of a period when eastern Nebraskans were too much concerned with the struggles for survival to give much heed to the sentimental.

Mari Sandoz, best known as the author of *Old Jules* (1935) and *Crazy Horse* (1942), who was an employee in the office of the Secretary of the Nebraska State Historical Society for a time and who served as assistant editor of the *Nebraska History* magazine, testifies that she knew stories of Antoine when she was a child. Miss Sandoz is unusually well versed in northwestern Nebraska history and legend.

He was a half-breed, the son of Michael Barada who was supposed to be of royal connections in Spain . . . . The town of Barada in Richardson County was named after Michael. Around 1934 when I was working at the State Historical Society, a letter came in seeking information on the Barada family, to settle, I recall now, an estate. Whether this was another

of the recurring Spanish inheritance hoaxes I don't know . . . .
There was also a Michael Barada in the Custer County region
for a while, I'm told.

An entry in *Nebraska Place-Names* (1925), compiled by Lilian
Fitzpatrick and published in the University of Nebraska *Studies
in Language, Literature and Criticism,* reads:

> Barada. This place is situated in Barada Precinct and it and
> the precinct were named after one of the first settlers, Antoine
> Barada (1807-1887), a French-Omaha half-breed whose wife
> was a French woman. He named the village after himself.

The year 1887 entered here as that of Antoine's death is
given in several other sources. And some state that the town and
precinct of Barada—the name has initial accentuation—were
named after Michael. It is likeliest, however, that they were
named not after Michael nor by Antoine after himself but by
others because of the residence of Antoine and his family in
the vicinity. The name Barada may suggest that he was Spanish-
Indian but there is no doubt that he was French-Indian, as
suggested by the name Antoine and as stated in most accounts
of his parentage. The statement that Michael Barada was "a
gay Parisian" and that his "romance" with a "pretty Indian
maiden, Laughing Water" was "one of the most beautiful in
the world" sounds as though it owes something to glamorous
furbishing, as will be seen.

There is one good source of information concerning Antoine
that seems in general to be overlooked, namely that in the biographical section, pp. 321-347, of the *Transactions and Reports
of the Nebraska State Historical Society,* II (1887). In this section are printed seventeen biographies of well-known Nebraskans; his is the fifteenth, pp. 343-346, and is given by no means
the briefest space. The secretary of the Society was then Professor George E. Howard of the Department of History of the
State University, a fine scholar, trained in Germany. The biographies may have appeared under his supervision, some perhaps
from his pen. The account of Antoine begins:

> Among the many noted Nebraskans gathered to their fathers
> in the past few years, there were none whose deeds of bravery

and adventurous life compare with those of Antoine Barada, who died in the summer of 1866 at the little town which bears his name in Richardson County . . . . His career as chief, captive, trader, scout and pilot deserves more than passing note.

In summary, the account states that he was born in 1807 near what is now Fort Calhoun in Washington County. His father Michael was a white man and represented the Omaha tribe of Indians at the conference which drafted what is known as the treaty of Prairie du Chien in 1836. His mother was a full-blooded Indian woman. At seven he was captured by Sioux in one of their forays on the Omahas but was spared the fate of his companions. After two years he escaped and returned or was returned to his parents. Colonel Rogers of the United States Army planned to place him in the Military Academy [West Point] but his aunt, Mme. Mousette, in St. Louis, persuaded him to hide and not go to the academy. From boyhood he exhibited extraordinary muscular powers. When employed in Missouri as superintendent of quarries he is said to have proved his strength by lifting clear 1,800 pounds. In 1832 he returned to his tribe to visit his parents. Again in St. Louis, he married a French woman, Josephene (Josephine) Veien in 1836. In 1849, the Gold Rush year, he went overland to California, meeting many adventures and exciting incidents on the way and when returning. He remained on the West Coast six years. He had often visited his mother's tribe in Richardson County. After his return from the West he finally settled there on a farm. He brought up a family of three sons [Michael, William, and Thomas] and four girls. He died in 1866 and is buried in the Catholic cemetery just east of the village of Barada. His biographer in the *Transactions* comments that he had the appreciation of "many friends, acquaintances and strangers for his kind words, good deeds, and generous acts."

This brief account of his life should be that which is most nearly authentic since it was written nearest the time of his death, whether he died in 1866 as stated in the *Transactions* (possibly a misprint for 1886), or in 1887, or in 1885, the year given on his tombstone. It nowhere states that his father was a Parisian Count or a member of a noble Spanish family. Nor is there any reference to his father's romance, "one of the most beautiful in history."

Some years later, in 1917, appeared another pretty dependable account. This is in Lewis C. Edwards' *History of Richardson County,* chapter VIII, p. 191. The author makes no claim to have known Antoine but he had information from members of the Barada family. Edwards states that Antoine was "born at St. Mary's near Fort Calhoun across the river from Omaha." His father Michael was an educated Frenchman from France employed by the United States government as an interpreter, and he served in that capacity in the making of the famous treaty of Prairie du Chien, negotiated in a town of that name in Wisconsin. The elder Barada and his wife "were stationed at Fort Lisa about 200 miles north of St. Mary's above Omaha." Here the lad was stolen by the Sioux and a ransom demanded of his parents. He was recovered six months later by the payment of "two ponies." Some soldiers promised to take him east to be educated at West Point Military Academy. He was taken down the river to Carondolet south of St. Louis. Here he was left stranded by intoxicated soldiers and found and returned to his aunt, Mrs. Moosac. Later he was employed in a stone quarry. He was a thick, heavy-set man of broad shoulders and prodigious strength. He married a French woman, Josephine Vierhen, who was familiarly known as Marcelite.

In Edwards' *History* of 1917 is a short paper headed "Pioneer Exploits by Antoine Barada," written by him, it is stated, in response to solicitations for sketches of early times. By 1917, Antoine had been dead many years. It hardly deserves the credence of preceding accounts for it goes astray in the second sentence, "My parents were of French descent and coming from New Orleans were called Creoles." The Louisiana Creoles were white persons descended from the French or Spanish settlers of Louisiana. Antoine's mother was an Indian, not a Creole. The account speaks of his having been reared "in every luxury of civilized life" but that he preferred adventure and entered as a mere boy into the employment of the Northwestern Fur Company and traveled back and forth to the mountains. In 1856 he settled on a farm, the second settler in the region, and the precinct was named after him. According to Edwards the inscriptions on the stones at his and his wife's grave say: Antoine Barada. Born August 2, 1807. Died March 30, 1885. Josephine Barada. Born March 22, 1817. Died May 8, 1889.

What is the source of the tale of the gay Parisian Count and his romance with the Indian maiden? How did it make its way into circulation? It seems to have emerged about 1933-34, perhaps from the Barada family, or from a lawyer, or from a friend and since then has been handed on. It was given prominence in the Sunday magazine section of the St. Louis *Post-Dispatch*, May 20, 1934. A preceding account, the initial appearance of the story so far as I have been able to learn, came from Edward Harlan, president of the Tribal Council of Omaha Indians, when the Thompson-Howard bill seeking to establish Indian rights was introduced into Congress by representative Edgar Howard of Columbus, Nebraska. Howard was United States Congressman, 1922-35. The bill provided for placing certain members of the Barada family, "descendants of Count Michael and Laughing Buffalo," on the official rolls of the Omaha tribe, in order to make them eligible for land allotments. The story of Michael's romance was included in the report made by the Committee on Indian Affairs which accompanied the bill pending in 1934. It would be of great interest to see this report in view of the light it might throw on the initial account of the Barada ancestry. One infers that the tale was helpful in the passing of the bill. Yet it is hard to see how Antoine's descendants of the 1930's could be expected to give altogether trustworthy information concerning Michael's coming to America. Without written records to fall back on, relying on story, how many of us in the twentieth century could tell much concerning the romances of our grandfathers in the eighteenth century?

Whoever was responsible for the launching or publicizing of it, the glamorous account by Keith Kerman of the Sunday magazine staff of the *Post-Dispatch* must have done much to float it into currency. It does not appear in the available printed accounts before 1934, so far as I know, but it does in all those written later. I am indebted for seeing a typewritten transcription of the St. Louis newspaper story to Mr. John Wiltse of Falls

City, the author of "Tales of Antoine Barada and his father Michael," a well-written paper prepared for a program and now in the files of the State Historical Society. It occupies four single-spaced pages. Here, in summary, is the tale of the romance of the Count and his Indian bride. It is so glamorous and far-fetched, yet stock, that one wonders at its unquestioned acceptance. Omitting many details it is as follows:

Young Michael Barada was twenty as he sauntered along a fashionable Parisian street, his sword in its jeweled scabbard swinging jauntily. In front of the house of a nobleman a rose dropped at his feet from a window. He looked up in time to see the face of a girl and fell impetuously in love. Returning to the scene the next day, he found that she had just left Paris to sail for America. She was an Indian girl who with others of her race had been brought to Paris by the French government that Parisians might see aboriginal Americans and they in turn might see France. The girl was Tae-Gle-Ha, or Laughing Buffalo. She was seventeen. The young gallant knew nothing of Indian tribes or the part of the country to which she had sailed. Nevertheless he took ship, landing in Montreal in the late 1780's. He had one clue in his search for her. It was that in the northern and western Indian languages the word *tae* meant buffalo. He held to his purpose and journeyed to many tribes in many regions. His stupendous search lasted ten years. At last he found Tae-Gle-Ha in a village of the Omaha tribe. She was twenty-seven and still unmarried—perhaps because of her glimpse long before of the young Parisian gallant. Two weeks later they were married, first by Indian ceremony and later by a Jesuit priest. Barada became a member of the Omaha tribe. They moved across the Missouri River with the Omahas into what is now Nebraska, living in the first house built by a white man in the region.

An account in the Falls City *Journal*, the leading Richardson County newspaper, written five years later than Kerman's of 1934 and reprinted in the Lincoln, Nebraska, *Sunday Journal and Star* of December 31, 1939, differs in a few details. One is this:

The French nobleman met Antoine's mother when the Indian girl was in school in France under the sponsorship of a rich and kindly French family which had taken a liking to her during a visit to the United States. Count Barada followed Laughing Water to America and married her.

The stories of Antoine agree that when a lad in St. Louis, after his return from the Sioux, he stayed with his aunt, Mme. Mousette (Moosac in 1917), living a civilized life in Missouri rather than a tribal one with the Omaha Indians. Obviously this aunt with the French name was Michael's sister rather than Laughing Buffalo's. How about her? She too, if Michael's sister, was of noble birth. How did she reach St. Louis? She did not accompany Michael on his ten year search but must have come to America later. If so, in view of her birth and position in Paris, why make the venturesome journey across the Atlantic, surely an unusual one for a French noblewoman of her day, or later, especially since it was to a pioneer region.

Doubtless Laughing Water (apparently echoing Longfellow's Minnehaha) is a more attractive name than Laughing Buffalo. Yet with the change goes the one clue that enabled the Count, in the story of his romance, to find his inamorata. He could find Laughing Buffalo (Tae-Gle-Ha) but never Laughing Water.

Finally, there is another consideration to be taken into account, an important one, too. If Michael Barada was a young gallant at the court of King Louis XVI, the late 1780's and early 1790's seem a strange time for him to desert the King and the court for his long quest of the once-glimpsed Laughing Buffalo, temporarily in France at that unlikely time. This was the period of the French Revolution and 1789 was a cataclysmic year. King Louis was beheaded in 1793, and the French nobility abolished. If Michael was really a Count, a likelier story would state that he came to our shores after the outbreak of the Revolution to escape French conditions. Landing at New Orleans, he penetrated into the central west and, like many white men, such as Manuel Lisa or Kit Carson, married an Indian girl. Given this situation, his patrician sister might more probably have followed him to the New World, coming from New Orleans to St. Louis. One doubts, however, that Michael Barada was a Count, and one surely doubts the details of his romantic quest.

Probably coming allusions to Antoine and Michael Barada will repeat the story of the gay young Parisian and his romantic winning of his bride. But how far should it be credited, in these days, and continue to be handed on as valid biography? Folklore is of interest and it has its degree of importance, but it should be distinguished from history.

Reprinted from *Nebraska History*, XXX (October, 1949), 286-294.

Olof Bergstrom: Swedish Pioneer

———————————— 𝖗 ————————————

Olof Bergstrom, an early settler in Dawson County, was a leader of Swedish immigrants in the Gothenburg region. It has often been remarked that his life and activities in the Nebraska of the later nineteenth and earlier twentieth centuries deserve at least partial chronicling.[1] Some day, if and when the history of the Scandinavian element in Nebraska is written, his will be a prominent place. Not only was he an influential colonizer; he was a colorful personality; and, before it is too late, some account of him should be made available. It is nearly too late now, for hardly anyone who knew him is yet alive. What information is to be had may well be brought together at the present time as a contribution to the history of Dawson County.

A German settlement preceded the Swedish in the Gothenburg locale. The Germans came mostly from the eastern states and they had in some degree resources to fall back on. They preempted the choicer locations for their homesteads. When the settlers from Sweden came, this in 1882, their alternatives were to homestead the less desirable land to the north and west of the present Gothenburg, or to buy land from the Union Pacific railroad, which had penetrated and crossed Nebraska by the late 1860's. The federal government gave the Union Pacific every

———————————

[1] For the suggestion that this article be written and for much or most of the information supplied I am indebted to P. R. Beath of Washington, D. C., and Don Holmes of the Gothenburg *Times*.

other section of land (the odd numbers) for ten miles on each side of the right of way. The railroad might then sell the surplus land to the settlers. Olof worked on the Union Pacific after coming to America in 1881 and he decided to homestead in the Gothenburg region, after a stay in the town of Stromsburg in Polk County of which his brother became a resident. He took his homestead in Dawson County in 1881. The original Bergstrom farmhouse was a dugout, the site a sheep pasture, and there was no house or building near. In the summer of 1882 a house of sun-dried brick was put up. The earlier farmhouse was used as a shelter for Swedish immigrants when they came until they were located on their own land.

Olof and the Plum Creek station agent, J. H. McColl, got the concession to sell land from the Union Pacific railroad. The railroad laid out eight blocks, now known as the Original Town, and built the first side track. The name Gothenburg given the site came from the Swedish city of Gothenburg (Göteborg) from which Olof had emigrated. In the spring of 1882 he went back to Sweden and induced a number of persons to come to Dawson County and to start the new town. He told them that they would soon be independent and he assured them that there was no need for them to learn English as this town would be made up of people from Sweden. When the Swedish settlers came in that same year, their alternatives, as already said, were to homestead the less desirable land north and west of the present Gothenburg or to buy land of the railroad at $6.00 an acre. More did the latter.

One of the Swedes coming in 1882 was Per Nelson, a preacher. He went again to Sweden and returned with another group of immigrants. He painted the Nebraska plains to them in glowing colors. Naturally those coming with him were disappointed when they found no town on arrival, but he told them to look forward to the future. Another of those coming from Sweden in 1882 was Dr. Vollrad Karlson. He worked in a Kearney drugstore, primarily as a pharmacist. The next spring he opened up his own drugstore in the second building to be built in Gothenburg, this in January, 1883. Dr. Karlson died while yet in his twenties; his was not a long life for one who played a large part in the early days of Gothenburg. Two citizens of Gothenburg state that their impression is that Olof Bergstrom himself made several trips to Sweden, three perhaps, to bring more immigrants to Gothenburg and Dawson County.

The Gothenburg *Independent* of 1885 had an advertisement of Olof Bergstrom and Company.[2]

> The above firm is engaged in the real estate business, and is composed of O. Bergstrom, Dr. Vollrad Karlson and A. S. Booton. O. Bergstrom, then senior member of the firm, is a native of Sweden and came to America in 1881, making Nebraska his first permanent stopping place. He secured from the U. P. railroad six townships of land, the same including the present site of Gothenburg. He returned to Sweden sometime during the same year, but in 1882 he again set sail for America, bringing with him a party of about 370 of his countrymen. The major part of the company settled in Phelps County, but few caring to stake their fortunes in Gothenburg and vicinity— although a large number of them have since moved here. Mr. Bergstrom is the founder of Gothenburg and, having implicit faith in the future of the town, has labored zealously for its welfare.

His "implicit faith" was to be borne out, but probably, at the time he expressed it, it was more qualified than he represented to his followers. Elvina Karlson, daughter of Dr. Vollrad Karlson's brother Frederick, said in an interview in 1944, quoting her mother, that "knowing the hardships and slim pickings of the years ahead, Olof reasoned that only the Viking spirit of high courage and self reliance could hew a homestead out of this camping ground of Buffalo and Indians." In the same interview [3] Elvina Karlson told more that she had learned from the talk of her mother of Olof Bergstrom. Mrs. Frederick Karlson was his contemporary and knew him well.

> In 1885 Mr. Bergstrom got up a petition for a Postoffice. The petition was accepted and Bergstrom was appointed Postmaster. Mail was brought to his house or homestead and anyone who wanted his mail called for it there. There was not

---

2 May 18, 1885.
3 Reported by P. R. Beath in 1944.

much mail, a sack coming in at a time. If no one was at the train to get the mail it was stuffed into a box used as a stepoff from the train. Sometimes the mail would remain there for days before some one from the Bergstrom's would walk down to get it. Bergstrom himself was seldom at home, newly arrived emigrants doing his work around the place. When the sack was brought back there was a general stampede for the key which hung on a nail, and the one getting the key was privileged to open the sack and dump it on the floor. The letters were then gathered and placed on a table. When people called for their mail they were invited to look through the mail on the table. In 1883 when Dr. Vollrad Karlson started his drugstore, the Post Office was moved there, on Front Street, and he served as mail clerk. Dr. Karlson conducted the Post Office in a more dignified manner. He went after the mail himself and tucked it away in a cigar box under the counter in the store. He sorted the letters and told the settlers if they had any mail.

Olof married a concert or opera singer as his second wife, and this seems to have had no little effect on his career. A soprano of considerable note, coming to this country from Sweden, she gave concerts in the East and had a wide repertory.

Inquiry sent to Mrs. J. A. Frawley, daughter of Lewis Headstrom, the founder of Stromsburg, brought the following information, in May, 1944. I am indebted for it to Chattie Westenius of Stromsburg, editor of the Stromsburg *Headlight.*

[As a child] I remember Olof Bergstrom's being spoken of as a revivalist type of Baptist preacher. . . . My parents attended some of these meetings, but he was never a guest at our house, either in Galva or Stromsburg. Then one day a letter came from him stating that he had just returned from Sweden and had attended a concert in Stockholm given by a beautiful and talented singer, and was told that she was very anxious to visit the U. S. A. and study for her career. So he conceived the idea that it might be a very profitable financial success if he could be her manager. He obtained an interview and arrangements were so made. He told her they would have to be married because in America it would not be proper for them to travel together except as man and wife. So they were married and lived at Gothenburg.

This is the account of her coming to America as told by Mrs. Bergstrom to Mrs. Frawley. The latter added that Bergstrom asked Mr. Headstrom to let his wife come to Stromsburg to give a concert, which she did, Mrs. Frawley playing her accompaniment. He had asked that the Headstroms sponsor her as their guest, and they did. This was about three years after Mrs. Frawley's marriage. Mrs. Frawley also remarked "Bergstrom's wife was a very pleasant and confiding guest but we never heard of either of them again."

The same issue of the Gothenburg *Independent* that printed the real estate advertisement of the Bergstrom-Karlson Company (May 16, 1895) contains, according to Don Holmes, "reports from Minneapolis papers about the Aklander-Bergstrom Concert Company of which Mrs. Bergstrom was the prima donna, with a soprano voice of remarkable strength, range and compass." Mrs. Frederick Karlson stated that "When they came back as bride and groom to Gothenburg, the Gothenburg band met the Bergstroms at the station, which was a platform merely with no building in sight as yet." Mrs. Bergstrom gave up concert singing. They lived in the home of sun-dried brick and entertained lavishly. In 1890 it became the scene of a killing.

Earlier Bergstrom had been deeply interested in temperance. According to Mrs. Karlson he even went to Sweden and organized there a Temperance Union called in Swedish *God Templar*. Finally, to continue Mrs. Karlson's testimony:

Mrs. Bergstrom, forgetting her good training in Sweden and Olof Bergstrom falling a devotee of liquor, they carried on in their house extravagantly. A few of Mrs. Bergstrom's friends met there one evening. One of those present was a jolly sort of fellow, always teasing. He agitated Olof Bergstrom that night so that he picked up a revolver. There is no evidence to prove that he did shoot, or who did it, as all present were in the same state.

The last sentences refer to what was the most conspicuous event in Bergstrom's life in Dawson County, his trial for the murder of Ernest G. Edholm. Records concerning the case are on file in the office of the Clerk of the District Court in Lexington, Dawson County [4] and in the Appearance Docket. The killing took place March 14, 1890. The information against Bergstrom was filed March 15 by Edwin Edholm. The judge examined the following witnesses at the preliminary hearing: Dr. W. P. Smith, Annie Dell, Amanda Ingram for the complainant and Mrs. Sarah Johnson for the defendant. The defendant was represented by Hinman and Garret. The trial began June 9. The defendant with counsel appeared in court and pleaded not guilty. In the interval between July 9 and July 14, the jury was decided on. The papers in the case that are existent tell of formal motions made by the parties concerned and preserve three sketches of the scene of the crime and a few subpoenas. There is no verbatim testimony and the motive of the crime is nowhere mentioned.

For a transcription of the charge (The State of Nebraska, Dawson County, in the District Court of the Tenth Judicial District vs. Olaf Bergstrom), I am indebted to Mr. and Mrs. Frank Johnson of Lexington. I hope I may be pardoned for printing a section of the document. It is more interesting, perhaps, as a sample of the legal language of the time (legal language is said to be much simplified today) than as throwing light on the Bergstrom case. The italics, punctuation and spellings of the original have been retained.

Be it remembered that T. L. Warrington, County Attorney in and for Dawson County, and in the Tenth Judicial District of the State of Nebraska, who prosecutes in the name and by the Authority of the State of Nebraska, comes here in person into the Court at this June term, A. D. 1890 thereof and for the State of Nebraska gives the Court to *understood* and be informed that Olaf Bergstrom late of the County of Dawson, on the *Fourteenth* day of March, A. D. 1890 in the County of Dawson aforesaid in and upon one Ernest G. Edholm, then and there being unlawfully, purposely and feloniously and of deliberate and premeditated malice, did make an assault with the intent him the said Ernest G. Edholm unlawfully, purposely and of deliberate and premeditated malice to kill and

---

[4] District Court Journal, 3, pp. 100, 123, 140, 141; Appearance Docket, 2, p. 237.

murder, that the said Olaf Bergstrom, a certain rifle then and there charged with gun powder, and one leaden bullet, which the said rifle, he the said Olaf Bergstrom, in both of his hands, then and there had and held, then and there unlawfully, feloniously, purposely and of deliberate and premeditated malice, did discharge and shoot off, to, at, against and upon the left breast of the body of the said Ernest G. Edholm, and that the said Olaf Bergstrom with the leaden bullet aforesaid, out of the rifle aforesaid, then and there by the force of the gun powder, by the said Olaf Bergstrom, discharged and *shott* off as aforesaid, then and there, unlawfully, feloniously, purposely and of his deliberate and premeditated malice did strike, penetrate and wound, with the intent aforesaid thereby then and there, giving to the said Ernest G. Edholm, in and upon the left breast of the body of him, the said Ernest G. Edholm, then and there with the bullet aforesaid, so as aforesaid discharged and shot out of the rifle aforesaid by force of the gunpowder aforesaid by the said Olaf Bergstrom, in and upon the left breast of the body of him, the said Ernest G. Edholm, one mortal wound of the depth of four inches and the width of which said mortal wound, he the said Ernest G. Edholm instantly died, and the said T. L. Warrington, County Attorney, as aforesaid upon the authority aforesaid does say that the said Olaf Bergstrom, him, the said Ernest G. Edholm, unlawfully, feloniously, purposely and of his deliberate and premeditated malice did kill and murder contrary to the form of the Statute in such case made and provided and against the peace and dignity of the State of Nebraska.

T. L. Warrington, County Attorney

The following persons were named as jurors: Charles Cook, Thomas Patton, J. P. Cahow, J. B. Donaldson, Howard Koch, John Lee, Ed Thomlinson, William Reed, George Bogett, Con Hammond, William Tallowell, Jer Kearns, who were duly impaneled and sworn according to law. They returned their verdict in writing as follows:

We, the jury in this case, being duly impaneled and sworn in the above entitled case do find and say that we find the defendant not guilty,

J. P. Cahow, Foreman

And therefore it is ordered and adjudged that said defendant Olaf Bergstrom be discharged.

A statement made by Howard Koch, one of the last jurors to survive, concerning the trial of Olof Bergstrom is of interest.[5] Koch was born in Philadelphia, he states, in 1865. His father homesteaded north of Lexington and Howard came from Philadelphia to join him in 1877. Koch said:

> One day in the spring of 1880 I came to town to get some repairs for my binder. The sheriff met me on the street. He said to me:
>
> "Hello, Howard. The judge wants to see you."
>
> "Not me," I said. "I ain't got no time to serve on any jury. My binder is one of the best in the country and I've got to get it fixed."
>
> "Well, come on in anyway," said the sheriff.
>
> So I went in the court house and there they were preparing for the trial of Olaf Bergstrom for shooting that fellow up in Gothenburg. Well, the judge picked me for one of the jury, and I guess I'm the only one of them left.
>
> Well, I had heard of Bergstrom before the trial, but I had never seen him till that day. He was a partner of Jack McColl. I bought my farm from McColl.
>
> As for the trial itself, as best I can remember, the testimony was that Bergstrom and this fellow Edholm were sitting there on the settee in Bergstrom's house examining Bergstrom's goose-gun. We called shotguns "goose-guns" in those days; the country was full of geese. Well, they got to quarreling about the gun and finally to wrestling and it went off and shot Edholm and killed him. Bergstrom said Edholm was one of his best friends. I remember one of the lawyers tried to bring in about this fellow fooling around Bergstrom's wife, but he didn't get anywhere with that line. His wife was at the trial and seems to me she testified the same as her husband did. I remember too, about a Swedish maid the Bergstroms had, but she wasn't at the trial. Right away after the killing, I believe, she went back to Sweden.
>
> Well, there was only one thing to do, so we set him free. He was a big man, fine looking and wore a moustache. We all wore moustaches in those days.

---

[5] Reported by P. R. Beath, 1944.

And after the trial, you know what? Bergstrom was so happy he took us into the back room and opened a little black bag he had and gave us each a $20 bill. Well, the trial was over, you understand, and he was happy to get free and wanted to do something for us.

According to Don Holmes, when the verdict came Olof Bergstrom was met at the train by the Gothenburg Silver Cornet Band and escorted to his home.

The best account of Bergstrom was obtained by P. R. Beath from Mrs. Frederick Karlson, Sr. It should be printed in full. It was written down in 1944 by Miss Elvina Karlson of Gothenburg from the conversation of her mother, Mrs. Frederick Karlson, Sr. A few sentences from it have been quoted in preceding pages.

I arrived in Gothenburg, Nebraska, the morning of June 18, 1885. In the afternoon I went to my brother's drugstore. Outside was Olof Bergstrom standing by his team of horses and buggy. He was all dressed up for the occasion to meet Dr. Vollrad's sister who had just arrived from Sweden. Dr. Vollrad Karlson was secretary to Olof Bergstrom and Company. Olof Bergstrom was a very handsome gentleman, fine physique, six feet tall, brown curly hair. He was dressed in a dark suit, white shirt, white vest. He was outstanding in his mannerisms. One characteristic was he always held his head on one side and had a pleasant smile. He possessed a fine personality. He spoke excellent Swedish; he was a Swedish minister from Göteborg, Sweden. He did not use much English because he contacted mostly Swedish people. His parents were very fine folks in Sundsvall, Sweden.

He lived in Göteborg, Sweden, before he came to America in 1880. He first went to Stromsburg, then to Gothenburg in 1881. He was a Real Estate agent for the Union Pacific railroad; he sold railroad land cheap. He was in the real estate business, sold railroad land and was agent for the homestead land. He was no relation to McColl. Mr. McColl, an attorney, was real Estate Agent at Plum Creek, Lexington, Nebraska, for the Union Pacific Railroad Company. Mr. Bergstrom would consult Mr. McColl on the many land deals. Bergstrom was no relation to E. G. West. They were business partners. Mr. West came with Mr. Bergstrom from Chicago.

He told them [his recruits in Sweden] that land was so cheap that they would soon be very independent. They would not have to learn to speak the English language because there would be just Swedes from Sweden. They could possess their own beautiful valley, he said, "the wonderful Platte Valley, the greatest agricultural valley in the world excepting the Nile in Egypt." To homeseekers he made the statement "The Early Bird Catches the Worm."

He was married twice, would have been married the third time but he left the bride "waiting at the church." His first wife was a very cultured woman. He had a beautiful daughter by this marriage. The daughter had a winning personality like her father. She studied music in Boston and Chicago. Mr. Bergstrom played the violin very well. The daughter died at the young age of twenty-five years; she grieved so much over the loss of her father's speculations in Chicago. His second wife was very homely but a fine dresser. She was an opera singer from Stockholm, Sweden. She sang in grand opera there. She received her education there. She gave concerts at the cities and towns in America. A pianist from Boston was her accompanist. Mr. Bergstrom's plans were that she would make a great deal of money with her mezzo soprano voice. I'm sorry to say Mrs. Bergstrom did not use her career to a good end. She died in the County Hospital at Omaha and sold her body for medical purposes.

Olaf Bergstrom was tried for murder but acquitted. The jury decided that under the circumstances Bergstrom could not be accused alone, because the other men in the party were drunk as well as Bergstrom. A minister from the East pleaded this case to this ending.

In later life Bergstrom lost all his wealth, probably through speculations in Chicago, and went to Tennessee. The late Ernest Calling who came to Gothenburg in 1889 and was at one time a partner of Bergstrom told P. R. Beath, July, 1944, that he bought the farm immediately north of Lake Gothenburg from Olof Bergstrom in 1906. This farm was the scene of the killing for which Bergstrom was tried and acquitted. Later Bergstrom returned from Tennessee and wanted Calling to trade for some Tennessee land the farm where he intended to spend his last days. Calling refused and Bergstrom returned to Tennessee. It was probably of the same occasion that Mrs. Karlson said, according to the account of her daughter in 1944, "Mr. Bergstrom lost all his wealth and returned the last time plain 'broke.' He went to Mr. Karlson's market and wanted to pawn his watch and chain, but Mr. Karlson said 'No.' He fixed up a nice lunch of meat, crackers and cheese etc. for Bergstrom. Olof's many friends helped him. He left for Tennessee and died there."

An article on Bergstrom is said to have appeared in the Chicago newspaper *Svenska Amerikanaren Tribunen*. Whether this was before or after his death I do not know. Elvina Karlson was unable to obtain from the newspaper the date of the issue in which it is supposed to have been printed.

In a few respects tales and anecdotes of Olof Bergstrom have affiliations with Nebraska folklore. When I first looked into his history I thought there must be something of legend associated with his attitude toward strong drink. Various sources of information mentioned him as almost a fanatic crusader for Temperance. Other sources mentioned his unique prowess as a drinker. My brother Roscoe, for instance, whose remarkable memory is well known, recalls stories of Olof's prodigious capacity as regards alcoholic potations. But in due time I realized that folklore was not involved in these contradictory reports. Both accounts of his attitude seem to have been true. A preacher, he started life in the United States as a strong advocate of temperance. Perhaps it was after his marriage to the opera singer that he surrendered to the attraction of alcoholic beverages, serving them liberally in his home and drinking with others as the custom was. The representations of Mrs. Karlson are relevant here and no doubt should be accepted. His change of attitude was fact; no lore entered into it. Beyond question, however, is Olof's relation to the folk stories of Febold, the Nebraska strong man. Paul R. Beath, editor of *Febold Feboldson: Tall Tales of the Great Plains* (1948), states that Febold was a reconstruction of Olof Bergstrom, though the name got itself applied to or mixed up with Bergstrom Stromsberg, the reputed grandnephew of Febold and the narrator of tall tales concerning him. The same testimony is given by Don Holmes of the Gothenburg newspaper in which many of these tales were originally printed and are still being printed. Olof played, then, a leading part in the genesis of the Nebraska Febold tales. A third bit of lore that has a degree of circulation by chroniclers of Febold is that, by transposition of syllables, the town of Stromsburg was named from Bergstrom. Olof's brother Andrew became a resident of Stromsburg, as mentioned already, but the town was founded by Lewis Headstrom in 1872, nearly a decade before Olof came to the United States. According to the historian of the place,[6] it took its name not from Olof Bergstrom but from its earliest inhabitant, Headstrom, -*burg* being added to the second syllable of his name (*Strom's burg*). The same explanation is given in *Nebraska Place-Names*.[7] Unmistakably the association of Olof Bergstrom with the naming of Stromsburg is folklore.

Reprinted from *Nebraska History*, XXXI (March, 1950), 64-74.

---

[6] Chattie Westenius, *History of Stromsburg* (Stromsburg, 1931), p. 2.

[7] Lilian Fitzpatrick, *Nebraska Place-Names*, (University of Nebraska, 1925), p. 117.

The Southwestern Cowboy Songs and English and Scottish Popular Ballads

――――――――――――――――― 🐾 ―――――――

This article was a pioneer venture questioning the then accepted position (the "Harvard position") of Professors F. B. Gummere and G. L. Kittredge then prevailing in American ballad literature. The Texas cowboys brought their songs to Nebraska when they drove their herds northward, but in general a large proportion of the Lomax songs which were current over the Central West and in Texas were adapted for local conditions from popular songs of the day. In addition to those of the Lomax songs I was able to identify, Phillips Barry of Cambridge found the sources of many of the pieces supposed to be of group emergency by canvassing old New England newspapers. The position taken in this paper of 1912 brought much criticism at the time but is now generally accepted with few dissenters adhering to the once enthroned "Harvard" belief.

Several writers recently have found analogy between the conditions attending the growth of cowboy songs in isolated communities in the Southwest, and the conditions under which arose the English and Scottish popular ballads—those problematic pieces which form so special a chapter in the history of English poetry. Mr. Lomax, the chief collector of southwestern folk songs,[1] notes, when speaking of western communities, how "illiterate people and people cut off from newspapers and books, isolated and lonely—thrown back on primal resources for entertainment and for the expression of emotion—utter themselves through somewhat the same character of songs as did their forefathers of perhaps a thousand years ago." Professor Barrett Wendell [2] suggests that it is possible to trace in this group of American ballads "the precise manner in which songs and cycles of songs—obviously analogous to those surviving from older and antique times—have come into being. The facts which are still available concerning the ballads of our own Southwest are such as should go far to prove, or to disprove, many of the theories advanced concerning the laws of literature as evinced in the ballads of the Old World." Ex-President Roosevelt affirms in a personal letter to Mr. Lomax [3] that "there is something very curious in the reproduction here on this new continent of essentially the conditions of ballad-growth which obtained in medieval England."

The parallel felt by these writers is worked out, with more specific detail and greater definiteness, by Professor W. W. Lawrence, in a passage prefixed to a discussion of the ballads of Robin Hood: [4]

> These men, living together on the solitary ranches of Texas, Arizona, or New Mexico, have been accustomed to entertain each other after the day's work is done by singing songs, some of which have been familiar to them from boyhood, others of which they have actually composed themselves. . . . These cowboy ballads are not the expression of individuals but of the whole company which listens to them, and they are, in a very real sense, the work of other men than the author. . . . The

---

[1] *Cowboy Songs.* Collected by John A. Lomax. New York, 1910. See also G. W. Will, "Songs of Western Cowboys," *Journal of American Folk-Lore,* XXII, XXVI.

[2] Lomax, *Cowboy Songs,* Introduction.

[3] *Ibid.,* Prefixed letter, dated from Cheyenne, 1910.

[4] *Medieval Story.* New York, 1911.

author counts for nothing, it will be observed; his name is generally not remembered, and what he invents is as characteristic of his comrades as of himself. . . . Here we have literature which is a perfect index of the social ideals of the body of men among whom it is composed, literature which makes no pretense to literary form or to the disclosure of the emotions of any one man as distinguished from his fellows. There are few communities of the present day which are as closely united in common aims and sympathies as these bands of Western cowboys, hence there are few opportunities for the production of verse which is as truly the expression of universal emotion as are these songs.

Such Western ranches reproduce almost perfectly the conditions under which the English popular ballads were composed. . . .

It is obvious from these passages that their writers find a real parallel between the conditions leading to the growth in our own time, in certain homogeneous communities of the Southwest, of fugitive folk pieces like those gathered by Mr. Lomax, and the conditions responsible for the rise in the Middle Ages of the traditional ballads of England and Scotland. For the student of both folklore and literature, the parallel so clearly set forth in the paragraphs last quoted has strong interest; and its possibilities of instructiveness are warrant for making it the basis for a brief special examination. Wherein does it hold? How far is it to be pushed? What, if anything, is indicated concerning the Old World pieces by their New World analogues? Of the two leading schools of thought concerning the genesis of the English and Scottish ballads, that which may be designated the "Harvard school" emphasizes the idea of real communal composition, as by a collective village community, and adheres to a definition by origins for genuine popular ballads; that which may be called the English school[5] defines by destination and style. For the mass of traditional English and Scot-

---

[5] See chiefly W. J. Courthope, *History of English Poetry*, I (1895); G. G. Smith, *The Transition Period*, vi (1900); W. P. Ker, *On the History of the Ballads*, 1100-1500 (1910); and T. F. Henderson, *Scottish Vernacular Literature* (1898); Introduction to Scott's *Minstrelsy of the Scottish Border* (1902); and *The Ballad in Literature* (1912).

tish folk-ballads it finds necessary the hypothesis of a higher origin than spontaneous popular collaboration. Which, if either, of these schools may find support in the parallel under discussion; if it be true, as Professor Wendell suggests, that the facts concerning western songs may "go far to prove, or to disprove, many of the theories advanced concerning the laws of literature as evinced in the ballads of the Old World," in which direction, if either, is the student of English balladry led?

Let us first examine, for the sake of the generalizations to be made, the subject-matter of the American pieces, and their style.

A certain percentage of the songs in the collection of Mr. Lomax are perhaps genuine cowboy pieces, approached from almost any point of view. Those which are most typical are related very closely to the life of the communities which originated and preserved them. Some of these, the editor tells us, the singers themselves composed. There are songs dealing with the life of the ranch, of the trail, songs of stampedes, of the barroom; but chiefly they deal with cattle and the cowboys who have them in charge. There are a few passing references to their "bosses"; but songs relating to these, or to the ranch-owners, songs of the lives of their employers and their families, do not appear. A few preserve the style of the ultra-sentimental or "flowery" period of American verse,[6] with doubtfully westernized setting, a few are ascribed to personal authors,[7] and some are plainly built on or out of well-known songs;[8] but these are not wholly typical. Of what may be termed the real cowboy pieces, the following verses, cited as representative by Professor Lawrence also, will give a good idea:

I'm a rowdy cowboy just off the stormy plains,
My trade is girting saddles and pulling bridle reins,

---

[6] "By Markentura's Flowery Marge," p. 224; or the story of Amanda and Young Albon, p. 271.

[7] "Night-Herding Song," p. 324; or "The Metis Song of the Buffalo Hunters," p. 72.

[8] "The Cowboy's Dream" (based on "My Bonnie Lies over the Ocean"), p. 18; or "The Railroad Corral" (see Sir Walter Scott's "Bonny Dundee"), p. 318. "The Little Old Sod Shanty on the Claim," p. 187, widely known in the Midwest, is an adaptation, it seems to the present writer, of the once very popular "The Little Old Log Cabin in the Lane."

Oh, I can tip the lasso, it is with graceful ease;
I rope a streak of lightning, and ride it where I please.
My bosses they all like me, they say I am hard to beat;
I give them the bold stand off, you bet I have got the cheek.
I always work for wages, my pay I get in gold;
I am bound to follow the longhorn steer until I am too old.
    Ci yi yip yip yip pe ya.

Or—

Come all you jolly cowboys that follow the bronco steer,
I'll sing to you a verse or two your spirits for to cheer;
It's all about a trip, a trip that I did undergo
On that crooked trail to Holbrook, in Arizona oh.

Or—

Bill driv the stage from Independence
Up to the Smokey Hill;
And everybody knowed him thar
As Independence Bill,—
Thar warn't no feller on the route
That driv with half the skill.

As might be foreseen, though picturesque and often forceful, these pieces are crude and nearly formless, without literary quality or individual touch.[9] Also they tend to be songs rather than ballads; they are more likely to express collective or individual feeling than to be verse narratives. There is an established manner, but it is crude; real poetical quality they can hardly be said to have. The *Stoff* is relatively unambitious and was found by the composers close at hand. No doubt it is compositions of this nature to which may fairly be ascribed the communal origin suggested by Mr. Lomax and sketched out by Professor Lawrence. These might well have found their origin in the improvisation of a community isolated and homogeneous; and they well reflect

---

9 It is more than likely that even these compositions are built from well-known songs, like those cited in the preceding footnote, i.e., are adaptations. Most of them follow the model of stall ballads, or "Come all ye's," as they are sometimes designated. Of course it would be only the framework, the suggestion that is so given; the rest would be the work of some adapter, or, it may be, series of adapters.

the life, the tastes, the themes, and song modes, of those among whom they are current. To reiterate, they deal as a mass with the life and the interests of the same class of people that originate them and sing them. And among this class, it is tempting to add, the pieces so composed are likely to die!

Suppose that we endeavor to distinguish, among the songs collected by Mr. Lomax, those which have found widest diffusion and greatest promise of permanence. They are not those which may fairly be thought to have originated on southwestern ranches, but rather those which may fairly be thought not to have originated there. Currency and diffusion, a sort of permanence, have been gained by a number of the better pieces; but they are pieces not peculiar to the cowboys or to the Southwest; they deal rather with outside life and topics. The very first, "O bury me not on the lone prairie," or "The Dying Cowboy," despite its title, is no communal cowboy improvisation. It has been recovered from oral tradition in Missouri, Kentucky, New England, Nebraska, and elsewhere. It is built, as is well known, on a sea piece, accessible in print,[10] "O bury me not in the deep, deep sea." The songs "Jesse James," "The Death of Garfield," "The Days of Forty-Nine," "The Texas Rangers," "The Boston Burglar," and others have been recovered in many states of the Midwest, East, and South.[11] So with "Young Charlotte," thought by Mr. Phillips Barry to have been composed by a rural poet in Vermont, about two generations ago.[12] "The Dreary Black Hills," has been recovered in Missouri, Nebraska, Wyoming, and elsewhere. A version of "Mississippi Girls," localized to suit quite different conditions,[13] is in the possession of the writer.

---

[10] A text appears in Fulton and Trueblood's *Choice Readings,* Boston, 1883; but the ascription of authorship there is probably not to be trusted.

[11] Additional instances are "Fuller and Warren," "Jerry, Go Ile That Car," "The Cowboy's Lament," "Macaffie's Confession," "The Little Old Sod Shanty," "The Wars of Germany," "Fannie Moore," "Betsy from Pike," "Rosin the Bow."

[12] "Native Balladry in America," *Journal of American Folk-Lore,* XXII, 365-373.

[13] The Old World ballad "The Two Brothers" (Child, 49), in a version in the possession of the writer—otherwise pretty faithful as regards narrative—seems from the surprising "way out in Idaho" of its last line to be well on its way toward becoming a western piece. A version of "Lord Randal"

For songs of the cowboy type quoted from earlier in this paper, a spontaneous origin on the trail may be a probable explanation, but not for those of the type enumerated in the preceding sentences. The latter are more likely to have drifted to than from the Southwest.[14] But be that as it may, it seems to be true that the group which has achieved currency and permanence did not concern itself with the local and the special in cowboy life, but with the general, i.e., with widely known and interesting events and persons. Some, like the ballads of Jesse James and Cole Younger, or of the death of Garfield, have or had a sort of nation-wide interest. Others have some striking interest of situation or climax, or have more sustained and "artistic" execution, as "Young Charlotte"; or they were perhaps floated into diffusion by special tunefulness.

Surely songs, or ballads proper, or both, are frequently improvised even now in remote or isolated homogeneous communities, as they were in greater degree in the past; but it does not seem that these are the pieces most likely to persist and to find permanent transmission. Behind these spontaneous and inevitably crude compositions there is too little *élan;* not enough quality, poetic style, "art," tunefulness perhaps, not enough universality of appeal.[15] It takes pressure, strong impetus, to "float" a piece into real transmission and diffusion. Even among the Texas cowboys, it is not their communal or improvised "dogie" songs which are likely to persist nearly intact among them for many decades. These rise and die, impermanent and fluctuating by nature. The better chance for life will be had by pieces like "Jesse James," or "Young Charlotte," too regular of rhyme and meter and too sym-

---

(Child, 12) recovered from railway camps in Colorado, under the name "Johnny Randall," has already become such. See *Modern Language Notes,* January, 1902.

14 The cowboys wandered into the Southwest from diverse regions and varying cultural conditions; they must have brought with them differing conceptions and models of verse, sung to diverse tunes. Mainly, however, their models would be of the stall or street ballad type.

15 Some songs of spontaneous local composition on Wyoming ranches are in the possession of the writer, and some of similar composition brought by emigrants from mining communities at Newcastle, England. All are crude in form, and show the same commonplaceness and lack of poetical quality as the cowboy pieces.

metrical of structure, though communal by preservation or destination, to be of communal origin. More likely yet, compositions of the character of "After the Ball," "There'll Be a Hot Time," "Juanita," or "Lorena," now belonging to folk-song though not originating as such, will linger among the cowboys long after their local improvisations have perished. The purpose in this paper is not to risk prediction, however, but merely to examine and contrast; and to this it is time to return.

What now of the general nature of the subject-matter and style, as related to the folk and their interests, of the English and Scottish traditional ballads? We have seen that the songs originated by the cowboys deal with the life nearest them and are couched in the rude and nearly formless style most to be expected. They deal with the lives and the interests of the people among whom they arose and by whom they were preserved. In the many discussions regarding the authorship of the Old World ballads, the relation of the themes of the songs to the singers has had curiously little emphasis.[16] Yet the subject-matter of the English and

---

[16] The matter is dismissed (in a note) in Professor Gummere's *Old English Ballads* (Introd., p. xxvii) with the sentence: "This homogeneous character of a ballad-making folk, by the way, is quite enough to explain the high rank of most personages in the ballads—princes, knights, and so on." But difference between the life and interests of the hall and of the village or rural throng was very marked in the Middle Ages. This class cleavage is reflected in Froissart. Chaucer realized it when he placed knightly matter in the mouths of his aristocratic pilgrims and bourgeois matter in the mouths of those of lower class. In *The Popular Ballad*, Professor Gummere, while treating many matters minutely, contributes on this topic only (p. 309): "The favorite characters of the old ballad of communal tradition are the knight and the lady, wife or maid, who were in the focus of communal view and represented the fairly homogeneous life of that day." As if, for example, the "poor folk in cots" of *Piers Plowman*, or other humble people, were responsible for the references in balladry to bowers and falcons and knightly life, while artisans, peasants, husbandmen, common soldiers, they mention not at all? Only in *The Beginnings of Poetry*, a book not primarily treating the English and Scottish popular ballads, is Professor Gummere (pp. 178ff.) much concerned with the characters and the material of these ballads. Here there is insistence again on homogeneous conditions, the "ballad community." He is content, by specific statement, with purely communal origin for the aristocratic "Edward," "The Two Brothers," and "Babylon."

How far is the hypothesis of the homogeneous character of the mediaeval community historically tenable? Cowboy society is much more homogeneous, tested by its poetry and by the general character of the life reflected, than

Scottish popular ballads, viewed as evidence concerning the nature of their origin, deserves from critics not incidental treatment as a side issue, but to be faced clearly as a main one.

Undoubtedly the shepherds, or knitters, or weavers, the "humble people" of mediaeval communal conditions, paralleled by those on western ranches, originated pieces of their own; as, according to the testimony of Mr. Lomax, the western cowboys occasionally do. A liking for or the gift of song may surely not be denied them. Of what would these songs treat? Would they not be most likely to deal with matters belonging to daily life; to reflect the tastes, civilization, characters, paralleled, say, by "Bill" or the "dogie" songs of the cowboy pieces? Would they not be genuinely, as regards both material and style, the "homely traditional songs of simple people," i.e., be the mediaeval counterparts of the crude pieces for which modern communal origin may be affirmed? Perhaps, too, they would more probably be songs than ballads, be lyric rather than narrative; though on this nothing special hinges. Yet folk life and folk themes are the one subject with which the English and Scottish traditional ballads do not deal. In direct contrast with our western pieces, the kind of people who are supposed to have preserved them are the very people who do not appear in them; much as though the cowboys sang never of themselves but only of their employers, or of those above them in the social scale. The subject-matter of the Old World pieces is aristocratic, whether they be romantic-domestic, military, or riddling; this is true, largely, even for the "greenwood" pieces. The English and Scottish ballads are well-wrought poetical tales, not crude songs, and they treat not of humble folk at all, but of kings, princesses, knights, harpers, of Lord Randal, King Estmere, Sir Patrick Spens, Young Hunting, Child Waters, Young Beichan, the Douglas and the Percy. This is true not only of a few special ballads but of the overwhelming mass, by numerical calculation. The half-dozen or so in which appear a mason, a ship-carpenter, a smith, a butler, are exceptional. The ballads are as aristocratic in their material as the metrical romances, or

---

was the mediaeval society which fostered the English and Scottish popular ballads.

as mediaeval literature in general. They have a distinctive style, too, and real poetical quality, blurred by the manner of their preservation; a quality that improvised pieces, unless adaptations, do not show. The folk preserved them, but did they originate them? Somewhere, as said earlier, behind the theme, story, or melody of the ballad which is to find perpetuation, there must be more than ordinary impetus; widespread interest such as that centering about outlaws like Jesse James or Robin Hood; in battles like those between the Texas Rangers and the Indians, or those of the Scottish Border; in national characters like Garfield, or like the Percy and the Douglas. The pieces that stand out as of better execution or more striking character are those that persist. Improvised origin at some homogeneous folk-gathering would not typically afford the *élan* to bring outside currency. In the ballads collected by Professor Child, those which are nearest to folk life and to folk style, as paralleled by the western pieces, those which might most plausibly have had the type of origin sketched by Professor Kittredge for "The Hangman's Tree," [17] are those farthest from the "good" type established by pieces dealing with aristocratic themes.

The ballad last cited, "The Hangman's Tree," is selected as typical to illustrate the probable manner of composition of the English and Scottish ballads, by both Professor Kittredge,[18] who bases his argument on an Americanized version, and Professor Gummere.[19] On the other hand, Mr. T. F. Henderson [20] urges of

---

[17] Introduction to *English and Scottish Popular Ballads*, pp. xxv-xxviii. Professor C. Alphonso Smith, "The Negro and the Ballad," in the University of West Virginia *Alumni Bulletin*, January, 1913, suggests as an example of modern communal composition certain Negro revival hymns and plantation melodies. "If one will attend a negro revival in the country or suburban districts of the South he can see and hear this process of communal composition, about which so much has been written and surmised." The illustrations cited by Professor Smith are simpler than "The Hangman's Tree." They are songs, not poetical narratives, and they deal with the familiar revival material of the Negroes. In general nature, in suitability to the composers and to the occasion, they are much what might be foreseen.

[18] Introduction to *English and Scottish Popular Ballads* (1904), p. xxv.

[19] *The Popular Ballad* (1907), p. 101; also the *Nation*, August 29, 1907; also *Democracy and Poetry* (1911), p. 193.

[20] *The Ballad in Literature* (1912), pp. 72-79.

this piece that it is far from a typical instance in that all ballads
are not fashioned on the model of this; nor are they by any means
so simple in plot or so inevitable in structure and diction. It may
be added here that in point of characters the ballad in question
is exceptional also. It is nearly the only piece in the collection in
which the main characters, at least in the older versions, do not
have perforce to be interpreted as people of rank. The versions
that we have of "The Hangman's Tree" are neutral; they do not
specify. Possibly then this particular ballad *might* afford an instance of humble people improvising about themselves, not choos-
ing some theme more germane to the harper and the castle hall
than to the cottage and the village throng. Yet it is as likely, or
likelier, that the ballad as we have it has descended from one of
definitely higher life; much as "Lord Randal" evolved into the
"Johnny Randall" of a Colorado railway camp, or "The Two
Brothers," Sir John and Sir Willie, of the Scottish ballad,[21] became merely "Two Little Boys" in their New World home. To
find a piece which might plausibly illustrate the unanimous village throng collaborating on a suitable theme, a composition was
chosen which instead of being representative was nearly the only
one of its kind to be found by canvassing the whole group.

We are told that "the ballad genesis is more plainly proved
for the Faroes than for any other modern people." [22] But those
originated by the Faroe Islanders, when they improvised ballads,
seem to be wholly of the expected character and general style.
Witness the narrative cited by Professor Gummere of the Faroe
fisherman and his boat,[23] or the folk tale of the girl carried off by
Frisian pirates.[24] Clearly, like the southwestern cowboys, the
Faroe Islanders improvised concerning the events nearest them,
and in equally crude style, no doubt. Nor is it proved of these

---

21 See note 13.

22 Gummere, *The Popular Ballad* (1907), p. 69. His position is, specifically,
that the popular ballad arises from communal beginnings, such as those
found among the Faroe Islanders, followed by an "epic development." When,
where, or from whom the latter comes, he cannot, or does not, clearly set
forth.

23 *Ibid.*, p. 24.

24 *Ibid.*, pp. 109, 150, etc.

pieces so created that they gained much currency.[25] The best ballads from the Faroes are derived admittedly from Icelandic literary tradition. They tell not of fishermen or girls carried off by pirates but of the deeds of Sigurd. They are pieces of high descent. Similarly with the songs of more contemporary communal creation in modern Europe brought together with painstaking erudition by Professor Gummere.[26] The pieces improvised concern the singers themselves, their own lives and daily work. They are songs rather than ballads, nor is there evidence that they ultimately developed into more elaborate form, or attained higher poetical quality; nor that they gained much diffusion. Like the Faroe pieces, they are on a par with the improvised cowboy songs rather than with the English and Scottish popular ballads. The soldiers who took part in the Battle of Otterbourne may have made their own songs of that battle,[27] but their songs would have had little chance to endure beside those made by the minstrels who are urged to "play up for your warison," [28] or those from some yet higher source. Once a good one was made, expressing "the mind and heart of the people," much, say, as did the "Marseillaise," "John Brown's Body," "Marching through Georgia," or "Auld Lang Syne," (does it matter much to those who sing these pieces who originally composed them?), public interest in, and memory of, the event and the song would furnish the necessary impetus for diffusion. From this point of view, if songs of the Faroe fisher folk, or of the toiling village throngs of modern Europe, or of the Texas cowboys, throw light on the manner of origin of the English and Scottish popular ballads, they point to a genesis for the latter of some much higher kind.

Nor, if the parallel of the western pieces be still followed out, is the style of expression of the English and Scottish ballads a

---

[25] Accessible in H. Thuren's *Folke Sangen paa Færørne* (1908). Mr. Henderson remarks of the Faroe fisher ballads that "they are very woeful specimens of verse, of interest only from their touching and almost childish naïveté; and they are not sung to native melodies of ancient fisher tradition or of new fisher improvisation but to lugubrious tunes borrowed, according to Thuren, from Protestant Psalmody."—*The Ballad in Literature,* p. 88.

[26] *The Beginnings of Poetry* (1901), pp. 202 ff.

[27] Gummere, *The Popular Ballad,* p. 265, but see also his admission, p. 260, of minstrel part in the ballad as we have it.

[28] Stanza 43.

style which we should expect to find shepherds or plowmen or weavers, "spinsters and knitters in the sun," evolving from crude collaboration. The older the version, the nearer to the original form, the better is the style likely to be. The latter, like the subject-matter, bears the hall mark of a high descent. In the oldest pieces, as "The Battle of Otterbourne," there are phrases and alliterative formulae recalling that fixed poetic vocabulary not used in ordinary speech (*bern, freke, byrd,* etc.) which Dr. Bradley reminds us was characteristic of a group of professional poets about the middle of the fourteenth century.[29] The diction of the older ballads preserves many of the stereotyped alliterative phrases of the metrical romances. To the present writer, another mannerism of ballad expression seems well worthy of attention, in the search for stable testimony as to origins.[30] The liking for "shifted" or "wrenched" accent (*Douglás, Londón, forést*) is familiar to all students of traditional English balladry. For explanation of this it would seem clear that we have to proceed from French loan words, preserving for a while their final accent (*certáyne, countrée, pité, menyé, chambér*), with occasional transfer of this accentuation, through confusion, to native words having properly initial accent [31] (*ladié, daughtér, mornnýge, lesýnge.*) The words so stressed were prominent words in the line, were often rhyme words, the most stable words in the stanza; hence the usage established itself as traditional and remained a persistent feature of ballad diction. But the origin of the practice is surely to be found in aristocratic French, not in the vernacular initial accent of the folk. The tradition was more likely to emerge from the rhyme modes of the higher classes, or from a profes-

---

[29] *The Cambridge History of English Literature,* I, chap. xix.

[30] Even Professor Gummere is troubled by the thought of an aristocratic origin for the ballad stanza, derived almost certainly, it was long believed, from the classical septenarius (*Old English Ballads,* xxx, note 3); but the whole subject of the genesis of the ballad stanza is too dark for very safe inference to be drawn therefrom. See Saintsbury, *History of English Prosody* (1906), for a recent discussion of the origin of the ballad measure.

[31] Some prosodists might hold that these "wrenched accents" are only instances of "pitch accent," and derive them from Old English. Others may feel that they are merely crudenesses, made possible by the fact that the ballads were sung not read. But the final accent is too clearly marked, and is used too definitely and too frequently, at least in the earlier pieces, to be explained as something merely casual or fortuitous.

sional singing fraternity, than from humble "spinsters and knitters in the sun." To judge from the character of the stories narrated and the life reflected, perhaps from the general nature of the ballad stanza, and of the expression, the English and Scottish pieces may well have been favored and fostered by the upper classes, as they almost certainly were in Denmark. They might well have been sung in the halls of castles or in the market place with harp accompaniment by accomplished minstrels.[32]

The parallel suggested by the writers quoted at the opening is as interesting as they promised; although conclusions from it, if they are to be made at all, are not to be made hurriedly. It is clear, however, that the better analogy for the Old World pieces is afforded not by those created by the cowboys themselves but by those which have drifted among them and found preservation there.[33] On the whole, if either of the two leading schools of

---

[32] The minstrel of the pre-modern era, that conspicuous figure of the mediaeval world, was a very different figure from the minstrel of the seventeenth and eighteenth centuries, "ruled out of court" by Professor Kittredge. The latter says: "There is no reason whatever for believing that the state of things between 1300 and 1600 was different [as regards minstrel transmission of ballads] from that between 1600 and 1800—and there are many reasons for believing that it was not different" (Introd. to *English and Scottish Popular Ballads,* p. xxiii). But the change from feudal to modern conditions, and especially the introduction of printing, would be quite enough to bring difference in the standing of minstrelsy and in the character of its song.

For the best account of mediaeval minstrels, the higher and the lower orders, the wide scope of their singing, their fondness for dialogue, and the like, see E. K. Chambers, *The Mediaeval Stage* (1903), I, chaps. iii and iv.

[33] It should not much longer be reiterated, at least without careful definition and restriction to a certain type, that the making of popular ballads is a "closed account." Already there has accumulated in outlying regions a considerable body of American ballads, somehow finding diffusion among the people and preserved in many communities by oral tradition. For a general survey of these, see H. M. Belden, "Balladry in America," in the *Journal of American Folk-Lore,* January-March 1912, and the bibliographical references there. The style of these American pieces is not that of the English and Scottish popular ballads; but that is no more to be expected than that modern book poetry should continue the style of mediaeval book poetry. Surely it should not be said much longer that folk-ballads or traditional ballads, "popular" ballads in the usual sense of that term, are no longer living things; that real folk-ballads are practically extinct. The distinction between "popular," "pure," or "genuine" ballads and "vulgar" ballads, the former ballad type the product of the people in a special sense, under social conditions no longer existing in England or America, the only type of ballad to be claimed for folklore, and a type now obsolete; the latter or so-called

thought regarding the origin of the English and Scottish ballads may be said to find support in the testimony of the latter's New World analogues, it is not that school which defines by origin in folk composition, but that which presupposes a higher descent, and defines by style and by destination. In the case of the New World pieces, we are dealing with genuine "humble poetry of simple folk"; in the case of the English and Scottish popular ballads we are dealing with poetry of aristocratic material, having traces blurred by time of an aristocratic manner. Working from both subject-matter and style, it would seem that among the cowboys of the Southwest are reproduced not the conditions which created the English and Scottish popular ballads but rather, it may be, some of the conditions which preserved them.

Reprinted from *Modern Philology*, October, 1913, 195-207.

"vulgar" ballad type written for the people, a low form of "literature" in the usual notation of that term, and not belonging to folklore—this distinction, so long insisted upon and held to be of such importance, serving for many as basic in ballad classification, is probably not sound; at least not in so far as it is based on *origin* rather than *style*. It would seem that there need be no difference between the kinds in origin; that one kind does not belong to folklore to the exclusion of the other; also that neither, despite the special pleading of Professor Gummere, need represent or be a direct continuant of primitive poetry.

Yet Another Joe Bowers

———————————————— ❦ ————————————————

Probably no American song in folk tradition, with the possible exception of "Frankie and Johnny," has had so many divergent origins attributed to it as "Joe Bowers," an overlanders' song of "The Girl I Left Behind Me" pattern. It was widely known in the Gold Rush era and still lingers here and there in folk memory. Some have thought Joe Bowers a real person from Pike County, Missouri, who crossed the plains to California with the gold seekers. Others believe him to be merely a typical figure of the time popularized by the ballad. "Joe Bowers" has been termed "the best-known song of its day" and as such its authorship has intrigued folklorists. By this time it has developed a sizable bibliography of newspaper, magazine, and other matter. Yet the facts of its composition and launching have never been established. Now comes yet another candidate on the horizon for acceptance as its composer and popularizer. His credentials are good but, as for other originators brought up, they are not final. Meantime, while looking for evidence regarding the hero of the ballad and its composer, I have found that the author of "Betsy from Pike"—often called its companion piece, the authorship of which has been termed unknown—can be stated with certainty; and also with certainty can be named the originator of the so-called "Molly group" of comic versions of the familiar old "Springfield Mountain" ballad telling of the death of a youth

171

from the bite of a "pizen sarpent." More about these two identifications later.

In two notes in the *Southern Folklore Quarterly*[1] I reviewed the ascriptions of authorship that had been brought forward for "Joe Bowers" and added a new one found in Merwin's *Life of Bret Harte* (1911). Perhaps it is in place here to repeat briefly in a preliminary way the leading possibilities hitherto advanced.

In the Pike County, Missouri, *News* of June 17, 1899, Judge T. J. C. Fagg of Louisiana, Missouri, identified as the composer of the song a man named Johnson, who was the head of a minstrel troupe known as Johnson's Pennsylvanians. Johnson was a composer and singer of songs and a comedian, and he was the author of a small paper publication, *Johnson's Original Comic Songs*. He states in the Preface of his first edition (1858, dated from the Melodeon Theater, one of the oldest in San Francisco) that his troupe toured the mining camps; this was in addition to their singing in the Melodeon Theater. This edition does not contain "Joe Bowers," but his second edition (1860) does, and this has been assumed to be its first appearance in print. Johnson's texts give words but not airs. In general the composers of popular songs of the day fitted their words to well-known tunes; the creators of the music need not be sought. Later, in a letter to W. E. Connelley dated October 5, 1906, Judge Fagg shifted his position from Johnson himself to a member of his troupe, a John Woodward, a variety actor and singer associated with Johnson's Pennsylvanians. Judge Fagg went to California early in this century and while there he tried hard to find the author of the song. He said he had the testimony in a sworn statement of an old actor connected with the Melodeon Theater who said that Woodward, a member of Johnson's minstrels in 1849 and the early fifties, wrote the song for Johnson and that it was first brought out in the Melodeon in 1850. The old actor declared himself to be well acquainted with Woodward, who was a variety actor and singer. Later Woodward sang the song up and down the coast. Fagg said that he got the same statement from another man connected with the minstrel troupe.

---

[1] *Southern Folklore Quarterly*, I (September, 1937), 13-15; and II (1938), 131-133.

To continue the list of conjectures, Harry Norman affirmed in the St. Louis *Republic* for May 27, 1900, about a year after Judge Fagg's first statement, that there was an ox driver Joe Bowers who did have a brother Ike and a sweetheart named Sally, as in the ballad, and who joined the Argonauts from Pike County. Frank Smith, he said, a fellow traveler, composed the song concerning Joe. Evidently Judge Fagg did not accept this account but, as just stated, transferred his ascription to a member of Johnson's troupe. Of late years Fagg's ascription has reigned in favor.[2]

Fullest treatment of the song is to be found in W. E. Connelley's *Doniphan's Expedition* to California and Mexico, an ambitious and rather ebullient book printed at Topeka, Kansas, in 1907. The first chapter is headed "Joe Bowers," whom Connelley characterizes as the hero of the era, personifying the typical qualities of the western adventurer.[3] Connelley even reprints a hypothetical, idealized picture of Bowers, made by the artist P. B. McCord for an article on Joe Bowers by the former Congressman from Missouri, Champ Clark (1851-1924) in the St. Louis *Globe-Democrat*. In a footnote to his first chapter Connelley states that William Kinkaid of Bowling Green, Missouri, told Clark that Joe Bowers was drawn from a man named Abner McElwee of Pike County who went to California in 1849. With him were two of his nephews, one of whom was the brother Ike of the song. The plot of the song, he said, was imaginary. Champ Clark himself felt sure that Mark Twain was the author, but his belief found no acceptance. Mark did not cross the plains until after 1861 and the song was already floated and popular before this; and he was not in California until 1864. Except for the dates he need not have been ruled out summarily; he could have composed the song from Pike County, Missouri, stimulus. There is no mention of the trek itself in the song. Mark composed humorous songs; but he was involved in other activities in the later

---

[2] See H. M. Belden, *Ballads and Songs of Missouri* (Columbia, Mo., 1940), pp. 341-343, and MacEdward Leach, *The Ballad Book*, 1955, pp. 751-752.

[3] In his enthusiasm for Joe Bowers Connelley wrote (p. 13): "Whether he ever lived or not, as a character in the history of the West Joe Bowers is the greatest Missourian."

forties and early fifties and did not yet have western interests. I have not been able to see Clark's newspaper article in the *Globe-Democrat,* or to learn its exact date, but I would like to know his grounds for his belief in Mark Twain's authorship. Had Mark written so well-known a song, mention of it would hardly have escaped his many biographers and bibliographers.

Connelley stated further in his footnote that Meredith T. Moore of Cedar City, Missouri, who crossed the plains in 1849 and again in 1852, heard the song at least as early as 1854 and perhaps a long time before that. Moore thought it possible that a man known as Squibob ("true name unknown") may have written the song. He also gave Connelley a statement by a friend of his that the song was written by a Piker Joe Bowers, whose name is not remembered and who went to California and Mexico with Doniphan; that it was sung by soldiers; and that afterward one English of New Jersey rewrote the poem, changing it to suit him, and retained the old tune that the Piker had used. He said further that the man from Pike County known as Joe Bowers is buried in Chillicothe, Missouri. Connelley could not verify this.

When reading Merwin's *Life of Bret Harte,* 1911, I came on a passage stating that a certain Frank Swift composed the song when he was a member of a party of two hundred from Pike County, Missouri. The organizer and leader of the expedition was Captain McPike and among the men was an ox driver named Joe Bowers, an "original," a "greenhorn," and a "goodfellow" who was seeking a fortune for his Missouri sweetheart. Frank Swift, who afterward attained a reputation as a journalist, made the song about Bowers during a day's journey. It caught the fancy of the party, was sung by them, and was carried to California where the men dispersed in all directions, carrying it with them. It was printed in cheap form in San Francisco in 1856 and was sung by Johnson's minstrels in the Melodeon. The date of the composition was 1849 and the date of its printing, in Merwin's account, is four years earlier than Johnson's printing of it in the second edition of his song book, 1860.

Merwin's account of the date of composition of the poem and Meredith Moore's account to Connelley agree well with that of Francis Withee of Stella, Nebraska, from whom I had a good text of the ballad in 1915. Withee crossed the plains in 1849 and later as a freighter on the Nebraska City–Denver trail. He said the song was certainly in existence as early as 1854 and was a freighter's favorite in the sixties.

Now comes still another candidate for whom a good case can be made as the singer and popularizer of the song. A letter from Mr. Robert E. Kerr of Lake Charles, Louisiana, suggested my writing for information about "Joe Bowers" to John W. Winkley of Walnut Creek, California, a Methodist clergyman who is interested in the history and lore of his region. Mr. Winkley is curator at the Pacific School of Religion at Berkeley and has been active in the California-Nevada Methodist Historical Society. From him I learned of a candidate with excellent credentials as the composer of "Joe Bowers"; yet difficulty as to dates and the failure to find the ballad included in his published songsters leave his authorship unestablished.

This candidate is John A. Stone, known as "Old Put" ("put it here, put it there"). His small group of singers called themselves the Sierra Nevada Rangers, toured the mining camps as did Johnson's Pennsylvanians, and sang at the Melodeon Theater. Stone issued two small paper songsters, printed in San Francisco, that contained his original songs fitted to popular airs. That the songs were unmistakably of his own composition is clear from his prefaces and from references to him as a contributor in the songbooks of others. Stone entered his booklets for registry, according to the practice of the time, established by Act of Congress.

Here is information given me by J. W. Winkley after my letter of inquiry.

I was surprised to learn that there was any question as to the authorship of the "Joe Bowers" song. The author is well established in the little town of Greenwood on the Nevada border and in that area of the Motherlode country as John A. Stone. Some years ago I knew some old people who knew and heard "Joe Bowers" sing his songs. He lies buried in Greenwood Cemetery. Until a few years ago a tiny slab of slate marked the grave. . . . It simply had three letters on it— J.A.S., for John A. Stone. I put a story in the Oakland *Tribune* Feature page, remarking that it was a shame that the grave did not have an appropriate headstone. A Monument owner wrote to me saying that if I would furnish the inscription for it he would provide a granite marker and erect it on the grave. This was done and I went with him to Greenwood where a small company of neighboring folk assembled. They knew through their parents of "Joe Bowers" and thanked me for obtaining the beautiful marker for his grave. My wording was as follows: John A. Stone, Early California Song Writer; Author of Put's Golden Songster, and Put's Early California Songster. Crossed the Plains from Pike County, Missouri in 1849.[4] Died January 23, 1864.

Many of his neighbors never knew that he had any other name. Once in a while "Joe Bowers" would take part in a community social affair for which he would put on a song and dance. His songs were sung by thousands of the gold miners at their work and in their lonely cabins.

A passage from the Preface to Old Put's *Original California Songster,* entered in 1854 and issued in 1855, repeated in his second edition, reads:

Having been a miner himself for a number of years, he (the author) has had ample opportunities of observing, as he has equally shared, the many trials and hardships to which his brethren of the pick and shovel have been exposed, and to which, and in general they have so patiently and so cheerfully submitted. . . . Hence ever since the time of his crossing the plains, in the memorable year of '50, he has been in the habit of noting down a few of the leading items of his experience, and clothing them in the garb of humorous though not irreverent verse. . . .

In conclusion he would state, that after having sung them himself at various times and places, and latterly with the assistance of a few gentlemen known by the name of the Sierra Nevada Rangers, the songs have been published at the request of a number of friends; and if the author should thereby succeed in contributing to the amusement of those he is anxious to please, enlivening the long tedious hours of a miner's winter fireside, his pains will not be unrewarded.

---

[4] Stone himself gave the date as 1850.

Margaret Kelly, deceased, of Greenwood, California, was said to be collecting material concerning Stone ("Joe Bowers") perhaps with a view to writing of his life and work. Her sister, living at Greenwood, stated that her manuscript was at an attorney's office at Placerville. Mr. Winkley looked it up in the summer of 1955 and found it to be mainly a copy of old songs which John A. Stone, under the names of "Joe Bowers" and, at times, "Old Put," sang at Murderer's Bar on the middle American River in the 1850's. Miss Kelly had collected them under the title "Murderer's Bar Collection of California Folk Songs as sung by John A. Stone." She briefly added the opinion of a number of old-timers in the Motherlode country that Stone, known everywhere as "Joe Bowers," wrote the song by that name but after the publication of his "Old Put" songsters. This seems unlikely since it would postpone the advent and currency of the song till near the sixties instead of in the earlier fifties.

The chief consideration barring ready acceptance of Old Put's authorship of "Joe Bowers" is that in neither his first songbook of twenty-nine pieces (1855), nor in its second edition (1858), which adds eleven new songs, nor in his *Golden Songster* (1858), made up of more new songs, does "Joe Bowers" appear. Apparently the song was first printed, by Johnson, in 1860. Old Put's songsters were very popular. His second edition of his *Original California Songster* advertises the first as selling 18,000 copies, and there was a fifth edition of his songs in 1868. Unlike other mid-century songsters, Stone's included no popular favorites of the period such as "Darling Nellie Gray," "The Dying Californian" ("by permission of Oliver Ditson, Boston"), "Marching Through Georgia," etc. Stone printed texts of his own authorship only. When "Joe Bowers" appeared in Johnson's booklet of 1860 it was capitalized in the Table of Contents as were a few other songs, among them Stone's "Poker Jim," a testimony, no doubt, to their especial popularity. "Joe Bowers" appeared also in *Pacific Song Book,* an independent publication in 1861. Both books printing it announced that songs by Old Put were included, but they did not state which were his or the airs to which they were sung. Old Put's pieces may be identified by their inclusion in his own publications.

If Stone wrote "Joe Bowers" after the publication of his song-sters then the testimony of Connelley's Meredith Moore who gave its composition as in 1849, of the Nebraskan Francis Withee, of the Merwin account, which assigned it to 1849 and its printing to 1856, and Judge Fagg's date for Woodward's singing of it in 1850 must be rejected. In view of its popularity it is hard to be-lieve that the song was not printed until 1860. The likeliest and most acceptable possibility, it seems to me, when all the conflicts of testimony are examined, is that the song was printed in the early fifties in broadside or penny song-sheet form; that is, printed independently, text, not air. This would account for Stone's omission of it, had he composed it, from his *Original California Songster* in 1855 and his *Golden Songster* in 1858. As stated already, he did not repeat what had been printed but in-cluded only his new songs. Or, of course, he might have omitted the song because it was not his, or not wholly his. Broadside ballads were printed liberally throughout the century. Even in our time I have seen them on sale here and there or have had single sheets given to me. With the coming of the radio and the phonograph the institution is probably obsolete now. And it is broadside ballad texts that perish soonest in comparison with those in songbooks. Accepting the hypothesis of its early printing, that so popular a song should be reprinted in a songbook of 1860 and in many later ones seems inevitable.[5]

The versions of the ballad gathered in our century from many western and southern states do not vary much. The song as re-covered has been pretty stable; the variations are mainly in length and language.[6] The texts might well derive from a single printed source which, though no longer preserved, launched it

---

[5] In his *Folk-Songs of the South* (Cambridge, 1925), J. W. Cox cites Pro-fessor G. L. Kittredge as informing him that "Joe Bowers" was printed as a De Marsan broadside, list 11, no. 483, by Wehman No. 455, and by A. W. Auner (Philadelphia). It appeared in *Singer's Journal*, I, 143; Howe's *Comic Songs* (Boston, p. 98), in all these not dated, and in *Carncross and Sharpley's Minstrel* (Philadelphia, 1860, p. 38), *Tony Pastor's Comic and Eccentric Songster* (cop. 1862, p. 39), *J. S. Comic Song Book* (cop. 1863, p. 60), etc.

[6] According to C. L. Sabin, *Buffalo Bill and the Overland Trail* (1914), p. 253. "There were so many verses that some bull whackers professed to sing 'Joe Bowers' all the way from Fort Leavenworth to the Rockies with-out a repetition."

into tradition. It seems unlikely that the ballad was of group composition such as is pictured in some accounts of it, an origin once believed in for most traditional folk pieces. If it was of spontaneous multiple composition by overlanders or miners it is possible of course that professional singers such as Woodward or Stone might have taken it over in its shifting, drifting state, given it stable and available shape, sung it up and down the coast, and popularized it. But songs of group launching and scattered regional traditionalizing result at best in such variable plotless pieces as the soldiers' "Hinky Dinky Parlez-Vous" of World War I. That "Joe Bowers" was floated by minstrel singers seems much more likely.

The songbooks that print "Joe Bowers" do not identify the air to which it was sung. The opening "My name it is Joe Bowers" follows a stock line in first-person narrative pieces, such as "My name it is John T. Williams," "My name it is Sam Hall," or "My name it is Charles Guiteau," in the later song on the death of Garfield.

Whether or not we can be certain that Old Put composed "Joe Bowers," it is certain that he composed "Betsy from Pike" which appears in his *Golden Songster* of 1858. He enters it as to be sung to the air of "Villikens and His Dinah." [7] Both "Betsy from Pike" and "Joe Bowers" were sung at the Melodeon by Old Put as well as by Johnson's Minstrels. It has long been noted by collectors that "Betsy from Pike" was printed in Old Put's *Golden Songster,* but it was not realized that this testified that the song was of his composition. It escaped notice that, unlike other songsters of the day, Old Put's included only his own pieces.

The "Squibob" mentioned by Champ Clark's friend Meredith T. Moore was not "a miner." He was, of course, George H. Derby, 1823-1861, who was known as a wit and practical joker and as the West Coast's premier humorist before Mark Twain. Moore's mention of him deserved following up, I thought. Derby

---

[7] Kittredge, *Journal of American Folklore,* XXIV (1911), 190, and XXV, (1912), 409, showed that "Villikens and His Dinah" was a parody popular on the variety stage in the middle of last century of "William and Diana," a tragic ballad. For humorous parodies of the old song of "The Frog and the Mouse" see the special study of this song made by Professor L. W. Payne, *Publications of the Texas Folklore Society,* I (Austin, 1916).

was a member of the U. S. Bureau of Topography. He was sent to California early in 1849 and he conducted several exploring expeditions in the gold country of California. In 1853 he went to San Diego and in 1856 he was transferred to the East. Some of his newspaper and other sketches appeared as early as 1853. He signed himself then as John P. Squibob. He printed characteristic sketches in *Phoenixiana,* published in New York in 1855, now signing himself John Phoenix. Other matter by him was published posthumously in *Squibob Papers,* 1864, in New York. Had Derby composed "Joe Bowers," however, it would not have escaped his biographers and bibliographers; and it would have appeared, since it was so popular, in either of his books, *Phoenixiana* or *Squibob Papers.* Curiously one of the papers in the former work was entitled "Life and Times of Joseph Bowers. Collated from the unpublished papers by John P. Squibob. By J. Bowers Jr. Vallecitos, Hyde and Seekim, 1854." This hoax piece seems to have no connection, however, save the name, with the Argonaut hero. Derby was quite capable of composing and floating the "Joe Bowers" ballad. He was interested in comic songs and composed some himself. In *Squibob Papers* was printed a comic version of the old "Springfield Mountain" ballad in which a youth died from being bitten by a "pizen sarpent." Seemingly Derby's travesty was the parent, or perhaps merely another example, of the "Molly group" (so-called by Phillips Barry) of comic variants of the ballad. The singing of parody versions of well-known songs seems to have had great popularity on the variety stage of the middle of the century. Another instance is the comic version of the old song of "The Frog and the Mouse." The ballad of "Young Charlotte" or "The Frozen Girl" long thought to be a "folk product" and treated as such by ballad specialists turned out to be—as shown by Phillips Barry, changing an earlier view advanced by him—the work, at least in part, of the professional humorist, Seba Smith.

Probably more attention should be given to Merwin's Frank Swift as a possible competitor for Old Put as the author of the western ballad. Swift seems to be, as we have seen, the same person as the Frank Smith of the St. Louis newspaper account of 1900. The *Missouri Historical Review,* XXXVI (January, 1942),

206-208, reprints in its section headed "History not Found in Text Books" an account previously published by R. S. Hawkins in the Independence *Kansas City Spirit* of March, 1909. Hawkins goes back to the St. Louis newspaper statement by Harry Norman in 1900 that the persons of the song and their story were real. Elaborating, he serves up a pretty and romantic story of Joe Bowers, aged 20, and Sally Black, aged 16, youthful neighbors along Salt River in Pike County. Joe, he said, joined the Argonauts in 1849, hoping to make a fortune for Sally. He started as a bull driver, but was soon promoted to be a sort of aide-de-camp to Captain McPike, organizer of the expedition. In the company, it is said, were "men of intelligence and learning such as Dr. James W. Campbell perhaps the most noted divine of his day in Missouri and Frank Smith afterward governor of California." The Merwin version of the story has, as we have seen, Frank Swift instead of the Frank Smith of Harry Norman. Young Joe told his troubles to his fellow traveler, Frank Swift, and the latter wrote the verses "perhaps as a joke on Joe." Judge Fagg (1900) and Connelley (1907) did not accept the early newspaper account but brought up other identifications; for instance, the naming by Connelley's friend William Kinkaid of an Abner McElwee, "a tall old bachelor" who went west with the Pikers and was the leader of the expedition and who served as the original of the hero of the ballad. The Merwin account, like that of Hawkins, named Captain McPike as the leader. It termed Joe Bowers, who joined the party, an "original," a "greenhorn," a "goodfellow," and stated that the song telling of him was made by Frank Swift, a brilliant youth, later a journalist, who recited or sang to a popular air the stanzas of the ballad.

Of especial interest is the naming in the Hawkins account of Frank Smith (Swift) as later a "governor of California." There never was a governor of California named Swift; but the *Dictionary of American Biography* recounts the life of a John Franklin Swift, 1829-1891, who was born in Bowling Green, Pike County, Missouri, who crossed the plains in 1852, became prominent and influential and was nominated for governor in 1880, losing the election by a few hundred votes. He was later ambassador to Japan. Swift was a regent of the University of California, 1872-

1888. The life of Ambassador Swift might well have further examination. One could understand that as a dignified political personage he might not care to play up his possible part in the composition and launching of "Joe Bowers." There seems, however, to be nothing in the materials about Swift in the California State Library to connect him with the popular ballad. Nor did California have a governor named Frank Smith.

Stone deserves his tombstone and epitaph at Greenwood, California, but whether he was called "Joe Bowers" by his fellow villagers for his authorship of the song, or because of his singing of it, or because all Missourians from Pike County were likely to be called Joe Bowers in those days is not certain. If it was printed in broadside form early in the fifties, as was more than likely, it could have emerged with especial appropriateness from the author of the later "Betsy from Pike." The tales of Frank Smith and Frank Swift are not far apart; they seem to be of the same person. Woodward may have been a stage name taken by a member of a minstrel troupe; witness "Old Put" taken by Stone. Both Woodward and Stone sang at the Melodeon in the early fifties; but they were more likely to have been rivals than the same person. Mark Twain is out, "Squibob" is out, English is out, Smith or Swift has never won acceptance. Stone now seems the likeliest candidate. Demonstrably a composer and singer of humorous songs of the Gold Rush era and of miners' life, with years of conspicuous recognition at Greenwood and now a tombstone there, he is well in the foreground. Since Judge Fagg's John Woodward had but two vouchers and Stone many times that number, the latter seems now to deserve primary recognition, with Woodward and Smith-Swift perhaps next in preference. Stone was easily eligible as a fertile composer of comic songs and, whether or not he made it, he certainly popularized the song.

Additional evidence may turn up some day. Or the real origin of the song may never be known. All that we can yet term established is that the floating of "Joe Bowers" is especially associated with the old Melodeon Theater in San Francisco, that it was remarkably successful on the minstrel stage, and that it made its way into many regions, carried there by professional singers and their broadsides and songbooks and by singing freighters, travelers, and soldiers.[8]

Reprinted from *Western Folklore*, Vol. XVI, No. 2 (April, 1957), 111-120, published by the University of California Press. Earlier notes in the *Southern Folklore Quarterly*, I (September, 1937), 13-15 and II (1938) 131-133.

---

[8] *The Overland Monthly*, II (June, 1869), 538-544, printed a hoax appraisal by J. P. Caldwell of the remarkably literary quality of the Lament of Joseph Bowers composed by the great American poet Jobouers, only a fragment of whose work, a song mourning the loss of Sallyblac, has been preserved. He is termed the Father of Lyric Poetry and his lament is made the subject of extravagant interpretation and eulogy.

In addition to the main articles and studies cited in this paper as dealing with the song or its author, passing mention or comment appear in the *Missouri Historical Review*, XXII (1928) and XXIV (1929), 135-137; Vance Randolph, *Ozark Folk Song* (1948), p. 191; Edna B. Buckbee's *Saga of Old Tuolumne*, 104-105; and the *History of Music Project: A San Francisco Songster, 1849-1939*. Dolph's *Sound Off* (New York, 1929), p. 314, includes the ballad as a soldier's song and adds, "It has been credited to Mark Twain, to a miner named Squibob, and to a man named English."

Some Old
Nebraska Folk Customs

The customs to be recorded here are from the nineteenth century, though most persist into the twentieth and are, indeed, familiar to the majority of us today. Some have been noted from as far back as the 1850's, when Nebraska was still a territory. It became a state in 1867. Most were gathered from comparatively late in the century. All are really much older than their appearance in Nebraska; in the main they are legacies from the British Isles or from the European continent. That they still exist among us is, however, no reason for excluding them. The Fourth of July celebrations and the political rallies seem those customs most indigenous to the United States; but of course political or civic festivities of much the same type have existed elsewhere, associated with other occasions.

As regards sources, a large part of what I have recorded derives from my own recollection or is of my own assemblage from oral sources. In the days when I was interested in folksong, its origin and transmission, I liked, for some reason, to gather other folklore matter as well, perhaps as background. But I owe very much to many individuals, notably to Dr. Ruth Odell, Mrs. A. H. Rulkoetter, Mari Sandoz, Grace Tear, and to student contributors, such as Ruth Milford, Florence Kellogg, Josephine Hyatt, Jeanne Allen, and others too many to name. Testimonies concerning frontier days I owe to various newspapers and documents, territorial and later, preserved in the Library of the State Historical Society. I have not attempted to make my assemblage exhaustive; but as a preliminary survey it may be complete enough to serve its purpose. Sometime in the future there may well be appropriate supplementation of my chroniclings, extending the records for Old Nebraska as contributing somewhat to its history as well as its folklore.

The customs regarding which I have gathered materials may be grouped for convenience under these headings: Civic Customs; Customs for Special Days or Occasions; Social Activities; Sports; Literary, Debating and School Activities; Singings; Play-Parties and Dances; Theatricals and Related Entertainment; Food; Addenda.

Civic Customs

Fourth of July

Among older civic customs, those of the Fourth of July may well take priority and should have treatment in considerable detail because of their historical place. Beyond question, the celebration of the Fourth was the great occasion of the year in frontier days. Stock features were the program, the big dance or dances, and the dinner. The whole region around about was invited to attend and take part. Settlers thronged in, coming in wagons horse-drawn or ox-drawn, on horseback, or even on foot. At times the vehicles were decorated with green boughs or with flowers. Often there was a dance on the night of July third, sometimes one outdoors "on the green" on the afternoon of the Fourth, and nearly always a large dance that night. The Fourth might be ushered in by the firing of salutes, or the ringing of bells. Children set off firecrackers or torpedoes, after these were to be had at stores. At about ten o'clock there was a march or procession, sometimes with the escort of a military company, to a nearby wooded place or grove where the formal program was held.

Preparations were often very elaborate. The Brownville *Adver-*

tiser of July 5, 1856, commented in its editorial column: "The Fourth Attendance from our own and adjoining counties of this Territory and Missouri was large . . . . Vocal music under the supervision of Captain Thurber and Lady was fine as we ever listened to. The Declaration of Independence was read by Mr. Lake in a clear, audible and impressive manner." Of the dinner it was remarked that "All the delicacies and substantials of the season weighed down the tables: Buffalo Meat, Venison, Barbecued Ox, Roast Sheep, Hogs and Pigs enough to have fed the whole Territory." "Sentiments" and "responses" were delivered. In the evening there was a "Ball in McPherson's Hall, a new and commodious building rushed through to completion for the occasion" . . . "The 'fiddle and the bow', the 'merry dance' continued until toward the 'wee hours' when all repaired to the large room below, where C. W. Wheeler had prepared a supper". . . . "The dance went on 'until broad daylight'. . . ."

Of the Fourth of July celebration at Nemaha City, the Brownville *Advertiser* of July 2, 1857, in its Weekly Review column gave as the program: "1st. Vocal Music, American Ode—by the Choir. 2nd. Prayer—by the Chaplain. 3rd. National Glee—by the Choir. 4th. Reading of the Declaration of Independence—by A. D. Kirk. 5th. Freedom's Choice—by the Choir. 6th. Oration—by C. E. L. Holmes. 7th. Star Spangled Banner—by the Choir. 8th Remarks—by Invited Guests. 9th. Dinner. 10th. Toasts. 11th. Dance on the Green." On July 11, the same newspaper commented: "The celebration of the Fourth at our sister town Nemaha City was a grand affair—we say without hesitation it was the most magnificent affair of the kind we ever attended. The table was four hundred feet long, and perfectly groaned beneath the weight of eatables placed thereon. There were over two thousand persons present, and after all were abundantly fed, there was yet 'enough and to spare'. There was a grand attendance of the fair sex . . . ." The celebration was held in the "new Hotel building." After the exercises, with numbers by the choir and an oration, there was a "dance on the green." In the evening "all hands adjourned to Brownville, where the merry dance was kept up . . . ."

The Nebraska City *News* of June 25, 1859, announced that the "Nebraska Harmony Singing Association have made arrangements to give a Grand Ball and Supper including singing, reading the Declaration of Independence, etc., on July 4. The Sidney Brass Band has been engaged for the occasion."

The Omaha *Nebraskian* of July 21, 1860, has among its Territorial Items: "The Cass County *Sentinel* estimates the numbers in attendance upon the Fourth of July celebration at Plattsmouth as from 1200 to 2000. Only two drunken men were in attendance." The same newspaper, July 7, 1860, tells of the Fourth at Omaha. The exercises "commenced at about nine o'clock by the presentation to the Hook and Ladder Company . . . of a magnificent ladder carriage." There was a presentation speech, a procession, an amateur band made music. At the grove there was the prayer, the reading of the Declaration of Independence, national songs were sung, an oration was delivered, and cannon were fired at the close. There was a "small display of pyrotechnics in the evening."

At these celebrations the dinners and toasts came at noon. At Bellevue in 1854 the toasts offered were as follows: "The Fourth of July," "George Washington," "President and Acting Vice-President," "Spartan Mothers of the American Revolution," "The Union," "Nebraska," "Our Friends Crossing the Plains," "The Press," "Bellevue," "The Ladies." Next came nine volunteer toasts to various persons, including the Indian Agent and the ladies who made ready the food.

In Lincoln from early times onward the Fourth was celebrated in much the same manner. There was the usual prayer by a minister, an oration, the reading of the Declaration of Independence, and songs were sung. Indeed, there might be speeches all day long. In many places in later decades of the century there might be an initial parade, with a pretty girl as Goddess of Liberty leading the floats. Or there might be a militia parade, a band concert, or a flag pole dance.

Staple sports, when these made their appearance, were ball games, horse races, foot races, wheelbarrow races, sack races, obstacle races, three-legged races, potato races, fat men's races, donkey races, greased pole climbings, and greased pig races.

On the Fourth, sometimes on other days, men might spin silver dollars at a mark, occasionally half dollars or quarters. Children sometimes imitated them with dimes, nickels, and pennies.

Picnics were often planned for the Fourth. For these there was often a Marshal of the Day riding a horse, with perhaps a large red scarf draped from shoulder to hip. Almost always at Peru, Nemaha County, a young girl, selected for her beauty, posed as the Statue of Liberty. Old soldiers' picnics were held on this day, sometimes on other days; at these reminiscences were called for. Or there was a big dinner or barbecue with buffalo meat, occasionally catfish, the main eatables. At night fireworks, mainly Roman candles, pinwheels, and rockets, became a fixed custom. In the 1880's balloon ascensions were a frequent attraction.

In the later half of the nineteenth century, "water fights" were part of the day's entertainment on the Fourth, or perhaps on Memorial Day or at the county fair. In towns too small to maintain full-time fire departments, fire protection was furnished by so-called volunteer fire departments. These developed not only into fire-fighting organizations but also into social, fraternal, and insurance benefit societies. Water fights were staged between teams of two to four men against teams of like number. Each had a hose into which water was turned at top pressure. The object was to drive the opposing team over a certain line by water. Not only did the contestants get thoroughly soaked but very often the spectators. Lincoln had local competing teams in the 1880's.

The celebration of the Fourth of July was resumed in Lincoln in 1946, after having lapsed with the outbreak of the Second World War. Out of town picnickers were present but there was no reading of the Declaration of Independence, no oration, no official prayer. There were qualifying trials for the Mid-West Championship automobile races, then the competitive races for $2,500. One man was killed in these. A night show was given in front of the state fair grandstand, revues and stage acts were presented by producers from Chicago, and carnival shows and rides on the midway preceded the fireworks.

Political Rallies and Elections

Political rallies were marked by torchlight parades. The marchers carrying torches wore rubber capes to protect them from sparks. If there was an evening program, it might be started off by Roman candles.

A testimony early in the present century from Hebron, Nebraska, told that when the polls are closed on election day, the clerk goes out on the main street and calls, "Hear ye, hear ye, the polls are now closed." This is the official closing. This custom was observed at Omaha and other places also.

Oysters were shipped into the middle states in November, and sometimes there were oyster suppers at churches for those who came down town to learn the November election news.

Oratory

My mother, who came from New York to Nebraska in 1869, crossing the Missouri River on the ice, was fascinated by the pioneer eloquence she heard in early Lincoln on the Fourth of July and sometimes at political and other gatherings. Here are two examples she often quoted "verbatim" to her children. She had the "fabulous memory" that my brother Roscoe inherited. The first was from a Masonic orator, I think:

> In the course of human events since man's earliest history each presents an embodiment of compartments subordinate to the result of an ultimate one grand temple.

The second was from a newcomer to Lincoln, a German, who seems to have known his Latin and accenting carefully his long penultimate syllables.

> The diffi'culties and excellen'ces of a man's charac'ter are never known till he is laid in his sepul'cher.

Curfews

A curfew was tolled in Central City by the city fire bell at nine o'clock in the summer and at eight in the winter. This practice is not now followed. The children were told that they must be indoors when the curfew rang, or the town police would "lock them in jail." At McCook a nine o'clock whistle was sounded as a warning that "small girls should be at home in bed." This was true in Lincoln for a time. An eight o'clock curfew was reported from Fullerton and a nine o'clock from Fairbury.

Special Days and Occasions

Customs for Hallowe'en, Thanksgiving, Christmas, New Year's Day, Easter, May Day, Decoration Day may be omitted as pretty staple, widely recurrent, and varying little and in minor matters. The once flourishing custom of New Year's calls at the homes of friends where cards were left and often drinks served died out with the coming of the twentieth century.

Arbor Day

Arbor Day, a day set apart for the planting of trees or shrubs, was instituted by J. Sterling Morton of Nebraska City who was later the United States Secretary of Agriculture. On his motion, it was founded by the Nebraska State Board of Agriculture January 4, 1872. Prizes were offered by the Board for the best essay on agriculture and for the largest number of forest and fruit trees planted on Arbor Day. It was devoutly believed in those days that "rain follows the plow" and that the way to ensure more rainfall on the western plains was to plant more trees and to break more land. The day originally fixed upon was the second Wednesday in April, April 10, 1872. In 1885 the Nebraska legislature changed it to April 22 and made it a legal holiday. The first Arbor Day proclamation was made by Governor Robert W. Furnas in 1874. Alabama, Maine, and other states took up the Nebraska idea and by 1890 it had spread over the United States and, indeed, to other parts of the world. Its observance now comes late in April or early in May. It is still a legal holiday, though less widely observed. Schools recognize it by programs or ceremonies.

Birthday Customs

In southern Nebraska near Red Cloud and the Kansas line a

neighborhood observed a birthday in a rather peculiar way. "It was unusual for a birthday to pass without a surprise party. Young and old gathered at the home of the family of the person whose birthday it was. As the high point of the party the unfortunate whose birthday was celebrated was thrown into the watering tank, usually none too clean. Cattle and horses might be frightened from their drinking as the shrieking person was tossed into the tank. Possibly this custom was of Kansas rather than of Nebraska origin."

It was the custom in some Nebraska towns to butter or grease the nose of a member of the family or a friend on his or her birthday. This was a Buffalo County testimony.

Occasionally it is the thing to pinch a person on the day after his birthday. Or, oftener, to pat or slap him on the back, or to paddle him, as many times as the years of his age "with one to grow on."

Gifts from the family were customarily placed under a person's plate at the breakfast table.

When a birthday cake is brought in, it is placed before the person whose birthday it is. On it are as many candles as the number of years of her life is supposed to be. If she blows out all the candles at her first trial she will be married within the year. If not, the number of candles left burning indicates how many years it will be before she is married.

Widely customary is the singing of "Happy Birthday to You," by those about the table, at the entrance of a person whose birthday is announced.

It was a pioneer custom for the mother to hold a child on each of its birthdays and rock it like a baby. A contributor testified that her mother always sang to her on such an occasion the lullaby she sang to her children when infants, Dr. Watts' cradle hymn, "Hush my dear, lie still and slumber."

Weddings

A familiar old custom is the shower of rice which usually takes place at the depot as the bride and groom depart by train. If they leave in a car, the shower comes as they leave the house.

The tying of an old shoe to the baggage, or of a white slipper, is supposed to bring good luck.

The bride throws her bouquet as she comes down the stairs to go away. The girl who catches it is supposed to be the next to be married.

A penny, a thimble, and a ring are baked in the wedding cake. The person getting the penny is to be wealthy, she getting the thimble will be a spinster, and the getter of the ring will be a bride.

The carriage, car, taxi, or automobile in which the newly married are leaving is placarded to let the public know of the wedding and bring embarrassment to the couple.

The saying that a bride should wear—

> Something old, something new,
> Something borrowed, something blue.

is not merely lore but is a custom religiously carried out by present-day brides.

In earlier days the "genteel" always had home weddings. In some rural sections there were no ordained ministers. The local justice of the peace often officiated. "The bride always had to have two dresses. Her second day dress, so-called, was to wear at the 'infare', which was always held at the home of the groom while the wedding was in the bride's home. The traditional gift of a farmer to a daughter was a cow."

"At some Bohemian weddings of Northern Nebraska, it is the custom to decorate the bridal car with streamers of the bride's chosen colors. The bridal party usually drives to the county seat for the marriage. The car with its gay decorations attracts immediate attention. Free dancing for the community is part of the wedding festivity. The town hall is frequently rented for a big free dance."

"A curious custom was followed till recent times in the German-Russian settlement at Lincoln. At the wedding dance the bride was the center of attention. She danced, not with her husband, but with other men. Each man who danced with her was expected to pin on her dress a bill. The money she collected in this strange way was used to pay the bridegroom, who customarily advanced the money for the bride's wedding finery. Feasting was another feature of the dance."

The Shivaree

In frontier days a wedding was always followed by a shivaree (charivari), and the custom is far from extinct. The shivaree took place at dusk or later, on the day of the wedding, or sometimes in the evening of the next day, at the new home of the couple. Friends or young people of the neighborhood gathered to serenade the bride and groom with the beating of tin pans, oyster cans, the ringing of cowbells or sleigh bells, with whistles, the blare of horns, firecrackers or shooting, or the utilizing of any other noise-making devices that might be available. This was kept up till the young couple appeared before the serenaders to treat the crowd. The crowd might be asked into the new home to be served pumpkin pie and watermelon or other eatables; or the groom might hand the men cigars. One contributor testified that sometimes he might actually "buy off" the boisterous crowd. Others doubted this. Another contributor wrote as follows:

I distinctly remember my first shivaree. I was six years old and had come to live in Gothenburg in the fall of 1912. The local druggist had just been married. After dark a crowd of boys gathered down town for a march on the newly-weds' home. As we progressed the crowd grew. Arrived at the house, we began to yell and beat upon cans and otherwise make a noise until in a while the bride and groom appeared on the front porch. Then the groom told us what we had been waiting for, that he had instructed the local candy kitchen to treat us to ice cream. As I grew up, in the next ten years, I participated in many more shivarees. At least once but occasionally more than once, a popular newly-wed couple was shivareed by the local youngsters. I recall only boys participated; it was a little bid rowdy and too late at night for little girls.

Belling and warmer are other words for the customs that were used in Nebraska in the 1870's. Mari Sandoz says that the latter is still current in the sandhill region. Calithumpian, a name often used elsewhere, has not been common in Nebraska.

See "Charivaria," by Mamie J. Meredith, in *American Speech*, VIII (April), 1933, 22-24. For instances of belling and warmer she cites the Lincoln *Daily State Journal*, January 1, 1878, and November 22, 1874.

The Nebraska shivaree is far from extinct. In 1936 the Louisville *Courier* of March 5 described a local shivaree on the preceding Sunday evening, and the Plattsmouth *Journal* of May 25, 1936, described another of local occurrence.

A news item from Hastings printed in the *Morning Journal* of Lincoln of June 16, 1946, read as follows:

There'll be no more of the old-fashioned charivari parties on Second Street here. They're getting out of hand, in the opinion of Police Chief C. W. Cawiezel.

Here's what has been happening, Cawiezel said:

1. The bride sometimes is placed on one fender of an auto and the groom on the other, forcing them to hold hands across the hood to keep from being thrown off.

2. The bridal couple is hauled in a small trailer, which is zigzagged and whipped, forcing the couple to hold on tightly to keep from being thrown out.

3. The newly-married pair is forced to ride on the running board of an auto.

The chief assured citizens the police will not interfere with "reasonable" community celebrations of marriages.

The shivaree has often been played up in western literature, for instance, in the play "Green Grow the Lilacs" by Lynn Riggs, given by the New York Theater Guild in 1931. This play was the predecessor or inspirer of the popular "Oklahoma."

The Infare

Another necessary accompaniment of frontier life was the *infare* (usually but less properly spelled *infair*) which took place on the day following the wedding. "It consisted of a visit of the bride and groom, the bride's folk and perhaps others of the wedding party to the home of the parents of the bridegroom." Sometimes the infare was a sort of housewarming or party of welcoming to their new home by the bride and groom and the bride's parents. Not infrequently the young girls attending rode horseback, riding behind their escorts, or on separate horses. Or the coming of the guests was by wagons.

In the frontier period an extended honeymoon was out of the question but sometimes "the couple loaded up a grist and drove gaily across the prairie to the mill, camping along the way while awaiting their turn. Or perhaps they took a two or three days trip to the County seat to buy a few articles for their scanty housekeeping."

Deaths and Funerals

A widespread custom at a death, as at Fullerton or Fairbury, was to toll a bell the number of years of the life of a dead person.

In early frontier days the corpse might be wrapped in a blanket or sheet. It was not unusual for caskets to be made from floors or cupboards if no lumber was to be had. In some instances coffins or rough boards were blacked with shoe polish, or lamp black or soot were applied to the coffin. When saw mills came coffins might be made to measurements. Such coffins were "somewhat triangular in shape, wide at the shoulders and narrowed to a peak at the feet." "In towns the casket for an older person was nicely covered with black alpaca, those for children with white cloth." If the death came too late in the day for burial, friends "sat up" with the body, keeping the face of the corpse wet with vinegar in order to delay mortification as long as possible. No actual "wake" was held. Neighbors came in and sat with the dead. "In our neighborhood," said an informant, "among the Protestants sitting up with the dead there was no drinking. Polish neighbors sat drinking at the home or drunk." If there was opportunity for formality or effort, all blackness possible was availed of for the burial. Usually little funeral equipment was to be had. There were services by the preacher at the grave as well as when the funeral was conducted at the home of the dead person.

While the family was at the burial many brought food to the home. In Nance and Thurston counties, for example, "a sort of elaborate dinner was given, with roast meat, fowls etc. provided. Everybody stepped in and partook and there was something of a reception afterward."

Throughout the century mourning was worn for months. Those not able to afford new mourning garments borrowed black garments in order to show respect for the dead. Horses in a funeral procession were always driven at a walk, no matter how great the distance to the cemetery. Letters from those in mourning must always be edged in black.

Whisker Vogue

Whisker vogue still characterizes the celebration of certain days. As a reminder of frontier times, men sometimes dispensed with barbers and let growths of whiskers, beards, "sideburns," handlebar mustaches, or goatees cover their faces. As late as August 18, 1935, for the Fiftieth Anniversary Picnic at Diller, Jefferson County, this practice was observed. For the same or similar occasions the daughters of pioneers went about the streets in garments of old style, poke bonnets, hoop skirts, lace mitts, such as their grandmothers wore. The Golden Spike Celebration at Omaha, April 26-29, 1939, honoring the anniversary of the completion of the Union Pacific Railroad, was made an elaborate occasion. It was marked by both masculine and feminine reminders of frontier days, whisker growth for the men and old fashioned apparel for the women. The shops too were made up to suggest pioneer times.

Social Activities

Church Occasions

When a new preacher moved to town there was a pound party. Everyone took a pound of something to a welcome party in his home. Hunters shot wild animals to provide meat for the winter for the preacher, as a deer or a buffalo. Such parties were held in Dawes, Thurston, and Nance counties and elsewhere. There were donation parties also, later, when the preacher seemed hard up. Those who called brought an offering of food or other gifts.

Church activities included Junior or Christian Endeavor groups, choir practice (the night when young persons dated), prayer meetings, missionary societies, Ladies Aid societies. Some churches had "socials," some "sociables," as did rival churches at Fullerton. In season these might be ice cream or strawberry socials (sociables) held on lawns, with Chinese lanterns lighting them. The Omaha *Times* of June 17, 1858, tells of a strawberry festival given by the Methodist Episcopal Church.

In all, there were five types of church dinners: ice cream festivals, strawberry festivals, oyster stews, mixed suppers, and box suppers. "Soliciters," always young girls and their "beaus," drove from house to house listing what each housewife would bring to the church.

Church "bazaars" and "raffles" were popular, though the latter were ultimately stopped, as were lotteries in general.

The Omaha *Times* of June 24, 1858 tells of a ladies' fair, at which fancy work, cakes, and edibles were sold.

On Sunday a child whose birthday had occurred during the week advanced to the front of the church and dropped in a box there as many pennies as the number of years of his or her life.

Other Customs and Social Occasions

A popular event was the box social or mystery lunch or supper box party. Boxes or packages were brought by the girls and bid for by the boys. Usually there was some secret means of identification, by the ribbons or other decorations, communicated to the escorts so that the right box would be chosen. At Columbus sometimes as high as fifteen dollars were bid. The money went to the church.

Taffy pulls were of frequent occurrence at homes, sometimes at school houses. The participants took turns at pulling boiled-down sorghum till it was thin enough to stretch out.

Pasture parties were held now and then in scattered places. These were a type of picnic given in what seemed at the time a preferable location.

Surprise parties had vogue in some regions. Merrymakers went by wagon or horseback to some cabin or isolated home in pioneer days. Hayrack riding was a popular institution and so was the bobsled party.

Quilting parties at which quilts were pieced were also popular. They were held at homes. "Log cabin quilts" reportedly 80 years old are said to be still in existence in Nebraska. Watermelon feeds also deserve mention.

Mari Sandoz tells of feather stripping. "A dinner plate was placed upside down in the lap of each person. My mother gave each one a little knife and paper sack to be held in the lap, or a 'poke' made out of an old newspaper. The child then reached in under the plate and took out one feather, (a handful of feathers had been placed under the plate), stripped it, and carefully dropped the quill on the floor and the strippings in a paper bag. Riddles and jokes were told during the feather stripping. When phonographs were had there was dancing to the music."

Miss Sandoz tells also of bean picking. A bushel sack was emptied at a table. The guests separated the good from the bad and refilled the sack. Merrymaking followed.

According to the Dannebrog *News* of October 8, 1936, the big social event of the early days was the housewarming when a new home was built. There were drinks, almost invariably punch, just after midnight, at which time numerous toasts were offered and songs sung and speeches made. This was for the men. The women were served coffee, chocolate, and cake. All the rest of the night until daylight, sometimes till sunrise, was devoted to dancing the rapid whirling muscle-exercising Danish round dances, with one or two quadrilles thrown in for American flavor. These sociables or dances were immensely popular.

In rural communities and small towns, the general store served as a meeting place or social center, and it still may.

Along the Missouri River, as at Nebraska City or Brownville, it was an exciting social occasion when steamboats, especially the first steamboat of the season, arrived. At Brownville the young people were known to desert even church services to rush down to the banks when boats came in.

Courtship customs were pretty standardized in early days in

Nebraska. Young persons "kept company." Sunday was "beau day." "In the evening a boy called upon a girl quite formally. He was shown into the parlor and there he and the girl spent the time, while the rest of the family kept away. He never stayed late. If he took a girl to evening church or to a party they were not to sit out in the buggy or sleigh after reaching her home, not if her parents were obeyed. He must bring her to the door but not enter. Neither must he come during the week unless for a brief call at the door. Mothers did not want their girls 'talked about.' "

"Long engagements were common, sometimes lasting for years. The engagement was never announced even to the parents until near the wedding day. The engagement ring was usually a carved gold band. It was not worn until a short time before the wedding and then served as wedding ring also. To be an 'old maid' was regrettable. To be a divorced woman was to be shamed, no matter what the provocation had been."

Sports and Games

Outdoor Sports

In the sandhill country the wolf hunt or coyote hunt has been described by Mari Sandoz. It was planned in advance. Sometimes a few friends took part. Sometimes it was a community affair.

Riding and hunting were popular over the prairies from the first. Horse races were arranged and aroused much interest. The natural prairie grass made an excellent track. Bets were made freely. Backers might place fifty or a hundred dollars on each side. Outsiders bet considerable sums as well as local men. When the horses were from different towns, citizens exhibited their "loyalty" by backing the home town. The races might be running or trotting races. Occasionally there were "ladies contests," these on side saddles, with side saddles likely to be the prizes.

Ball was played in simple form from the first. By the early '70's baseball had appeared and prairie towns had their competing teams. Milford played Seward a game lasting from 2:00

till 6:00, August 18, 1871. Baseball was a well organized competitive sport by the 1880's.

Pitching horseshoes (quoits) was common from early days.
Croquet came rather late.

The bicycle arrived in the 1880's, and the vogue of roller
skating reached Nebraska in due course.

Traditional outdoor games played by young persons were:
hide and seek; pom pom pullaway; run sheep run; dare base;
steal sticks; old witch; London bridge; farmer in the dell; drop
the handkerchief; ring round Rosie; pussy wants a corner; crack
the whip; cross tag; shinny; one-two-three o'cat; tin tin. Over
fallen snow, fox and geese or dog and deer were played.[1]

There were contests in broad, high, standing and running
jumping and in wrestling and racing. Men's races on special
occasions might include a three-legged race, sack race, fat men's
race, potato race, peanut race, and wheelbarrow race.

Indoor Games

Popular indoor games were: postoffice; hide the thimble; cha-
rades; guessing games; spin the platter. Card games were euchre,
poker, hearts, high five, five hundred, flinch, and there was
some duplicate whist played at the turn of the century. Auction
and contract bridge belong to the present century. Authors
were played and checkers, more rarely chess. Parchesi and tid-
dledewinks, etc., were transient amusements.

Statuary (one person strikes a pose. Others guess who or
what he is supposed to be) was played either indoors or outdoors. So was paying forfeits. ("Heavy, heavy hangs over your
head. What shall the owner do to redeem it?" The judge, seated
in the circle, asks, "Fine or superfine?" The person holding the
forfeited object answers "Fine" if it belongs to a man, "Superfine" if it belongs to a woman. The penalty or sentence is
then pronounced by the judge.)

---

1 These were played in the standard ways, with local variations. For the
"rules" see such a book as *Active Games and Contests*, by Bernard S. Mason
and Elmer D. Mitchell, New York, 1935.

Literary and Debating Societies and School Activities

These had various names, Literary Society, Lyceum, Debating School, or Debating Society, and Athenaeum. Leading citizens, ministers, lawyers, and others participated in the debates, which offered good experience for youths. The Brownville *Advertiser* records that on February 8, 1857, the territorial legislature incorporated the Brownville Lyceum, Library, and Literary Association, intended to promote interest along these lines. The capital stock was $50,000, to be sold at $5.00 a share. The membership fee was $1.00 a season. The *Advertiser* had a notice of a meeting of the Library Association in its issue of September 9, 1859, and of a meeting of the Lyceum, December 12, 1859. In 1864 the Society raised $400 to improve the building in which the meetings were held. The Nebraska City *News* records a Library Association there December 4, 1858. The *News* of December 3, 1859, mentions the Webster Debating Society "composed of young gentlemen connected with Mr. Raymond's school." The Falls City *Broadaxe* tells of the Richardson County Lyceum in the issue of January 1, 1861. The Omaha Lyceum was organized in 1860. The Omaha *Nebraskian* announced, December 12, 1860, as a subject for debate December 22 at the Congregational Church, "Resolved that the Legislature of Nebraska has the right and it is its duty to prohibit slavery in the Territory." In 1876 in Harmon's Grove on the Nemaha River was debated, "Resolved that Water Baptism Is No Part of the Plan of Salvation." In general, questions concerning governmental and economic topics were debated, such as "Popular Election of Presidents," "Missouri Compromise," "British Colonial Policy." Other questions debated were "Resolved that the Nebraska Legislature should pass a law releasing persons from debts outside the Territory after a residence of 60 days in the country," "Resolved that the Legislature should pass a herd law restraining all kinds of stock from running at large," "Resolved that men and women should be equal before the law in respect to legal rights and liabilities."

Often lecturers were invited to meetings to present some special subject.

Some topics discussed at Brownville in the days when Brownville College had been planned were: "Manifest Destiny," "Philosophy Greek and Roman," "The Historian, Statesman, and the Divine." These and other topics were mentioned in the *Advertiser* of February 25, 1857. The place of meeting was the Methodist Church.

As a rule, meetings of literary societies were held in schoolhouses. The programs were made up of debates, declamations, dialogues and music, and there was usually a paper telling "jokes" about those present.

Spelling Bees

These were popular among grown-ups in the '60's and '70's and they are still popular for children as an educational exercise. Words were given out by school teachers or other available persons. Marks for spellers were registered as points for each side. At the end of the evening tallies were counted for each side, where two or more groups competed. The person who lasted longest before missing "spelled down" the others. Friday afternoon was the usual time for spelling contests for schools. McGuffey's spelling book was relied upon and memorized by the zealous.

Bret Harte described a spelling contest in his "The Spelling Bee at Angels, Reported by Truthful James." It was organized by grown-ups who sat around the bar-room stove. "The Spelling Bee" was reported as a new game in Frisco. The schoolmaster said he knew the game and would give instructions. The words he called for were: separate, parallel, rhythm, incinerate, phthisis, gneiss. Bret Harte's bee ended in a shooting affray.

A district spelling contest (these are no longer called "bees") was held at Wilber, Nebraska, April 9, 1946. There were written and oral contests, each won by a girl.

Figure downs were held at times on Fridays after school hours. Arithmetical problems were placed on the board and pupils strove to finish first.

General school exercises might be held Friday afternoon also, with recitations, dialogues, essays, songs, etc., featured.

A school exhibition ended the school year. This was more

elaborate than the "last day of school" program. It was often given at night and in a church or hall to accommodate the large crowd. A basket dinner served in the schoolhouse, a "surprise for the teacher," was a frequent event on the last day of a country school.

Singing

There was much more singing in Nebraska in the early days and through the nineteenth century than there is now, though instruments were few. The liking for music had to be met by singing. As time went on there might be a violin, accordion, banjo, guitar, or organ for accompaniment, or alongside the singing. Pianos were almost unknown for some decades. The songs were of two groups, sacred music, religious songs, and "opry songs," as they were sometimes called. The religious songs often sung were "Amazing Grace," "On Jordan's Stormy Banks I Stand," "Beulah Land," "Bringing in the Sheaves," "Throw Out the Life Line," "Pull for the Shore," "Work for the Night Is Coming," and other gospel hymns from the books used for church or Sunday school. There was more group than individual singing. Groups gathered Sunday afternoons, especially at homes where there was an organ. There were also singings at country school houses, and sometimes "teams" from whole counties or from various communities sang in rivalry.

Testifying regarding the early songs reaching the old sand-hill region in the northwest section of Nebraska, an old buffalo and cattle country, Mari Sandoz states that Indian songs came first, of course, then those of the French fur traders, mostly French-Canadian dance songs. The Texas cattle trail group came next. Few of theirs could be called "cowboy songs" (songs of the open range) today. The real trail songs were softly melancholy spirituals and ballads, sung with no accompaniment beside animal bawlings and howlings. Then settlers from the East came with their songs. They brought copy books full of pieces, many similar to those of the Texas trailers. A Scotch-Irish family from Kentucky sang "The Cowboy's Lament," at a literary, a dance, or a shivaree. Later came "The Old Chisholm Trail," "Old Paint," "When the Work's All Done This Fall," "Little

Joe the Wrangler," "The Little Old Sod Shanty," "The Lone Prairie," "Nebraska Land," and, alongside these, current popular songs such as "Puttin' on the Agony, Puttin' on the Style," "The Unfortunate Miss Bailey," and sentimental pieces.

The Frontier County Scrapbook, II, p. 96, in the State Historical Society Library, tells that at the Kester Schoolhouse, Arch Heater was accustomed to sing "The Steam Arm," "Shelling Green Peas," "Putting on the Agony," and other pieces. At Morrill Schoolhouse Andrew Johnson sang "When I Ride My Little Hump-Back Mule." He said "oomp" and "mool."

The Dance

Dance parties of various types in pioneer and later days were given various names, "barn dances," "hops," "stepping bees," and, for play-parties in certain regions such as the Sandhills, "bounce arounds." "Hoedowns," "shindigs," or "shindies" were rather rough and boisterous yet were occasions having some standing. "Hog wrassles," on the other hand, were characteristically cheap and rowdy. In Nebraska newspaper usage, nineteenth century dances might be alluded to as "terpsichorean performances" or "pigeon-wingings" or gatherings for "tripping the light fantastic" into the "wee small hours."

In many small towns and rural communities the "best families" never danced. One contributor told of being a guest at an infare party. She did not dance, but her Methodist minister told her that she was unfit to enter his church, and from that day she never did. In pioneer times gambling, dancing, saloons, and vice were always closely associated and hence were banned by the church.

The play-party games popular into the present century over the western plains thrived in regions where dancing was thought improper and was tabooed by the church. Neither the participants nor others ever called them dances. They were a lively and zestful species of social diversion for young persons in country regions or isolated towns and villages. They were at their height so long as there was little other amusement. In patterns they showed little change from those of the traditional

English and Scottish games from which they descended. As communities became less isolated, and dancing floors, management, and musicians were to be had, such games waned in popularity, disparaged by city dwellers as childish or rustic. From their accepted position as a popular feature of social custom, the recreation of grown-ups, they passed into the tradition of the schoolhouse and playground and now linger in the dramatic games of Nebraska children played in open spaces outdoors.

Primarily the dancing was to song only. Largely the Nebraska play-party games were circle or ring dances or long line reels, with someone who knew the songs and tunes serving as leader. Later, various musical instruments, the fiddle, guitar, banjo, harmonica, even the organ or piano were availed of. The tunes were those handed down. When the older traditional songs, ballads or narrative songs among them, were utilized, they tended to shorten, disintegrate, or merge. As time went on, the texts and tunes became more and more westernized and more and more use was made of indigenous American tunes. The conduct of play-party games was noisy, but lively and spirited rather than boisterous. Additions to the songs were introduced and local matter or allusions improvised.

Play-parties might be held in front rooms, or yards, in schoolhouses or schoolyards, or in barns. They were characteristically open to all in the region round about. They were especially enjoyed on moonlight nights outdoors. Participants might come from a dozen or more miles away. Cider or lemonade or coffee with doughnuts was served. Intoxicants were not favored. The main refreshments were cake, cookies, roasted apples, pies, etc. Men wore shirts of various colors, sometimes stiff collars and cuffs of celluloid. Women were in long dresses of calico or gingham with shawls. As quadrilles or square dances replaced the play-party for group dancing, and when dances were held in hotels or halls, there was more formality in dress and refreshment.

Among the inherited songs that were popular were "Needle's Eye," "Oats, Peas, Beans, and Barley," "Farmer in the Dell," "The Miller Boy," "Green Gravel." American of origin were "Buffalo Gals," "Old Dan Tucker," "We'll All Go Down to

Rowser's," etc. Nebraska's most popular play-party game seems to have been "Skip to My Lou," ("Maloo," "Malue," etc.).

Changed conditions and a more tolerant attitude on the part of the church gradually weakened the taboo on dancing which had given vitality to the play-party. The lessening of community isolation and the growing competition of other forms of amusement helped to break it down. Such dances as the waltz, polka, schottisch and two-step, and square dances (quadrilles, lancers) gained favor. The later play-party games were influenced by and finally replaced by them. Early in the present century the play-party was still fairly common in outlying places, but it is hard now to find it surviving. The present revival of folksong and folkdance in general, especially of the square dance, has brought with it the revival of many dances of the old circle and line type, and it may bring the renewal to some extent of the play-party. But if so, it will be conducted in more sophisticated surroundings than in pioneer days with the accompaniment of music.

Theatricals and Other Entertainment

With the coming of "opera houses," visiting troupes reached the larger towns. They played such dramas as "Uncle Tom's Cabin," "East Lynne," "Ten Nights in a Barroom" and "The Count of Monte Cristo." Amateur theatrical societies were often formed which sometimes attempted to play Shakespeare. At Nebraska City a dramatic society was organized as early as October, 1859. An item in the Nebraska City *News* of December 31, 1859, read, "The Dramatic Society gave its second representation. Mr. J. G. Abbott as Othello, and Mr. Story as Cassio sustained the characters excellently." The Dramatic Society of Brownville gave its first performance April 23, 1876. At Fullerton amateurs presented "Othello," "Macbeth," and "The Merchant of Venice."

Frank A. Harrison wrote an account of "Nebraska History Plays" in *Nebraska History and Records of Pioneer Days* (1918), in the State Historical Library. Mr. Harrison tells of his first experiment in Garfield County, a spectacle play in which Indian battles were acted out. Some weeks later he gave one at Belle-vue, and a year later he gave a history play at North Platte. The Omaha *Nebraskian,* June 2, 1860, mentions the Phil-harmonic Society as in its sixth year.

At times a director was imported to a town and a cantata or pageant of some type was locally presented by local children.

The coming of the professional circus with its morning parade and its afternoon and evening performances was always a great event. Also, somewhat later, the street fair and the carnival.

Children got up imitative dramatic performances which they wrote, directed, and acted themselves. They gave circuses also. Admission to these affairs was usually by some fixed number of pins.

Food

Buffalo meat and venison were early forms of meat pro-vided by hunters, and sometimes catfish were caught. Wild duck and turkey and geese were plentiful and so were prairie chickens and quail. Codfish and mackerel were brought in later. Jerked (dried) beef and salt pork became staple. Canned oysters were a real delicacy. Other staple food consisted of po-tatoes, hominy, cornbread or johnny cake, flapjacks, pancakes, buckwheat cakes. Sorghum gravy was made by browning flour and lard together, adding water, and boiling. Dried apples and navy beans were relied on, as were barley coffee and sorghum mo-lasses. Occasionally a bee tree gave up a store of honey. Fruits were choke cherries, ground cherries, wild plums, wild grapes, mulberries, gooseberries and crab apples. Ice cream and the sundae were late delicacies. The sundae and its name made their appearance at about the end of the century.

Mrs. Kittie McGrew, writing of "Women of Territorial Ne-braska" in the nineteenth volume of *The Nebraska State His-torical Society Publications,* left a description of a pioneer log cabin built in 1855 which was superior in many ways to the majority in the locality. She said of the kitchen (pp. 97-98):

> The kitchen was a very attractive place, with a good stove and other conveniences not usually found in pioneer cabins.

Its walls were hung with strings of red peppers, mangoes, popcorn and some choice seed corn tied with the husks and slipped on slender sticks. A great variety of gourds hung from wooden pegs driven into the walls. Some of the gourds were used for dipping water and some, with openings near the slender handles, held rice, dried corn, berries, or other household necessities and made fine receptacles. A sputtering two-lipped grease lamp, with cotton flannel wick, or perhaps candle wicking gave a fitful and feeble light . . . . In the yard was a well with a long wooden beam from which hung a chain and the old oaken bucket, a gourd dipper conveniently near, and a huge excavated log for a watering trough. Nearby was the great ash leach or hopper where the lye could be run off into the log trough to be made into a choice brand of soft soap. Near the kitchen door stood a split log bench where the family might have the tin basin for an early morning wash. There were great iron or copper kettles, suspended on poles or forked sticks, which were used in making soap and hominy and for heating water for the family washing and for butchering. All these were considered necessary adjuncts to a well regulated pioneer household.

Addenda

It is customary when a boy or girl shows up with a new pair of shoes for other boys or girls to spit on them.

Deserving of mention are the pioneer photograph album and the autograph album. In the latter, sentiments or verses were written as well as signatures. The vogue of collecting autographs lasted through the century.

Water-witching, attempts to find water by a divining rod, have been reported at various times, for instance from Platte County and Jefferson County. Rather peculiar old men searched for water with a forked stick of willow or other wood. The stick was much like a "sling shot" or "nigger shooter." It was held by the two forks and the point was supposed to point downward at the sought for spot.

Abridged somewhat from an article asked for and read in part at the Sixth Annual Folklore Conference at the University of Denver, July 11, 1946. Reprinted from *Nebraska History*, XXVIII (January-March, 1947), 3-31.

APPENDIX

Folklore and Dialect

1

Folklore and dialect have been less closely associated, in the past, than they should be. Surely dialect is a species of folklore, though the two subjects are usually treated independently. Dialect, in the sense in which we now ordinarily use the word, is *lore,* linguistic lore, and linguistic lore exists in tradition alongside the folk beliefs and folkways, the folk legacies that we usually term lore.

Among English-speaking peoples interest in folklore arose earlier than interest in dialect. It emerged, indeed, as an offshoot of the European Romantic Movement of the late eighteenth and early nineteenth centuries. Its beginning is probably to be dated from Jacob Grimm's *Deutsche Mythologie* (1835). If Grimm was the founder of Germanic Philology, as generally recognized, he was also the inspirer of interest in traditional customs, legends, superstitions, and beliefs preserved among the common people. The influence of his *Mythologie* came slowly, rather than at once. It was preceded by his collection of popular children's and domestic tales, Grimm's *Kinder- und Hausmärchen* of 1812-1822. He aroused interest in fairy tales, animal tales, legend, folk song before he stimulated scholarly interest in mythology and philology. After him Northern European interest in lore has never lapsed. It was perhaps at its height before the outbreak of the Second World War, and not only in Germany, the Scandinavian countries, Finland, and France but in many other areas.

In England scholarly impetus to the study of folklore did not come in the wake of the Romantic Movement but rather through the rise of the Anthropological School, the school culminating in the twelve volumes of Sir James G. Frazer's *The Golden Bough* (1907-1915). Though it did not originate the science of folklore (a distinctly romantic and humanitarian science, if it is one), England must have credit for originating its name. It was in 1846, as is well known, that W. J. Thoms, writing in the *Athenaeum* of August 22 (pp. 862-863) under the name of Ambrose Merton, began his contribution with the words, "What we in England designate Popular Antiquities, or Popular Literature (though, by the bye, it is more of a lore than literature, and would be most aptly designated by a good Saxon compound, 'Folk-Lore'—the lore of the people) . . . ." The new name was taken up at once and became accepted over Europe and the two American continents. Europe formed its international society known as the *Folkloristische Forscherbund* or "Folklore Fellows" and Latin America has such publications as *Folklore Americas* and *Associación Folklórica Argentina*. Some objected for a time to the name folklore as designating both the science and its content; but the same objection might be made for other sciences, such as history and language, for which the usage has become established. The Folklore Society of England, when it was organized, 1878, discussed calling itself the Society of Popular Tradition, but this designation seemed unwieldier and less definite, and Mr. Thom's suggestion was preferred. In France, however, the *Société des Traditions Populaires* was founded, 1886, and Italy published the quarterly *Archivio per lo Studio delle Tradizioni Populari*. In both countries the name folklore is now liked. Witness, for example, the *Manuel de Folklore Français Contemporain* of Arnold van Gennep, 1937-1938.

Mr. Thoms when coining his name hyphenated it, as was to be expected, and such was long the usage in this country as well as in England. Occasionally one comes upon the words written separately (folk lore) in popular writing, but of late it has become customary to omit the hyphen and join them. This is the usage of the *Southern Folklore Quarterly* from its establishment in 1937, and, since its change of format, about 1941, the *Journal of the American Folklore Society* has given up its original hyphenation. The *California Folklore Quarterly,* established in 1942, follows the newer practice. The conflation of "folk song," though parallel, came more slowly and has arrived with less finality. "Folk song," was preferred by Olive D. Campbell and Cecil J. Sharp in their *Folk Songs from the Southern Appalachians* (1917). Newman I. White in *American Negro Folk-Songs* (1928) preferred the hyphen. John A. and Alan Lomax entitled their work of 1934 *American Ballads and Folk Songs,* omitting the hyphen. A. H. Hudson, *Folksongs of Mississippi* (1936), wrote the compound as one word. In the July, 1944, issue of the *California Folklore Quarterly,* Bertrand H. Bronson writes of folk music and folk singers but of British folktunes; and under the heading Folklore News in the same issue appears *folk songs.* The *Dictionary of World Literature* (1943) heads its article on the subject *folksong.*

The English Folk-Lore Society of 1878 preceded the American by a decade or more. Active among its foundation members were such men as Andrew Lang, E. W. Tylor, Alfred Nutt, G. L. Gomme. Its first Annual Report appeared in the *Folk-Lore Record,* vol. 2, 1878. The *Folk-Lore Journal,* superseding the *Record,* at first a monthly and after 1885 a quarterly, was published from January-December, 1883, to Volume VII, 1889. In March, 1890, it was united with the *Archaeological Review* to form *Folk-Lore,* which describes itself as a quarterly review of myth, tradition, institution, and custom. Another new periodical of the end of the century was the *Journal of the Folk-Song Society,* seven volumes of which were published, 1899-1926. The American Folk-Lore Society was founded at Cambridge, January 4, 1888, with Francis James Child as its first president and W. W. Newell its first secretary. The first volume of its publication, the *Journal of American Folk-Lore,* was issued in that year.

2

As for dialect, it concerns itself with local and regional peculiarities of language, traditionally handed on and therefore lore. It was not an outgrowth of the Romantic Movement nor of

Anthropology but of the new science of Philology. Scholarly examination of older dialects, those of Old English, Middle English, and later, preceded interest in our current substandard language. The common speech, folk language, as over against that accepted in educated circles, gained attention in Germany, France, England in the last half of last century. Somewhat later the academic world of America, too, turned to the unexplored linguistic fields about it and collectanea and study began. The British Dialect Society started at Cambridge in 1873, with W. W. Skeat and Joseph and Mary Wright among its active spirits. The monumental *English Dialect Dictionary* in six volumes, edited by Joseph Wright (1898-1905), remains a treasure house of information concerning the dialect vocabularies of England.

The American Dialect Society was founded in January, 1889, by such men as Edward Sheldon, C. H. Grandgent, L. R. Briggs, G. L. Kittredge, all of Harvard, and W. W. Newell, president of the newly founded Folk-Lore Society. Professor F. J. Child, the distinguished ballad scholar, was its first president and C. H. Grandgent its first secretary. It announced as its purpose, in 1894, the publication of a large dictionary of dialect and regional words and localisms. The first volume of *Dialect Notes* was issued in 1896. The Society had a fairly vigorous existence for a number of years, fostered by such succeeding secretaries as O. F. Emerson, W. E. Mead, W. G. Howard, Percy W. Long. Originally a quarterly, *Dialect Notes* came to be issued irregularly. In the 1930's its most valuable work was the printing of unpublished material collected by Richard H. Thornton and stored in the Harvard Library, this capably edited by M. H. Hanley. When I was president of the Society, 1939-1941, I suggested its expansion through the partitioning of its activities into different groups, such as Regional Speech and Localisms, Place Names, Linguistic Geography, Usage, Non-English Dialects, Semantics. These were adopted and, with the addition of New Words and of Proverbs, are in the hands of able chairmen. I also suggested and encouraged the publication for practical use of an *American Dialect Dictionary*, edited by Dr. Harold Wentworth, the first for the United States. America is a large country compared to

England and its dialects less clearly marked and less static than the English. The making of an exhaustive cooperative dictionary of the scope of the Wright *English Dialect Dictionary* will have to wait many years for completion. In the half century since it was projected no adequate start has been made. Inquiries for such a work came to me constantly as an officer of the Dialect Society and an editor of *American Speech,* especially from writers of fiction and drama; yet, though many glossaries of slang have been printed long since, no American glossary of folk speech existed. Dr. Wentworth completed his difficult task, exhibiting excellent scholarship, in minimum time and as exhaustively as the limits of his volume permitted. It was published in 1944 and has already seen wide use.

From 1925 onward, *American Speech,* dealing with many phases of oral and written language, became the avenue of expression for many collectors and contributors from all parts of the country. Under the editorship of Secretary E. P. Wilson, the Dialect Society has resumed the occasional publication of word lists and other matter and more may be expected to emerge from the Society's group activities. In 1931 the important Linguistic Atlas was begun, under the auspices of and financed by the Council of Learned Societies and under the guidance of Dr. Hans Kurath. Well equipped for the phonetic recording of speech, its workers completed their survey of the Atlantic States from Maine to South Carolina (the original thirteen colonies) before the end of the Second World War period.

When the *Journal* of the American Folk-Lore Society was founded (1888), the relation of dialect to folklore seemed to be felt. The first few volumes had a section, "Wastebasket of Words," in which selected New England terms were commented on. Examples from its list are "delightsome," "dreen" (ebb-tide), "coast" (slide down a snow-covered slope in a sled), "give him jessy" (from *jess* in falconry, used to punish a bird), "mammock" (paw), "cod" (hoax, or make fun of a person by giving him false information). This section was included for several years and then dropped. There were a few linguistic articles in the old issues of the *Journal of American Folk-Lore.* George Patterson of New Glasgow, Nova Scotia, wrote "Notes on the Dialect of the

People of Newfoundland," which was read at the meeting of the Montreal Branch of the American Folk-Lore Society, May 21, 1894, and published in the eighth volume of the *JAFL*. Reginald Pelham Bolton had an article on "The Cockney and His Dialect" in the ninth volume, 1896. "More Notes on the Dialect of the People of Newfoundland" came also in the ninth volume, and "Algonkian Words in English," by Alexander F. Chamberlain, in the fifteenth (1902). A leafing through of later volumes showed no further linguistic contributions, for other avenues of publication became available.

3

In any discussion of folklore, folk song, or dialect, something should be said of the "folk." Europeans have sometimes remarked that Americans have an obsession for definition and classification. One hopes this is true. Certainly definite, not loose, usage of terms is essential and should be encouraged. "Folk" especially has been used very loosely, and so too have been "ballad" and "tradition." For "ballad," there are at last acceptable dictionary definitions, since the old "definition by origins," with its insistence on emergence from the dance and its overemphasis on creation by the "peasantry," has been given up by scholars abreast of the times. Since we do not know the origin of most of our traditional pieces, this old-time insistence on a single type of origin (Professor Gummere's ring-dance improvisation and belief in the power and vitality of folk improvisation in general) would bar almost the whole mass of traditional ballads (such as "Lord Randal," "Edward," "Sir Patrick Spens," "Barbara Allen") from our college anthologies. Our best matter would have to be excluded. Similarly, questionable definitions of folklore and folk song have lingered till recently in text books and some dictionaries. Many, even before the abandonment of "peasant origin" as a fundamental conception, still retained it for folklore and folk song. For instance, even the scholarly author of a recent *Science of Folklore* (Dr. A. H. Krappe, 1930), though he distinctly gives up peasant for literary origins in his work, still defines a folk song, when opening his chapter on the subject, as a "lyric poem with melody which originated anonymously among unlettered folk in times past and remained in currency for a considerable time, as a rule for centuries." A minor dictionary of the 1930's defined a ballad as "essentially rhythmic, originating among the common people," and a folk song as "a song originating and traditional among the common people." Similarly, it describes folklore as originating and handed down among the "peasantry."

Fortunately, as regards dialect, there has never been parallel sweeping insistence on peasant origins. Such an assumption if brought forward would make no headway. Dialect has not been associated with one vague assemblage of persons, the "masses," the "folk," the "peasantry," the "common people," as has so often folklore in general. We have anchored it to specific groups, occupational or class or racial, and to specific periods. Our vague conception of the folk, folk song, folklore in general should be delimited, as for dialect, this especially when the question of folk origins as well as folk preservation is brought up.

Surely theorists and dictionary makers should know by this time that there is no mysterious national "folk," "the masses," the "common people," of the old folklorists. Dr. B. A. Botkin once emphasized this when he pointed out that all oral tradition is necessarily regional or group lore, a generalization too often overlooked. There is never one folk from the point of view of folklore, but instead many folk groups, as many as there are regional cultures or occupations or racial groups within a region. That is, groups of people, homogeneous—not of mixed races— have a body of traditions peculiar to themselves, Swedish, German, French, Spanish, Czech, Negro, Indian. And there are also groups by classes or occupations, such as J. A. Lomax's cowboys, Franz Rickaby's loggers, Joanna Colcord's seamen, George Korson's miners. Cosmopolitan folk groups have no folklore traditions or songs or common dialect. They have individual lore but not lore belonging to the whole group until the group has become homogeneous. My personal definition of folklore would omit all delimitations of origin, characterizing it simply as lore traditional among homogeneous groups. Such traditional lore may be beliefs, superstitions, tales, legends, magic rites, rituals,

institutions, as generally recognized, and it should include linguistic usages too, that is, the dialect of the group, or the occupation, or the class, or the race. As said already, we are ignorant of
the parentage of most of this lore when we collect it. Yet there
has been overlong insistence that traditional lore must have had
its start among the unlettered and that this start was oral, not
printed. Folklore and folk song and the peculiarities of folk
speech or dialect start in many ways, from many sources, among
many classes, and in many regions, and they should no longer be
defined by hypothetical anonymous beginnings among the lowly.

4

As we have seen, the native English term *folklore,* or at least
the first element of the compound, deserves no little examination
and definition. *Dialect,* from the Greek, needs less comment. It
made its appearance in the English language in Renaissance
days. "E.K." commented to Gabriel Harvey in the dedication of
Spenser's *Shepheardes Calender* that "neither everywhere must
old words be stuffed in, nor the common Dialect and manner of
speaking so corrupted thereby that, as in old buildings, it seems
disorderly and ruinous." When he wrote this, E.K.'s *dialect*
meant the standard language. When S. Clark wrote in 1740,
"The lawyer's dialect would be too hard for him," his reference
was to the speech of a class, class dialect. A similar instance is
"the dialect of the theological society" (1805). A quotation from
the middle of the nineteenth century reads, "They lay aside the
learned dialect and reveal the unknown powers of the common
speech." All these uses are standard. To be taken into account,
too, is the use of the word in a wider sense as applied to a particular language in relation to the family of languages to which
it belongs, as when we characterize Attic, Doric, and Aeolic
Greek as dialects of Ancient Greek.

In the sense in which the Dialect Society oftenest employs the
word *dialect,* and that basic in this paper, the reference is not to
the standard language but chiefly to local or regional peculiarities
of vocabulary or usage, those diverging from the accepted usage
of the educated. Dialect is usually thought of as substandard,

though it is sometimes rather hard to draw the line of demarcation between the illiterate, semiliterate, and the standard. Probably the speech of any individual may be considered dialect of some type or another, but it is better not to take individualisms into account. Until recently the Dialect Society and its publications have given little attention to the dialects of various foreign languages spoken in America, or to the dialects of class or occupation. *American Speech* (1925), established later than *Dialect Notes,* has, on the other hand, welcomed from the first material dealing with special jargons, technical or colloquial. The characteristic vocabularies of railroad workers, telephone employees, librarians; terms used in shoe shops, beauty parlors, hotels; the peculiar language of summer employees at Yellowstone Park; the speech of foreign races in the United States, Italian, Greek, Yiddish; all these and more have had attention in its pages.

The relation of dialect to literature is a separate subject and one that can have but passing mention here. Robert Burns, poet of the Scottish vernacular, was the conspicuous inaugurator of conscious literary use of dialect in poetry, although behind him lay an attractive body of Scottish lyric verse, much of it traditional. Burns's American admirer, Whittier, did not try Yankee dialect in his poems of rural New England, though he fell now and then into dialect rhymes, often archaic. The real American promoter of dialect in verse was James Russell Lowell, whose *Biglow Papers* are perhaps the most original of his works. There had been sporadic prose employment of it in plays and fiction of his day, but it remained for him to furnish the real impetus to its use by literary men. In the second half of the nineteenth century humorists, such as Artemus Ward, Josh Billings, P. V. Nasby, relied heavily for their effects on unlettered dialect spellings. Dialect reigned in the short stories of Mary E. Wilkins and Sarah Orne Jewett and their successors. The Indiana poet James Whitcomb Riley used to recite his dialect pieces with great prestige in tours of the country. In our own day, reliance on dialect for humorous effect has been outrivaled by the popularity of slang, colloquialisms, and colloquial conflation of standard words, often of the "gotta," "useta," "dincha" brand.

The question is often asked, Is slang dialect? Properly it is not, or not at least until it has lasted long enough to become lore. Slang is characteristically ephemeral, dialect not. It is its transiency that differentiates slang from dialect. Most current slang soon wears out, to be replaced by something newer. When, however, it supplies a real need, it is likely to find permanence. Often, too, it may make its way upward into accepted or semi-accepted speech. Witness instances such as "bogus," "jazz," "toe the mark," "bosh," "poppycock," and the miner's slang, "peter out," "down to bed rock." Or, slang terms may remain in the language but remain as dialect, not making their way upward. This has been the fate of such "folk words" as "lummox," "skee-zicks," or "sockdologer," transposed from "doxologer." Expressions of this type are often recorded in larger dictionaries because of their persistence; but they are not recognized as standard. On the whole, slang locutions, the clichés of the day, phrases or catchwords that spring to popularity gayly and are then worn to death, although they are of cognate character, do not belong to the dialect field. Both slang and dialect, however, have interest for those who concern themselves with the mother tongue in all its phases, and both as associated with the life of the folk.

Folklore is an expansive field of investigation and study, with extraordinary catholicity of content. In its legacies from the past belong mythology, folk tales, folk song, legends, proverbs, riddles, ritual, beliefs in witchcraft, magic, medicine. Germane to the subject also are music, festivals, games, dance, folk drama, art crafts, architecture, dress, adornment, lore about food and drink, patterns of living and thinking. Dialect, too, is an expansive field of investigation and study, but in a lesser degree. It has concern with such subjects as local and standard idiom, usage levels, changes in acceptability, substitution of other for standard forms, the relation of colloquial to literary usage, of American to British speech, non-English dialects in the United States and their influence on the vernacular. Dialect may be studied in the light of history or racial stocks, or the study may be geographical, social, professional, or technical. For all my preceding remarks regarding their close relationship, I would not like to see the two societies, the Folklore and the Dialect Society, with their now carefully partitioned fields, merged into one. The Dialect Society might indeed be a branch of the Linguistic Society as appropriately as of the Folklore Society, and the latter might occupy a niche in the Anthropological Society. It is good for each to preserve its individual angles of approach. Each has enough rich soil of its own to till, and it is ground that can be better tilled if they are kept separate.

Abridged and somewhat modernized from an address given at a dinner of the first Western Folklore Conference, at the University of Denver, July 22, 1941. Reprinted from the *California Folklore Quarterly*, Vol. IV, No. 2 (April, 1945), 146-153, published by the University of California Press.

The Scholarly Study of Folklore

1

As the folklore conferences and folk festivals held in many places over the United States in these days testify, interest in folklore is now very high. It is strong not only among scholars but among nonprofessionals, amateurs devoted to search for the old and the "quaint," to use one of their terms. Teachers, clergymen, attorneys, writers, and others often feel prompted to hunt out the traditions, legends, songs, and tales of their own region. Why not? Such persons are of much the same type as those who search for antique furniture, old glassware, and the like. Some may call them dilettantes, but surely their hobbies are acceptable enough; and often, too, their activities are helpful to specialists. Indeed, popular traditions seem to me more laudable for collection than do many of the objects now often gathered ardently, such as match covers, pictures of ball players and cinema stars, and, among children, of backs of playing cards and even of colored milk bottle tops. Still other groups of folklore enthusiasts are devoted to the singing of old songs and the telling of old tales, or they may enjoy—and how many do these days—taking part in traditional dances and games; this wholly for the enjoyment of it. Again, why not? Such groups leave to scholars the relation of their findings and practices to anthropology, the science of man, to ethnology, the science of race, to history, religion, sociology, psychology, with all of which folklore has affiliations. Amateurs take conscious pleasure in what they find or take part in. Scholars

222

struggle over problems of origin, dissemination, classification; or they try to trace the life history of special items of lore. And, unlike amateurs, not all scholars find pleasure, *per se*, in what they investigate and theorize over.

2

In scholarly inquiry the "historical approach" is usually the proper one, and it is appropriate for the present discussion. Conscious interest in what we now call "folklore" arose early in the nineteenth century in the wake of the Romantic Movement. Its foundation was laid by the eminent German scholar Jacob Grimm, helped by his brother Wilhelm. The Grimms' pioneer *Kinder- und Hausmärchen* (I, 1812, II, 1815) was and remains a classic. The English translation of this book (1864) entitled *Household Tales* is generally known as "Grimm's Fairy Tales." Grimm's tales together with his *Deutsche Sagen* (1816-1818) and his *Deutsche Mythologie* (1835) brought him the title of "father of the science of folklore." He also laid the foundation of philology, the science of language, in his four-volume *Deutsche Grammatik* (1819-1837), another landmark book, and his *Deutsches Wörterbuch,* of which the first volume appeared in 1854. Grimm got his predilection for history and antiquities from Friedrich Karl von Savigny, the investigator of legal antiquities and Roman law at the University of Göttingen, whose lectures deeply impressed him. Incidentally, the so-called "communal" theory of the origin of law and social institutions and even of song not from individual minds but from a "mass mind" came from Savigny, as I found when following up the history of the term "communal" in the 1920's. This mass mind idea influenced German thought for a time and even came to the United States where it persisted into the middle of the present century, at least as regards the traditional ballad.

Grimm's folklore activities had little influence at first, but this influence did not wane but grew stronger. He aroused interest in fairy tales and animal tales and in folk song before he turned to mythology and to Germanic philology and lexicography, in which he also pioneered. In a few decades his enthusiasm for folklore spread over north Europe; Scandinavia and Finland as well as Germany took up collection and study. Ultimately materials were gathered in Lithuania, Lapland, Flanders, Bohemia, Sicily, Greece, and Russia. An especially strong impetus to the international study of folklore came from Finland. Not only did it record its traditions systematically but its contribution to folklore classification is unmistakable. The influence of Finland's folklore activities continued through the period of World War I and inspired among others, chiefly European, our leading American scholar Stith Thompson of Indiana University, who had his start in folklore at Harvard.

In England, scholarly interest in folklore did not come in the wake of the Romantic Movement as in Germany. Instead it is to be associated with the rise of the anthropological school, culminating in the many-volumed *The Golden Bough* (1907-1915) of Sir James G. Frazer. The anthropologists broadened and made more exact study of folklore, its collection and investigation, through their exploration of the life and lore of primitive peoples. They showed that in tribal lore are often exhibited cultural stages and cultural traits; indeed his lore was part of early man's science and religion. In these and other ways anthropologists helped toward the designation of folklore as a "science." One of the conceptions they brought forward, however, namely, that of the parallel development of culture all over the world, the belief that all races ultimately went through the same stages, the same changes, has now been given up.

The name "folklore" itself was originated, as often pointed out, by an Englishman, W. J. Thoms. The older English name was "popular antiquities," cumbersome and not quite exact. "Antiquities" includes too much. Thom's new name was accepted promptly. Germany, Scandinavia, and the United States employ it. Mexico, Argentina, and other South American countries now interest themselves in *folklórica*. France holds to the name *traditions populaires*, an excellent one that places the emphasis where it belongs, on tradition. Before World War II, north and south Europe had an international society, the *Folkloristische Forscherbund* (Norwegian *Folkeminne Forskning*,

Danish *Folkminde Forskning,* the compound Scandinavian term meaning research or science of popular memories).

The English Folk-Lore Society was founded in 1878, some decades after the advent of the Grimms. Among those instituting it were Andrew Lang, G. L. Gomme, Alfred Nutt, and E. B. Tylor. Tylor was the leading anthropologist of the group, author of the landmark book *Primitive Culture* (1871). The society first published a pamphlet the *Folk-Lore Record* in 1878, superseded by the *Folk-Lore Journal,* 1885, which merged with the *Archaeological Review* into *Folklore* in 1890. The latter is still issued, and there arose other publications representing other fields, such as a journal of folk song.

In the United States, a Folklore Society was established at Cambridge, Massachusetts, in January, 1888, half a century or more after the advent of the Grimms and ten years after the English society, which probably inspired it. The American organization formulated as its objects the collection and preservation of fading traditional lore in the United States, including survivals of older English lore, songs, tales, and superstitions; also the assemblage of the lore of Negroes and of Indian tribes, their myths and tales; also the lore of French Canada, Mexico, and foreign settlements such as Swedish and German. These purposes it has carried out in the sixty-three years of its existence. The first president of the new American society was Alcée Fortier, professor of romance languages in the University of Louisiana. The second president was Francis James Child of Harvard, maker of the historic ten-volume collection of *English and Scottish Popular Ballads.* Among other members were W. W. Newell, collector of the *Songs and Games of American Children* (1883), and G. L. Kittredge who inspired so many scholarly folklorists at Harvard, among them Archer Taylor, the proverb and riddle specialist. Alice Fletcher, the Indian specialist, was also an early member. The late Alexander Krappe published *The Science of Folklore* in 1930, a work literary in character and quality. Professor Franz Boas of Columbia University gave unmistakable impetus to the collection and study of tales from the North American Indians and to American anthropological scholarship in general.

Two men deserve special mention for their present activities and contributions. One is Stith Thompson who began his career with a doctoral dissertation on *Tales of the North American Indians* (1928) at Harvard, and who is the recent author of *The Folktale* (1947), a comprehensive scholarly treatment of the subject. Of incalculable use to the student wishing to check some special motif and its distribution is his six-volume *Motif-Index of Folk-Literature* (1932-1936), its basis and inspiration Finnish. It provides a model of classification and makes available an extraordinary mass of information. Another American scholar not to be omitted in an appreciative account is Ralph S. Boggs, a pupil of Archer Taylor. He is now a director of the Hispanic-American Institute at Miami and a professor on the teaching staff of Miami University. His annual bibliography of North and South American folklore publications for 1950 reached 107 pages. It is printed in the spring issue of the *Southern Folklore Quarterly*.

In a sketch such as the present one, it is of course impossible to mention all the leading folklorists who are doing distinguished and valuable work. The United States has by this time four well-established regional quarterlies in addition to the pioneer *Journal of American Folklore* founded in 1888.

3

What does the vast mass of traditional material now available include by this time? What are the kinds of things handed down from the past and interesting the present? The Grimms started with folk tales and set collectors at work all over Europe. Of all varieties of folklore perhaps the prose tale has accumulated the largest returns in assemblage and analysis, although the narrative song, the ballad, was soon in the foreground, too, and for a time it had the greater emphasis. Animal tales are a leading early type, the classic example coming from historic times, *Aesop's Fables*. In mediaeval times Reynard the fox was a conspicuous animal. He has a counterpart in southwestern American lore, the coyote. Tales of the bear, the snake, the raven, and the crow occur widely. To take a hasty inventory: in the world's traditional lore are wonder tales, merry tales culminating in some humorous situation, religious tales, romantic tales, local legends allied to features of landscape, family legends of ghosts and spirits and other types of supernatural beings such as deities, demons, giants, ogres, vampires, witches, fairies; and there are tales of heroes and of tricksters and their moron victims. Other species that interest collectors are weather and plant lore, lore of minerals, good and bad luck signs, charms, spells, and exorcisms, lore of courtship and marriage, of wish-making, dream lore, physical signs such as burning ears, white spots on the fingernails, jests and anecdotes, proverbs, counting-out rhymes, skipping-rope rhymes, traditional games and dances. Some favorite Old-World legend themes are of dragon fights, bottomless pools or lakes, sunken cities, leaps from precipices, buried treasure, supernatural adversaries, and various kinds of tests. Present-day counterparts of many of these are found in our own country. Our American Indian lore emphasizes especially animal tales, creation myths, adventures of heroes, supernatural beings, and transformations. A notable extension in the scope of folklore, made by the Scandinavians and Germans, is the inclusion of folk arts and crafts illustrating the life of the people, called by the Germans *Volkskunde*.

Obviously some comprehensive index of these materials ultimately became necessary, and for even a single species, the folk tale, this proved a gigantic task. It has now been carried out, however. It is recognized that the best classification for them is by what the French call *motif*. The complete tale is made up of a number of motifs, or salient features, such as the participants, or single incidents, or details of background. Folk-tale classification was promoted by Karle Krohn of Finland, who devised a preliminary system. Next Antti Aarne of Finland used the system of index approved by Krohn in a motif-index of folk literature. He brought together for comparative study materials from many lands, indexing hundreds of European and other stories in the folk literature of the world and grouping them according to types of character, kinds of action, happenings and environing circumstances, i.e., by motifs. America's Stith Thompson revised Aarne's *Types of the Folktale* in 1928 and in 1932 to 1936 came Thompson's comprehensive six-volume *Motif-Index of Folk-Literature* which is of immense help to the student of comparative folklore, whether he is interested in general aspects or in some single motif or story.

4

Not having the background of assembled materials, earlier folk-lore theorists evolved what seem to us now strange ideas concerning them. Most persons are interested in stories and hence the folk tale was the species first subjected to zealous attention. Early cultural theorizers, beginning with the Grimms, were greatly concerned with natural phenomena, as dawn, sunset, wild storm, the behavior of the heavenly bodies. A reigning theory for some time was that folk tales were broken-down myths, survivals from primitive times. That even the English Beowulf narrative was so derived by nineteenth-century German scholars and literati seems nearly incredible to us today. For example, Beowulf was explained by some as a wind hero, the storm spirit of autumn. Grendel and his mother were accounted as representing the plagues of the marshy Frisian coast during the summer months. The dragon is the mist on the heights that Beowulf frightens away. One scholar stated that the dragon is winter that in autumn stifles all life in nature.

Another reigning belief for a time alongside the myth hypothesis was that since similar or the same folk tales were found among peoples of different races and regions they must have descended from a common Indo-European ancestry, were survivals from a distant past. In 1859, Theodor Benfey, a notable scholar in the wake of the Grimms (*Kleine Schriften zur Märchenforschung* and *Pantschatantra*) launched the position that common European tales had their origin in India whence they reached Europe. After the British conquest of India and the resulting discovery of Sanskrit, antedating in its forms Greek and Latin, the conviction arose that India was the ancestral home of the Indo-Europeans and therefore the home of the earliest tales. In later times the ancestral home of the Indo-Europeans has been moved farther north.

Joseph Bédier (*Les Fabliaux*, 1893), an eminent French scholar, contested not only the mythological and Indianist theories but the position of G. L. Gomme, the English scholar who maintained that folklore is an aid to establishing historical fact (*Folklore and Historical Science,* 1908). Nowadays, like Bédier, we do not believe that folklore is a trustworthy contribution to history proper. It is not fact but represents only human ideas and their expression in tales and songs. Possibly a legend preserves the germ of some happening, but it should not be relied upon as genuine history. Another French scholar, Arnold van Gennep, emphasized the utilitarian character of early tales, among them animal tales. He pointed out that primitive myths and tales conveyed lessons of conduct or they were helpful in some practical way. Already mentioned is the belief of von Savigny that the creation of tales and songs, as of social institutions and laws, emerged from a "mass mind" rather than from individuals, i.e., they were of "communal" genesis.

Today all these theories are pretty much discredited. One of the contributions of Professor Franz Boas of Columbia University was to show that neither the myth nor the tale had priority among primitives. Van Gennep and the German Hans Naumann were among those holding, as we do now, belief in the multigenesis, the origin in many places, of motifs and stories, and in the idea of dissemination. It is recognized that the same motifs may arise independently in various regions from the same simple and natural situations, that people tell of them, and that they borrow lore from one another. The general position is now that no one explanation, no one formula of origin, mythological, Indianist, anthropological, historical, literary, geographical, will do for all folk tales or for general folklore. Broad generalizations have been discarded here and abroad.

5

As regards procedure for the scholarly collector of material, one need hardly repeat that it must be as accurate as possible. Phonographic recording of tales and songs, proverbs, anecdotes, jests, and whatever else may be germane, is supremely desirable but by no means always possible. The practical collector must try to learn first of all the persons most likely to know the lore he seeks and then get down in writing, or by phonograph, the results of his interviewing. The latter, the interviewing, usually requires much patience and tact. The experienced have found that it is usually older or middle-aged persons who are the best sources. The assemblage of many variants is often important, at least for stories. Their migrations and the geography of their distribution are to be taken into account. Indeed, anything that may throw light on the item of lore in hand is not to be overlooked. All this helps the scholar in comparisons and classifications. By the comparative method may sometimes be determined the archetype from which the variants have sprung. Occasionally one can trace the life history of a particular legend or tale or song or belief. This latter is what I have attempted in many preceding papers such as "The Nebraska Legend of Weeping Water," "Nebraska Legends of Lovers' Leaps," and "The Legend of the Lincoln Salt Basin." Once more, then, after collection, of interest and importance are such matters as analysis and comparison of versions or variants, attempts to make out their relationships, the examination of geographical data and of the changes in the course of dissemination.

In the preceding pages we have seen how the amassing of folklore materials, begun more than a hundred years ago, has made collectanea from many countries available for study and comparison, through international cooperation. Sounder methods have been arrived at and better patterns established. The assembling of traditional material continues to be swelled by both professionals and amateurs. To be taken into account, too, is the arrival of late years of the musicologists. Beginning with primitive music recorded among remote peoples, musicologists seek to preserve the manner of utterance of singers and their types of music. The musicologists are to be welcomed unqualifiedly. They have increased the accuracy and the extent of our knowledge of traditional music.

Indeed, by the mid-twentieth century, the scope of folklore has not only been greatly broadened but greatly popularized. In our period we seem to be collecting as folklore—rather unexpectedly to scholars—material that involves little if any antiquity. One assumed that we had reached a point where tradition and anonymity and accurate recording were accepted as criteria for determining what is folklore. But it sometimes seems now as though folklore had become merely lore of the folk. To many "folklore" seems to be anything "folksy." How far should this broadening go? What are the limitations, if there are such? Comic strips, cartoons, assembly-lined "westerns," manipulated parleyings of rural characters, hillbilly songs, political or propaganda songs, are these folklore? To me "traditional" is still the key consideration. My three tests of genuine folk songs, for example, have always been: they are handed down in tradition orally or in print, their form not static but continually changing; they are anonymous, their authorship and origin lost to the singers; they have retained their vitality through a fair period of time. Slang, for instance, is not folklore until it has been handed down. In the latter case it either becomes dialect, a branch of folklore having the permanence which slang, which fades quickly, has not; or, if it fills a need and is retained, it wins recognition in standard dictionaries. My own position is still that all that is folksy, all that is lore of the folk is not folklore. Is this becoming a minority position?

One other matter. Surely it is time that dictionaries revised their definitions of folklore, folk song, folk tale, and folk dance in the light of modern scholarship. They should no longer persist in their determination of folklore by origin among the lower classes. We know now that it has many origins, on many levels, among many types of human beings. In a representative dictionary of 1926, the Winston, folklore is defined as "popular traditions, customs, beliefs handed down among the peasantry." Since the United States has no peasantry this definition would bar it from having folklore. The unabridged Webster of 1935 has an acceptable definition of folklore, "traditional beliefs, customs, tales or sayings"; but it serves up the old criterion of origin for folk song, and folk tale; and the new unabridged dictionary of 1950 makes no alterations. Folklore is entered as before; folk song is still a "song originating and traditional among the common people" with the addition that "from their more or less impersonal origin folk songs are in general contrasted with art songs which are the known work of individual composers." A folk tale is "a tale handed down by word of mouth among the common people." A folk dance is a dance "originating among and characteristic of the common people of a country and transmitted from generation to generation like the folk song." To quote one more dictionary, the popular *American College Dictionary* of 1947, folklore is the "lore of the common people: the traditional beliefs, customs, legends etc. of the people." Folk music is "music originated and handed down among the common people." Folk song and folk tale are assigned the same origin and preservation among the "common people."

This assumption that folklore and its various species originated among the "peasantry" or the "common people" and is their private property is by this time itself folklore. Some scholars, indeed, such as Bédier and the cosmopolitan Russian-German-Estonian Walter Anderson, sometime professor at the University of Dorpat, take just the opposite position, namely that there is usually debasement from a higher to a lower level in folklore. The process is one of sinking rather than ascent. We know now that much lore is the detritus of older science, astrology, medicine, religion, older customs, and rites. The game of tag, now traditional among children, was played by maids of honor at the court of Queen Elizabeth. The traditional singing games of children, such as "Ring Round Rosie" or "Here We Go Round the Mulberry Bush," descend from the outdoor ring dances of mediaeval patricians. Some of our most preposterous folklore cures derive from ancient medical science.

As for traditional preservation among "common people," those on higher levels, uncommon people too, have their lore. Professors have been accused of having theirs, as of types of examinations, modes of grading and of teaching, and, in any case, as regards their anecdotal lore. Joe Louis is no common person yet he has his lore of the prize ring. Hitler had his lore, and Thurman Arnold wrote of the folklore of capitalism. Unmistakably folklore has many origins, exists on many levels, and circulates among uncommon as well as common people. Should not dictionaries drop their inevitable qualifying adjective before "people," or, better perhaps, content themselves merely with "folk," a word liberal of application?

I wish to protest, too, against the stock contrasting of the poetry or other creations of "art" and the "artless" creations of the folk, a contrast repeated as regards folk song in the Webster unabridged dictionary of 1950. The antithesis is really between traditional folk songs and those of culture. Art and culture are not identical. The most primitive people have their own kind of art and they adhere to its patterns. Primitive art, peasant art, common people's art is no less fixed than the art of higher circles. The distinction between the art of individual composers and the artlessness of the simple product of the folk is a familiar and a traditional one, but not, I think, valid. I urged long ago that it be given up, earliest perhaps in my *American Ballads and Songs* of 1922.

Read at the meeting of the Colorado Folklore Society held in connection with the Eleventh Annual Western Folklore Conference at the University of Denver, July 12-14, 1951. Reprinted from *Western Folklore*, Vol. XI, No. 2 (April, 1952), 100-108, published by the University of California Press.

American Folksong

Origins, Texts and Modes of Diffusion

In the descriptive Introduction to my *American Ballads and Songs* published by Scribner's, 1922, I attempted to characterize American folksong for the earlier nineteenth century. For our later period, an excellent individualizing account of *Native American Balladry*, "a descriptive account and a bibliographical syllabus," by Dr. G. Malcolm Laws, Jr., appeared as the first number in the Publications of the American Folklore Society, Biographical Series, 1950. This he supplemented by his "The Spirit of American Balladry" in the April-June issue of the *Journal of American Folklore*, LXV, 163-169. These fields have been well taken care of, and this "report" will be a generalizing one, dealing with folksongs as well as ballads and emphasizing no special phase or phases of its subject.

Interest in America's singing past is very lively in these days, both as regards older pieces descending in tradition, their provenience unknown to their singers, and older popular pieces of known authorship and history. The gathering of forgotten songs goes on apace among both amateurs and scholars. Though to lovers of popular song in general they may seem unimportant and negligible, to specialists the beginnings of the songs they collect are of great interest. The days are past, however, when searchers try to distinguish between "genuine" ballads, of the traditional type, and the so-called "vulgar" (or common-

234

place) stall ballads printed on broadsheets or in "songsters." Discrimination of this kind is no longer attempted; the two have existed side by side in the repertory of singers. And dictionaries should no longer define a folksong as "a song or ballad essentially rhythmic, originating among the common people," although most dictionaries still do. If the "peasant origin" insisted upon by early scholars were valid, the United States would have no folksong or folklore, since it has no peasantry. Belief in a single test for genuineness, such as ascent from below, has been given up for folksong as for folklore in general. Like folklore, folksong originates in many ways on many levels.

Individual pieces orally handed on and therefore sought by collectors have been recovered from many sources. American songs and ballads have been gathered from logging camps, mining camps, cottonfields, cattle ranches, or wherever available local singers are to be found. The best texts come, as to be expected, from the literate, the worst from the illiterate. Most valid and desirable of course, after these became available, are the texts and melodies recorded with phonographs. Traditional pieces have been had from rural persons and from city dwellers, from grandparents, from mothers and fathers, from college and high school students and even from children who learned them in schoolhouses. Often desirable texts have been retrieved from newspaper columns of "old favorites"; or found on single sheets sold by itinerant singers; or on broadsheets sold along streets; or in "songsters," small books of various types offered by vendors. Collectors have jotted them down from informal gatherings, temperance gatherings, camp meetings, crossroad stores, and at times from taverns and barrooms. "Western" songs have been obtained at Old Settlers' picnics, or at social occasions on farms or ranches and at the oldtime "play parties." In the nineteenth and earlier twentieth centuries, of special help to preservation and vitality were the manuscript books once widely kept in which favorite songs were recorded. These have yielded many good texts.

As a result there are now available collections of songs of American mountain people, cowboys, loggers, miners, sailormen, railroaders, prison inmates, Okies, W.P.A. workers, and those of racial groups such as Negroes, Indians, Mexicans, French-Canadians, Scandinavians, and others. There are no limitations as to regions, topics, classes, and occupational or racial groups. Religious and homiletic pieces, slave songs, temperance songs, journalistic pieces, game songs, children's songs, all are grist to the mill of the present-day folklorist. This liberality of inclusion contrasts with the earlier limitations imposed on themselves by folklore scholars before and after the turn of the century. American collectors sought then mainly the "genuine" English and Scottish pieces in America, neglecting their background in tradition of masses of folksong of other kinds and histories.

Imported pieces of the ballad type assembled by Professor F. J. Child and their affiliates seem to have had many origins. Some among the large body of English and Scottish ballads made available by him were originated by composers of older periods; some of the early religious pieces emerged no doubt from or under the influence of clericals; others came from the minstrels of great baronial houses such as the Percys, the Stanleys, the Howards (probable instances are "The Battle of Otterburn," Child No. 161, "The Rose of England," No. 166, "Sir Andrew Barton," No. 167), and they glorified the heroes of these houses. In the later sixteenth and seventeenth centuries and into modern times many surely came from professional entertainers and writers for the stage and for special occasions. To begin fairly far back, some testimony remains concerning English ballads sung in the period preceding the coming of the English to America and in that when the colonizing of America began. Some idea can be had of the audiences hearing them and perhaps of impetus to their diffusion.

The earliest reference to "The Fair Flower of Northumberland" (No. 9) is in Delaney's *Pleasant History of John Winchcombe,* 1633, in which it is termed "The Maiden's Song" and is sung before "the King and Queen." It was probably of professional origin. Fletcher's *Knight of the Burning Pestle,* 1611, mentions "Fair Margaret and Sweet William" (No. 74) and also "Little Musgrave and Lady Barnard" (No. 81), both of which survive in America, and also the religious ballad "The Romish

Lady," not a Child ballad but an old one found occasionally on this side of the Atlantic. "The Three Ravens" (No. 26) was included in the anthology *Melismata*, 1611, which was printed as "fitting the Court, Cittie, and Countrey Humour." "Barbara Allen's Cruelty" (No. 84) was heard by Samuel Pepys as sung by an actress on the London stage in 1666 and it may have made its début on that occasion. Phillips Barry is reported to have been working on it at the time of his death, with a promising outlook for determining its seventeenth century start. This song is very current in the United States though unstable of text and melody, as to be expected. "Lord Bakeman" (No. 53), liked by Dickens, was utilized with success in a popular play *Rosedale* and has had vitality over here. In the 1880's "Gypsy Davy" (No. 200) and "The House Carpenter" (No. 243) were widely sung in this country and texts are still recovered here and there. "Lord Lovel" (No. 74) was taken up by the American comic stage in the second decade of the nineteenth century. It appeared, says Barry, as a comic song on the playbills of the Warren theater, Boston, December 1834. He has also shown that "Sir Andrew Barton" (No. 167) was sung by Mme. Biscaccianti (Eliza Ostinelli) to enthusiastic audiences at Portland, Maine, about 1859. My Nebraska variant, however, came directly from Ireland, brought here by an immigrant about 1880.

Like the imported pieces, American pieces that are indisputably indigenous have a variety of origins and of agencies promoting their circulation. As said at the opening, criteria of origin for songs in folk tradition are not dependable, as once thought, nor is the degree of currency any criterion. Instead, emphasis, whatever the ultimate source of a piece, should go to its entrance into and preservation in tradition and its transmission through a fair period of time. It used to be held that if a song is to be termed traditional its vitality should have lasted through several generations. Now inclusion has been so liberalized that persistence for a relatively short time seems enough to allow a piece to be arrayed among folksongs if it has other major characteristics enabling it to be termed folklore.

Although, as said already, the Child ballads were long espe-

cially sought for in this country, many other types have come
from the Old World and are still to be found in the Appalachians, the Ozarks and many other regions. Some instances are
"Bonny Black Bass," a Dick Turpin song, "The Butcher's Boy,"
"The Rich Merchant of London," "The Drowsy Sleeper," "The
Farmer's Boy," "Mary of the Wild Moor." The Irish "Come All
Ye's" which reached America in some abundance have served
as models for many indigenous American pieces. Imported
songs, Child ballads and all, generally accommodate themselves
to their new homes. They domesticate themselves in agreement
with the characteristics of the regions they enter. Thus "Lord
Randal" became Johnny Randall in a Colorado mining camp
and Johnny Randolph in Virginia. "Edward" is Son Davie and
"Sir Andrew Barton," which has an affiliate ballad "Henry Martin," became Anders Bardien in Nebraska and Bollender (Bold
Andrew) Martin in Nova Scotia. Traditional songs are still
brought over occasionally from the Old World but soon will be
crowded from the folk memory by our present ever-changing
transitory "hit" songs for the radio, phonograph, and juke box.

Since not fixed for the singer by print, traditional songs,
whether indigenous or imported, are characteristically in a state
of flux. They shift in the mouths of different singers and, indeed, in the mouths of the same singers. The changes are rarely
deliberate unless there is intention to localize; they are instinc-
tive, unconscious. There are slips of memory, additions, subtrac-
tions, alterations of stanzas and phrasing. The names of the
characters and the place-names are influenced by the personal
experiences and tastes of the singers. Nor are the shiftings likely
to be for the better; more likely the converse. A piece may cross
with other pieces, disordering it or leaving it merely a heap of
confused materials. There may be any number of variants; witness the multiple texts of such pieces as "Barbara Allen," or
"The Two Sisters." The situation is more dependable than the
tune for the identification of a ballad. In general, the influence
of folk transmission is leveling. Whether a piece is imported or
indigenous its fate is degeneration unless it is taken up by some
gifted humorist or journalist or professional singer or composer.
Instances of texts so improved are one version of "Springfield

Mountain" and one of "The Frog and the Mouse," in which the older texts are transformed into effective comedy.

When printing their texts popular collectors sometimes quite frankly combine their best fragments, recovered from various sources, of a single song, although the song may really have no more stable form than "Hinky Dinky Parlez-Vous" ever attained. Folk singers manipulate what they sing, dropping many notes in melodies to fit their words or juggling their words to fit the melodies. Sometimes an editor helps out defective pieces on his own, as Sir Walter Scott did so successfully where passages seemed over-crude or were missing. The texts of many of the songs of J. A. and Alan Lomax are said by them (*Cowboy Songs*, 1938, p. xxix) to be composites made by selecting and putting together the best lines of their best fragments.

In addition to oral transmission and shifting texts and fair duration, another characteristic of the species of folksong that is folklore is that its past is uncertain to its singers and hearers; sense of its authorship is lost. Sometimes careful research can bring to light the composer or can fix or approximate its date; sometimes all efforts fail. "James Bird," for example, an unexpectedly persistent piece, was the work of Charles Minor of Wilkesbarre, Pennsylvania, and was printed by him in his newspaper. "Young Charlotte" or "The Frozen Girl" was formerly ascribed by Phillips Barry, that indefatigable searcher for origins, to an itinerant singer from Vermont. Later he found that its author was the professional humorist Seba Smith (1792-1868). Incidentally, one text I have of this ballad was supplied by a youth in Lancaster County, Nebraska, who stated positively that he composed it. Any collector of folksong is likely to come upon spurious claims of this type. A singer adapts some traditional piece to his own locality, then claims to be the author of it.

The absorption into tradition of songs by known authors, composers of the book or literary type, is no infrequent phenomenon. This has been true of some of Sir Walter Scott's songs and of Longfellow's. My prize example of what may happen to a song in this stanza recovered orally from a Wyoming ranch. Plainly it is the beginning of the once popular "The Spanish Cavalier."

The Spanish Cabineer
    Stood under a tree
And on his gautar
    Played a tone, dear.

The popularity of the so-called "Westerns" over the radio and in films has given impetus to the revival and repetition of old "cowboy" and pioneer pieces and to the composition of new. The best of the older ones recovered from Western singing are those made over from well-known songs of recognizable identity. An instance is the well-liked "O Bury Me Not on the Lone Prairee," adapted with changes from "The Ocean Burial" ("O bury me not in the deep, deep sea"). The words were printed under the name of the Rev. E. H. Chapin, a well-known Unitarian clergyman, in the *Southern Literary Messenger,* 1839. The music was copyrighted by George S. Allen in 1850. The Western adaptation seems to have been made in the early 1870's and it has been ascribed to several different persons. Another instance is "The Little Old Sod Shanty on My Claim" which I found, when I was interested in it about 1913, to have been made over with a few changes from a song my mother had, "The Little Old Log Cabin in the Lane," by Will S. Hays, which was copyrighted in 1871. The Western text was reported to have been sent about on postcards for pioneer gatherings in the Central West. "The Cowboy's Lament" was found by Phillips Barry to be an adaptation of an eighteenth century English or Irish song, "The Unfortunate Rake," but, as long since pointed out, it was not adapted consistently since the military funeral which gives rise to the refrain ("Beat the drum slowly, and play the fife lowly, Play the Dead March as you carry me along") and which is appropriate in the original, is out of place in a cowboy song. Among the ballads of the Meeks murder in Missouri in 1894 is one made over from and sung to the tune of "Little Nell of Narragansett Bay," with the refrain "Toll, toll the bell." George Meeks, the author of it, said he was also the author of the well-known "I Wish I Were Single Again."

In general ballads locally composed by neighborhood singers, whether adaptations or original of text, are a very ephemeral type. Ephemeral too are bits of spontaneous improvisations such as

are sometimes heard today in square dancing. Songs of improvi-
sational origin and handling are too loose and shifting to endure. They have no stories to hold them together and, like
"Hinky Dinky Parlez-Vous," they do not or cannot develop
plots. They are likely to be threaded on some striking refrain
to which they owe such popularity as they gain; but they never
get beyond the stage of shifting material. The chances of improvised compositions to survive are slight unless some popular
entertainer, comedian, or humorist takes them up, improves
them and makes them known. To the late John A. Lomax is to
be credited the popularization of such songs as "The Old Chisholm Trail," "Good-by, Old Paint," and "Whoopee Ti Yi Yo,
Git Along, Little Dogies." Other Westerners such as cowboy
Jim Thorpe may have given impetus to individual songs. "Home
on the Range" with its attractive melody was overlooked till
its appearance in Lomax's *Cowboy Songs* of 1910, in which it
was an outstanding piece. The late President Roosevelt's liking
for it also swelled its popularity. The verses were written by Dr.
Brewster Higley of Smith Center, Kansas, in 1883. The original
tune was supplied by Dan Kellogg, a neighbor of Higley.

How are songs old and new floated? Special impetus to their
circulation in this country has been given not only by itinerant
singers and printed sheets and "songsters" but by vaudeville
which in its heyday in the later nineteenth century and succeeding decades was a great medium of song exploitation and
survival. Barber shop harmonizers may also have played a role.
Today all these have been largely replaced by films involving
songs and by musical plays and phonograph records. As already
implied, a popular song may be given impetus to diffusion by a
singer or band or in concerts or in plays; various agencies contribute to its vitality. The public must hear and eventually
learn a melody and its words if it is to persist. "The Baggage
Coach Ahead," sometimes still found in oral circulation, was
composed by Gussie Davis, a Negro, and was popularized by
being thrown on slides at vaudeville programs. Another of
Davis's songs entering oral tradition was "The Fatal Wedding."
Joe Howard's "My Mother Was a Lady" was also made into a
slide song. The comedian Joe Flynn's "Down Went McGinty"

which he fitted into his vaudeville act was a great moneymaker but has been less well remembered by the folk mind. Nor did "Ta-Ra-Ra-Ra-Boom-De-Ay" find the vitality in tradition to be expected of it. "Two Little Girls in Blue" by Charles Graham is still recovered here and there. "Jesse James" of undetermined origin was a favorite in tavern singing. Charles Harris's "After the Ball" was popular everywhere. Its inclusion in Hoyt's play "A Trip to China Town" took it all over the country and even to Australia.

A further source of oral and other currency of folksongs in the nineteenth century was the "Old Folkes Concerts" popular in the '60's. A leader among these was "Father Kemp's" which toured the country in that decade. Eventually some fifty Old Folk's Troupes went about the States, or came into static existence here and there. First, amateur festivals were put on by groups, then performances established on a professional basis and traveling troupes might be formed. Another instance of such a group was the Peakes who became leading entertainers. They were succeeded by the Hutchinson family whose favorite balled "Johnny Sands" gained amazing vogue.[1] "Joe Bowers," popular in the Gold Rush era, has been ascribed to various authors. The likeliest is John Woodward of Johnson's Minstrels in San Francisco, who sang it in the old Melodian Theater there in 1850 and took it up and down the coast.

In these days the phonograph, radio, juke box, and musical plays largely replace variety shows, minstrel shows, and other stage productions and replace also circulation by itinerant singers and by the vending of printed broadsides. The commercializing of songs has brought many "folksy" pieces into prominence and helped them to a degree of currency. The exigencies of supplying non-copyrighted songs led recently to a revival of

---

[1] For "Father" Robert H. Kemp (1820-1897), who originated the unique institution, see the *Dictionary of American Biography*. P. D. Jordan's *The Singin' Yankees* (The Hutchinson Family), 1946, has the following passage, spoken by a member of the Hutchinson family: "You know we're not the only family troupe on circuit—There's the Bakers and the Rainers and the Peaks and the Cheyney family from Vermont. There are old folks troupes and Ethiopian serenaders and white-faced black minstrels. Barnum can get 'em by the dozen, all he wants."

many old favorites. How long will the currency of either the old or the new pieces last? According to an article of February, 1950, by Josephine Ripley, Americans write and copyright at the rate of more than 1000 a week. These compositions come flooding into the office of the Library of Congress in an endless stream. The same song, sung in the same way by the same singer, may be heard by every listener and can be bought by him from a music dealer in printed or in phonograph-record form. So many "hit" songs are launched in succession that few are likely to be remembered and handed on apart from print. As time goes on there will be less and less preservation in oral tradition. It is the attractive higher class songs authored by composers of acknowledged standing that will have better staying power, and these are preserved in static form: they are not folklore. In popular song today memorable tunes have been superseded to a large extent by rhythm. Jazz, boogie-woogie, swing, B-Bop do not rely on tunes of taking quality but replace them to a degree that many think regrettable.

Asked for and read before the Comparative Literature section II (Popular Literature), of the Modern Language Association of America, Detroit, December 29, 1951. Reprinted from the *Southern Folklore Quarterly*, XVII (June, 1953), 114-121.